T5-AWA-346

COMMUNITY AND FORESTRY

SOCIAL BEHAVIOR AND
NATURAL RESOURCES SERIES
Donald R. Field, Series Editor

Community and Forestry: Continuities in the Sociology of Natural Resources, edited by Robert G. Lee, Donald R. Field, and William R. Burch, Jr.

Social Science in Natural Resource Management Systems, edited by Marc L. Miller, Richard P. Gale, and Perry J. Brown

Economic Valuation of Natural Resources: Issues, Theory, and Applications, edited by Rebecca L. Johnson and Gary V. Johnson

Social Science and Natural Resource Recreation Management, edited by Joanne Vining

COMMUNITY AND FORESTRY

CONTINUITIES IN THE SOCIOLOGY OF NATURAL RESOURCES

EDITED BY
Robert G. Lee,
Donald R. Field, and
William R. Burch, Jr.

WITH A FOREWORD BY
Cecil D. Andrus

WESTVIEW PRESS
Boulder, San Francisco, & London

Social Behavior and Natural Resources Series

This Westview softcover edition is printed on acid-free paper and bound in library-quality, coated covers that carry the highest rating of the National Association of State Textbook Administrators, in consultation with the Association of American Publishers and the Book Manufacturers' Institute.

All rights reserved. No part of this publication may be reproduced or transmitted in any form or by any means, electronic or mechanical, including photocopy, recording, or any information storage and retrieval system, without permission in writing from the publisher.

Copyright © 1990 by Westview Press, Inc., except Chapters 6 and 15, which are works of the U.S. government

Published in 1990 in the United States of America by Westview Press, Inc., 5500 Central Avenue, Boulder, Colorado 80301, and in the United Kingdom by Westview Press, Inc., 13 Brunswick Centre, London WC1N 1AF, England

Library of Congress Cataloging-in-Publication Data
Community and forestry : continuities in the sociology of natural
resources / edited by Robert G. Lee, Donald R. Field, and William R.
Burch, Jr.
    p. cm. — (Social behavior and natural resources series)
    Includes index.
    ISBN 0-8133-7837-0
    1. Forestry and community. I. Lee, Robert G. II. Field, Donald
R. III. Burch, William R., 1933–   IV. Series.
SD387.S55C66   1990
333.75—dc20   89-14634
                                                                    CIP

Printed and bound in the United States of America

⊗ The paper used in this publication meets the requirements of the American
National Standard for Permanence of Paper for Printed Library Materials
Z39.48-1984.

10   9   8   7   6   5   3   2

WIDENER UNIVERSITY
WOLFGRAM
LIBRARY
CHESTER, PA.

Contents

About the Series   ix

Foreword   xi

Preface   xiii

I. Overview   1

1. Introduction: Forestry, Community, and Sociology
   of Natural Resources
   Robert G. Lee, Donald R. Field, and William R. Burch, Jr.   3

2. Some Contributions of Sociology to the Study of
   Natural Resources
   Walter Firey   15

3. Toward the Stabilization and Enrichment of a
   Forest Community
   Harold F. Kaufman and Lois C. Kaufman   27

4. Human Choice in the Great Lakes Wildlands
   Samuel P. Hays   41

II. Wood Products Industry and Community   53

5. Sustained Yield and Community Stability in American Forestry
   *Johannes H. Drielsma, Joseph A. Miller,
   and William R. Burch, Jr.*   55

6. Community Stability: Issues, Institutions, and Instruments
   Con H. Schallau   69

7. Sustained Yield and Social Order
   Robert G. Lee   83

8. Forest Industry Towns in British Columbia
   Patricia Marchak   95

9. The Changing Structure of the Forest Industry in
    the Pacific Northwest
    Andy Brunelle   107

10. Mill Closures in the Pacific Northwest: The Consequences
    of Economic Decline in Rural Industrial Communities
    Edward C. Weeks   125

11. Occupational Community and Identity Among Pacific
    Northwestern Loggers: Implications for Adapting to
    Economic Changes
    Matthew S. Carroll and Robert G. Lee   141

III. Forest-Based Communities in a Service-Based Society   157

12. Social Bases for Resource Conflicts in Areas of
    Reverse Migration
    Dale J. Blahna   159

13. Power Plants and Resource Rights
    Louise Fortmann and Paul Starrs   179

14. Depopulation and Disorganization in Charcoal-Producing
    Mountain Villages of Kyoto Prefecture in Japan
    Hisayoshi Mitsuda   195

15. Community Stability as Social Structure: The Role of
    Subsistence Uses of Natural Resources in Southeast Alaska
    Robert M. Muth   211

16. Building Trust: The Formation of a Social Contract
    Margaret A. Shannon   229

17. Counties, States, and Regulation of Forest Practices
    on Private Lands
    Debra J. Salazar   241

IV. Conclusions and Implications   257

18.   Community Stability and Timber-Dependent Communities:
       Future Research
          Gary E. Machlis and Jo Ellen Force   259

19.   Conclusions: Past Accomplishments and Future Directions
          Robert G. Lee, William R. Burch, Jr., and Donald R. Field   277

Profiles of the Authors   291
Index   297

About the Series

The *Social Behavior and Natural Resources Series* is about human adaptation to natural resources and the constraints these resources place upon institutions and work and play in everyday life. Natural resources, after all, are products of society. The very definition of natural resources arises from the interaction of population, culture, and the biophysical environment.

Biological and physical scientists are providing us with a clearer picture of the nature of species and habitats and the requirements of systems to function under varying management regimes dedicated to conservation and preservation. Social scientists are providing complementary information about the human species, our habitat, and how social systems respond to a wide range of resource management policies.

The integration of social science with biological and physical science is the focus of this series. The present book is about the relationships of human communities to forest environments.

Resource management issues are human problems which can only be solved with social science knowledge in combination with knowledge from the other sciences. The utilization of these different types of knowledge within the resource management arena depends upon the establishment of a partnership between scientists and managers. Sound management requires agreement on what information is pertinent, how information should be collected, and how information should be employed in decision making.

Here the social sciences can help. Social scientists have a keen appreciation of the power, as well as the limitations, of science to resolve policy conflicts. This is important for understanding how managers filter the concerns of competing constituencies and their own professional cadre while managing the natural resources under their charge.

There are many applied science volumes in sociology, anthropology, and political science that deal with communities, but this volume is original in its exclusive attention to forest-dependent communities. *Community and Forestry: Continuities in the Sociology of Natural Resources* represents the beginning of a new branch of an old intellectual tradition in applied social science.

Foreword

With only the two exceptions of serving my country—in Korea and in Washington, D.C., as Secretary of the Interior—I have spent my life in the Pacific Northwest. This region contains expansive forests which are unparalleled in producing commercial forest products for housing and paper, outstanding water quality that supports anadromous and resident fish populations, and a vastness that allows for unconfined outdoor recreation for its citizens. The Pacific Northwest offers a life that we love and guard with care.

As a logger, businessman, and public official I have experienced the way of life in our forested communities from many standpoints. I have focused much of my career as a public official on issues related to our natural resource industries and the environment in which they operate. Citizens in our forest-based communities are concerned about the future of their communities, and I share their concern.

As Governor of Idaho, I concern myself daily with issues that affect the vitality and future of the forest-based communities in our state. The forest industry must deal with issues including wilderness, forest plans, log exports, and water quality, all of which affect communities in Idaho and the Pacific Northwest. Forest-based communities have additional concerns that a Governor tries to address: education, economic development, health care, and transportation. These community concerns are inextricably linked to the relationships these communities have with the surrounding forests and the timber industry.

Our forests in this region, and the communities which depend upon them for their economic support, are in transition. Other forested regions in the United States and in other countries have experienced the social and economic changes that come with exhaustion of the resources that were present when an area was settled. But the change in the Pacific Northwest is different. It comes at a time when technologies in forestry and manufacturing have advanced to a point that will allow the region to adapt to the changes in the resource base. Just as important, our view of the importance of communities in our forested regions has also evolved. The societal effects of boom and bust on single-industry towns are a public issue. No longer are we willing to accept the notion that a community and all its institutions are built and destroyed on the whim of an individual corporation.

This volume represents a cross section of current research on how communities in forested areas develop and change. Sociologists are continuing to better define communities, understand how they function, and arrive at ideas that assist communities in adapting to changing economic circumstances. The diversity of opinion and research on the topic of communities and forestry contained in this volume stands as a testimony to this important effort.

The publication of this book is timely. Questions of forestry technology will be resolved by science, either in the laboratory or on the ground. However, the questions society has to deal with, such as dependence on the forest products industry, community stability, and conflict over the preservation and utilization of natural resources, will be answered in the political arena.

These fundamental questions about communities are value judgments and as such have no easy answers. As a public official, I encourage maintaining stable, productive rural communities as a legitimate social and economic goal for the United States. I am convinced that most Americans do want employment opportunities to exist in smaller towns, and they do want the chance to pursue a rural lifestyle if they choose.

This book represents the first step in describing the importance of the relationship of forestry and its dependent communities. It will serve to move the debate to forward-looking solutions that will protect both the economic and social structure of our communities as well as the natural resources, timber, fish, wildlife, clean air and water, and recreation that are produced from our forests.

Governor Cecil D. Andrus
Boise, Idaho

Preface

The papers assembled in this volume represent a complex ecology of ideas. Four intellectual generations are represented among the authors. Walter Firey, Samuel P. Hays, and Harold F. Kaufman, among others, pioneered the development of independent studies of natural resources by social scientists. Their work inspired William R. Burch, Jr., Donald R. Field, and others to extend sociological studies to a wide variety of natural resource problems and issues. Several foresters were in turn drawn to sociological work, especially after Burch was appointed to the faculty in the Yale School of Forestry and Environmental Studies. While studying at Yale, Robert G. Lee was the first among an emerging generation of foresters to see the necessity for expanding forestry to encompass concerns with human social organization and values.

These concerns were passed along to students, including Margaret A. Shannon, when Lee was appointed to the forestry faculty at the University of California, Berkeley and later extended to Matthew S. Carroll, Robert M. Muth and Debra J. Salazar (who is applying political science within forestry) when Lee joined Field at the College of Forest Resources at the University of Washington. Burch also inspired Johannes H. Drielsma and Gary E. Machlis when they were forestry students at Yale, and, through Patrick West, now at the University of Michigan, influenced Dale J. Blahna. This network of ideas has in recent years grown horizontally to include, among many kindred spirits with concerns about forest-based communities, Louise Fortmann, Con H. Schallau, Patricia Marchak, Joseph A. Miller, Hisayoshi Mitsuda, Edward C. Weeks, and recent students including Paul F. Starrs and Andy Brunelle.

Development of a sociological focus within forestry has not been an easy task. As implied in many papers in this volume, forestry has been a resource-oriented profession and has only slowly come to see the necessity for including consideration of people in resource management decisions. Political conflict over the allocation and use of forest lands has in recent years forced both foresters and their critics to consider people when addressing resource issues.

Three leading forestry schools anticipated these issues and took the risk of incorporating sociological expertise on their faculties years before the profession felt the full force of social change. In 1968 the Yale School of Forestry and Environmental Studies, under the leadership of Dean Francois Mergen, appointed William R. Burch, Jr. In 1970 James S. Bethel, Dean of the College of Forest Resources at the University of Washington, attracted Donald R. Field along with the establishment of a National Park Service Cooperative Park Studies Unit. In 1978 Bethel and Field enticed Robert G. Lee to join the faculty to extend the sociological focus to studies of forest communities and forestry institutions. The School of Forestry and Conservation at the University of California, Berkeley, under the leadership of Dean John A. Zivnuska, had appointed Lee to the faculty in 1973 and continued this commitment to sociology with the appointment of Louise Fortmann.

The Berkeley and Yale commitments to sociology were inspired by Berkeley Professor Henry J. Vaux, who had served on the visiting committee for the Yale School of Forestry and urged broadening of its faculty beyond resource economics. In addition to promoting sociology in the leading forestry schools, Bethel and Vaux were successful in exercising national leadership that contributed to a widespread recognition of the need for all forestry institutions to incorporate broader social science capabilities. How ironic that a wood technologist and a forest economist would break hard ground in forestry institutions and plant the first seeds of sociology. But such was the genius of their academic leadership.

Others contributed significantly to this book. The Western Rural Development Center, located on the campus at Oregon State University, and the School of Forestry and Environmental Studies at Yale University have provided support for the preparation of this volume. The College of Forest Resources at the University of Washington generously made available its typing and editing services. These institutions foster research and policy analysis on the interaction of social and biological systems, including the interdependency of forests and human communities.

Jean Matthews of the National Park Service Cooperative Studies Unit at Oregon State University kindly edited early manuscripts. Outstanding service by the staff of the Institute of Forest Resources in the University of Washington College of Forest Resources transformed the manuscripts into camera-ready copy. Cecilia Paul skillfully edited the manuscripts and provided valuable advice on formatting. Margaret Lahde turned our scribbles into beautifully typed drafts. Bev Anderson advised on structure and formatting and, together with her successor, Mary Smith, assured responsive service of the highest quality. We are indebted to all these individuals for both the quality of their products and the pleasure of working with them.

Robert G. Lee
Donald R. Field
William R. Burch, Jr.

I

Overview

1

Introduction: Forestry, Community, and Sociology of Natural Resources

Robert G. Lee
College of Forest Resources
University of Washington

Donald R. Field
School of Natural Resources
College of Agriculture and Life Sciences
University of Wisconsin

William R. Burch, Jr.
School of Forestry and Environmental Studies
Yale University

The future of human communities in forested regions is a growing concern among politicians, social scientists, land managers, and most importantly, community members themselves. The rapid growth of a national economy primarily dependent on service-based industries has had dramatic effects on economic regions historically dependent on natural resource extraction and primary manufacturing. Logging, sawmilling, and other resource-dependent industries have declined in their relative contribution to local economies in all forested regions; and there has been absolute decline in these industries in most regions.

Yet many forested regions with declining extraction and/or manufacturing industries have also experienced economic and population growth associated with tourism, recreation, and retirement settlement. Small towns with attractive natural amenities and relatively easy access to metropolitan regions have often been rejuvenated by such service-based activity. After seventy years of population decline, many such rural settings have again become attractive residential environments (Bradley, 1984; Herbers, 1986). Such reverse migration startled demographers and brought social and cultural change to isolated communities (Bradshaw and Blakely, 1979). But these new residents also restimulated declining local economies with the income they received from pension funds, investments, other transfer payments (Salazar, Schallau, and Lee, 1986), and "footloose" businesses such as consulting and computer-assisted sales and management. Tourists and outdoor recreationists attracted by places with exceptional natural amenities have further diversified local economies. As a result, traditional images of the rural logging or sawmilling town seldom match reality. There is great variation among communities in forested regions.

The impact of a service-based economy on communities in forested regions is expressed in both temporal and spatial variation. Some places have grown quickly, with local businesses rejuvenated by service-based industries. Major investments in resort facilities can produce the most dramatic growth and can be quite disruptive to the lives of long-term residents. Other communities have declined either slowly, or suddenly, when sawmills closed or logging operations were terminated. It has been difficult to predict how and when a particular community might be affected; there are few stable patterns for making generalizations about forest-based communities.

This volume was assembled to address the need for a better understanding of recent changes in forest-based communities. Unprecedented patterns of growth and decline, together with the complexity of the social and economic processes causing these changes, require a broad description of communities and the changes affecting them. Traditional stereotypes of forestry and the human communities that depend on it will no longer suffice. The primary purpose of this volume is to represent a spectrum of changes affecting people in communities. We did not address policy alternatives for attempting to manage such changes. A subsequent volume will be devoted to policy issues and action strategies. Our present objective is limited to describing changes in communities and the economic activity upon which they have depended. We have given special attention to the need to define forestry and community, and to show how natural resources sociology can be used to study the linkage between forestry and community.

FORESTRY

In conventional discourse, forestry is generally assumed to involve the growing and harvesting of trees for commercial wood utilization. Many foresters committed to wood production above all other forest values have perpetuated this relatively narrow definition. Forestry is actually far broader, and the forestry community—including practicing foresters, forestry educators, and researchers—

must expand its concern to understand and articulate the multiple functions of forests. Forestry involves the management of forests and the land on which they grow to serve a wide variety of purposes. In addition to providing wood, forests serve society by providing water, forage, wildlife, fisheries, scenery, and opportunities for recreation. They are also an important source of oxygen and sink for atmospheric carbon. The land upon which forests grow may also serve society in a variety of ways. Subsurface deposits of minerals, oil, gas, and coal are important requisites for industrial activity, transportation, and residential energy consumption. Special designations of land for wilderness or other natural or cultural features serve a need for land areas unavailable for commodity production. Such "ceremonial" uses of forest lands are increasingly important social functions.

Although forestry connotes a concern with tree-covered lands classified as forested, the land management issues and management problems on other wildlands (nonurban and nonagricultural) are similar enough to be handled by forestry professionals. The management of wildlands is the primary focus for the training and education of foresters. Land managers are generally well prepared for biological, physical, and technical problems. They are less prepared to address social problems. Aside from economics, for which expertise is readily available if not part of a professional's repertoire, social science preparation for land managers is generally inadequate. Hence, the broader social consequences of land management decisions are generally not appreciated or understood.

The forestry community has paid little attention to the human resource upon which its activities depend. People who work in forestry organizations will have a substantial influence on the future of the profession and its capacity to adapt to changes in the multiple functions of forests. A wide spectrum of occupations is involved, ranging from people who harvest and transport wood to those who market final products, develop land use plans, and translate legal and political issues into management directions.

Diversification of the workforce, especially in federal agencies, will bring substantial changes in work routines, expectations, and values. The increasing numbers of women and ethnic minorities will prepare forestry organizations for meeting the challenges of the twenty-first century by reflecting the concerns and values of a diverse population. But a diversified work force will also change relationships between forestry organizations and small resource-dependent communities. People representing the larger society will bring a new face to local branches of forestry organizations. They will become agents for cultural transfusion in isolated rural communities, as well as serve to diversify forest land management.

Correspondingly, the people who are engaged in utilizing forest resources, and who may live adjacent to forests, shape the relations between forests and local communities. Yet we understand little about how local workers feel about forests, or how forests are important in sustaining local ways of life. Sustained yield has recently again become a potent symbol for local workers whose ways of life are threatened by reductions in wood supplies.

The many competing demands placed on forests have illustrated the futility of ignoring the human components of forest ecosystems. Communities are especially important forms of social organization within these broader ecosystems. The community is the vehicle by which human values are established, nurtured, and shared; it can help us define those values with respect to forests, and to understand them, both in harmony and discord. The subjects covered in this book provide a brief sketch of community that helps to define the social concerns involved in managing forest ecosystems.

COMMUNITY

A basic definition of community will help students and practicing professionals to understand how people are organized in relation to the utilization of land and its associated resources. A subsequent introduction to the sociology of natural resources will demonstrate how the linkage between natural resources and human society can be studied systematically. Land managers are somewhat familiar with economic approaches for analyzing forest-dependent communities (Machlis and Force, 1988; Schallau and Alston, 1987). They are relatively unfamiliar with sociological approaches.

Review of sociological definitions of community show that there have been three general approaches (Hillery, 1955). One definition is community as locality—a human settlement with a fixed and bounded local territory. This is the definition used by most economists who analyze local areas where people reside and work. However, it has limited sociological meaning, since there is no consideration of relationships among people or patterns of social interaction. While it suggests there is a relation between geographic location and social life, it does not elaborate on that relationship.

Another definition is community as a local social system involving inter-relationships among people living in the same geographic area. Attention is focused on the pattern of social relationships, but not on the content or qualities of these relationships. This definition goes beyond geographic location to attend to networks of interaction and interpersonal knowledge. It is not important whether there is harmony or conflict, loneliness or sharing; all that matters is that people interact in some predictable ways.

A third definition is community as a type of relationship, especially a sense of shared identity. This definition most closely matches the conventional wisdom in which the essence of community is a "feeling" or "spirit." A shared sense of identity does not require a geographic basis for social interaction. Members of such a community may be widely dispersed, as in the "environmental community," "forestry community," or "loggers' world." Moreover, people need not ever have met or interacted in order to belong to such a community. Some sociologists refer to community morale when talking about community as a sense of shared identity. Communities of "interest" or "affiliation" represent types of relationships.

Sociologist Kai Erikson (1986:9-10) touched upon territory and identity when he described community in terms of people who

> ...spend most of their lives in close contact with one another, sharing a common sphere of experience which makes them feel that they belong to a special "kind" and live in a special "place." In the formal language of sociology, this means that communities are boundary maintaining: each has a specific territory in the world as a whole, not only in the sense that it occupies a defined region of geographical space but also in the sense that it takes over a particular niche in what might be called cultural space and develops its own "ethos" or "way" within that compass. Both these dimensions of group space, the geographical and the cultural, set the community apart as a special place and provide an important point of reference for its members.

Erikson (1986:11) emphasized the central importance of social norms and networks of interactions for maintaining community boundaries—both geographical and cultural:

> Members of a community inform one another about the placement of their boundaries by participating in the confrontations which occur when persons who venture out to the edges of the group are met by policing agents whose special business is to guard the cultural integrity of the community.

Everything from criminal trials and excommunication hearings to gossip and shunning demonstrates "...where the line is drawn between behavior that belongs in the special universe of the group and behavior that does not" (p.11).

These three dimensions, although separated for purposes of analysis, are generally condensed into one global sense of community—especially when talking about rural settlements. People have often romanticized isolated rural settlements and assumed that locality, a local social system, and a sense of communion are unified in a rural community. The fact that these three dimensions may rarely coincide completely creates heterogeneity in the social life of both rural and urban settlements. Much of the above mentioned variation in contemporary forest-based communities could be captured by such social analysis. The persistence of a sense of identity as a "timber town" in a "bedroom" or tourism-dependent community is just one such example of how social relationships and community identity may fall out of phase.

Community, however defined, provides scholars and forest managers an opportunity to understand the direct linkage between humans and their natural environment. Community, in contrast to other forms of social organization focuses primarily upon social structure—the network of institutions providing order to human affairs. The knowledge of process and structure in sociobiological systems is critical to understanding the persistence and change of these institutions and ultimately the cultural fabric of community. It is a community's social structure that ebbs and flows with the resource cycle.

Harold Kaufman (1939) in his master's thesis titled "Social Factors in the Reforestation of the Missouri Ozarks" deserves credit for one of the first quantitative and systematic studies of values and attitudes toward forestry among residents of small rural communities. He discusses the problems of deforestation in the Ozarks and the barriers to reforestation. The barriers, according to Kaufman, reside in the culture and a conflict between old forest folkways (such as woods-burning practices, timber "scrapping" and livestock grazing) and forest conservation practices. His discussion of assimilation of reforestation practices documents the importance of social relationships and human attitudes as key determinants for new forestry practices to arise within a community. He suggests changes in forestry practices will be best promoted by an understanding of the human process of adoption and diffusion of new knowledge among residents of communities.

Paul Landis (1938) in *Three Iron Mining Towns* provided what is perhaps the earliest comprehensive examination of the process of resource extraction in relation to community social structure and change. Landis' work traces the discovery, exploration, establishment, and development of iron-ore production in the Mesabi Range, Minnesota. At each phase of resource extraction, Landis discusses the nature and kind of human population present and the community institutions formed—economy, government, education, religion, and family. He further documents change in such institutions during different periods of ore production, and suggests that changes in the structure of community are directly related to each stage of resource extraction.

Forest-based resource communities follow a similar pattern of community formation, establishment, and contraction during phases of forest exploitation. Social and biological cycles interact. Technological changes in timber production, including new silvicultural practices, cropping systems, computer assisted logging, and robotics in sawmilling, are transforming an industry and the community institutions that support it.

The chapters presented here provide a picture of forest communities in transition. Most focus on a period of the industry's restructuring during the late 1970s and early 1980s, but a picture of community in its broadest sense is portrayed. For example, migration of people out of a community following the loss of forest products employment affects the age structure of a community. Young people, including the emerging leadership cadre that sustains local institutions are often lost, draining talent from government and civic organizations. The mobile community of independent loggers migrate from place to place as logging locations shift. The loggers' community takes on new dimensions as it widens its geographic area. These increasingly dispersed communities of shared identity can provide institutions that their members rely on to voice opinions and gather community consensus regarding natural resource issues. But if community institutions are in flux and leadership is mute or missing, a community position may be nonexistent and resource development strategies hard, if not impossible, to define.

Communities are the basis for the social order of human populations. Human attitudes and values are vested within community and definitions of resources emerge from community. A central thesis of this volume is that an understanding of community enhances the development and implementation of natural resource policy. These articles provide a snapshot of different views or perspectives of community interaction with forest ecosystems.

SOCIOLOGY OF NATURAL RESOURCES

Previous work on forest-dependent communities has seldom drawn upon accumulated knowledge in rural sociology—especially its subdiscipline of resources sociology. Rural sociologists have long been studying rural communities dependent on agriculture and ranching (Field and Burch, 1988). Natural resource sociologists interested in forestry have provided an essential body of knowledge on forest systems since 1964. They have sought to understand the adaptative strategies people use as they harvest forests, live within and adjacent to forests, and recreate upon lands set aside as forest resources. Such scholars have studied behavioral dimensions of human-caused fires, forestry/agriculture connections, wildland recreation, and associated issues of carrying capacity, including volume and patterns of use and recreation lifestyles. Underlying all such studies, however, is a recognition that forests are social as well as biological systems. Many of the authors in this volume draw upon this stock of knowledge to address problems of forest-based communities. To link this volume to the older sociological traditions in rural community and natural resources studies, we have reprinted two papers.

The first is Walter Firey's unusually insightful review paper entitled "Some Contributions of Sociology to the Study of Natural Resources." Firey discusses fifty years of studies on the interactions of people and natural resources and notes persistent themes that have gone relatively unrecognized by generations of researchers. Since these themes are reflected in many of the papers contained in this volume, we have placed this paper in the beginning section. Firey identified the following sources of unity in a wide variety of studies: (1) a sociological view of natural resources as a whole that encompasses both physical and sociocultural phenomena, (2) a conceptual framework in which either physical or sociocultural phenomena can be treated as independent variables, and (3) congruence between the concept of a "resource system" and the concept of "social system" that has been systematically examined by sociologists.

The second paper in Section I is a condensed version of Harold and Lois Kaufman's 1946 report on two forest-dependent communities in Montana: "Toward the Stabilization and Enrichment of a Forest Community." This is an especially noteworthy report, since it was the first empirical study of a forest-dependent community by a rural sociologist. We prefaced the report with an editor's preface and segments from an exchange of letters between the Assistant Regional Forester for the study area and the study's principal investigator to illustrate the sensitivity and novelty of the sociological approach to community within the forestry profession. Although limited in scholarly presentation, most of the insights and recommendations in the report are as valid today as they were in 1945. Especially noteworthy in light of contemporary conflicts between residential use and forest management is the Kaufmans' concern with dispersion of rural settlement patterns. Equally important is the balanced emphasis given to economic conditions, participation, and community pride as contrasted with exclusive reliance on material factors such as wood supply and jobs.

A third theme-setting paper was included in Section I to describe the historical context of contemporary forest-based communities. Samuel P. Hays', "Human Choice in the Great Lakes Wildlands," has in a few pages captured the patterns of historical change affecting forest-based communities in most of the United States. He chronicles how consumption patterns shifted from an emphasis on material supply to conveniences, and then in recent years to amenities. The choices people make about forests and their management is influenced by the perception and meanings associated with these consumption patterns. Hays ends his paper with a discussion of how communities are affected by these changes in the way humans value forests.

Themes developed in these three lead chapters are reflected in the original contributions to follow. Section II contains a collection of papers describing how communities have been affected by changes in the wood products industries. Economic and technological change in wood products extraction and manufacturing are given special attention. Instability in the wood products industry has had a pronounced influence on community welfare in many rural towns—especially in the western United States, Alaska, the Lake States and Maine, as well as in Canada, Japan, and other industrialized nations with vast supplies of wood resources.

The linkage between community stability and sustained yield wood production is examined from a social history viewpoint by Drielsma, Miller, and Burch. They identify the importance of replacing the idealistic commitment to a sustained yield doctrine with understanding of the realities of community life and the practical measures for improving community welfare. Schallau uses an economic perspective to examine the same topic. He finds similar faults in adherence to sustained yield and suggests how an understanding of economic processes could help managers regulate wood harvests to better serve economic interests of local communities. Lee's discussion challenges the economist's interpretation of sustained yield as a product of stable, isolated communities in feudal Europe. He argues that sustained yield was adopted following periods of rural community instability which suggests that it has been used as an instrument for restoring stability rather than as a vestige of feudal economic organization. As a result, its functions in stabilizing communities dependent on forests for products and services other than wood deserve greater attention.

Changes in the structure of the wood products industries are examined in the next two papers. Marchak describes how isolated communities in British Columbia have been affected by large corporations. She emphasizes that temporary and unstable communities are found in remote logging and sawmilling settlements. As was common early in the century, establishment of permanent communities remains uncertain when large corporations with absentee ownership control local investment decisions. Brunelle comes to similar conclusions about the recent instability of local investments by large corporations, but notes that significant shifts toward ownership by regional and local firms could bring greater employment stability. His structural analysis of sawmilling and plywood plants reveals that disinvestment by large national corporations has been followed by a more flexible and aggressive set of investors.

The effects of plant closures and sustained unemployment on communities are examined by the final two papers in Section II. Weeks looks at the local social impacts of plant closures in rural Oregon towns and notes significant disruptions in community life and changes in population structure that reduce community viability as younger people leave. This parallels subsequent observations Mitsuda makes in his analysis of declining Japanese communities. Carroll and Lee examine loggers and describe how the social organization of logging conforms to patterns of community defined by occupational identifications. They identify difficulties loggers face in shifting to other jobs when embedded in social relationships and identifications defined by logging culture. The emphasis on problems of maintaining community boundaries anticipates Section III.

Section III contains papers focusing on the interaction of forests and communities in an increasingly service-based society. The first three selections discuss changes in forest-based communities that accompanied decline in wood utilization and increased settlement by urban migrants. Blahna looks at patterns of social conflict between new migrants and traditional locals. He finds that cleavage lines do not conform to the conventional view that newcomers and locals are on opposite sides of community boundaries. Newcomers can quickly assume significant leadership roles in mobilizing a community against an externally induced change such as timber harvesting by a federal or state agency. Fortmann and Starrs observe similar patterns in conflicts between locals and outside interests seeking to develop wood-fired power plants. Urban migrants are especially adept in articulating the claims of locals to firewood resources and environmental quality. Mitsuda compares declining and rejuvenating charcoal-producing villages in Japan in discussing processes of community disorganization and reorganization. He suggests that urban migrants play a significant role in the reorganization of declining mountain villages. His work indicates significant cross-cultural similarities in the processes of rural community adjustment to the emergence of service-based economies.

Muth's study of subsistence use as a persistent social structure in southeast Alaska demonstrates the stabilizing influence of local institutions. Unlike areas subject to resettlement through reverse migration, southeast Alaska has been exploited by outsiders for its fur, fish, timber, and oil. Subsistence on fish, game, and fruits has remained a predictable source of support for locals following the collapse of each of these boom and bust industries. Muth's work reinforces the importance of conserving local knowledge and opportunities for resource utilization in other regions subject to unstable resource extraction cycles.

The final two papers in Section III emphasize the increasing importance of forests to people living in dispersed locations. Communities defined by shared interests in special places or even large tracts of forest land play an increasing role in forest planning and management. Unlike traditional local communities where the geographic boundaries of residential settlement delimited community, a common concern with particular areas of forest provide boundaries for community of affiliation based on common interests; patterns of social interaction and a shared "ethos" or "way of life" obtain for both residentially-based and interest-based communities.

Shannon explores the way in which U.S. Forest Service planning has facilitated informal agreements between national forests and both local residential communities and communities defined by affiliated interests in forest land. Salazar examines how communities defined by shared interests participated in formulating forest practices regulation on private lands. She uses counties as community units and shows that counties with an economic stake in timber production will not seek local forest practices regulations adverse to the interests of private landowners. In contrast, counties where timber production is of lesser importance will respond to broader environmental protection interests and seek to impose stricter regulations.

The volume concludes with a review of the issues associated with future research on forest-dependent communities. Machlis and Force's chapter discusses research on timber-dependent communities. A concluding chapter by the editors of this volume suggests how greater attention to spatial and temporal scales can help advance the accumulation of knowledge about the interaction of communities and their biophysical environments.

CONCLUSION

Some of the papers in this volume contradict one another on important factual issues. One of the most obvious contradictions involves the issue of whether large companies with substantial assets and branches are more stable sources of economic support than smaller, less well-endowed firms. There are also important differences over how communities are affected by external and internal conditions. We could have used editorial license to eliminate these differences. But to have done so would have been to cloud the existing state of knowledge with an aura of agreement that does not exist. We have left the reader with the task of assessing the relative validity or plausibility of contradictory factual claims and perspectives. Such is the actual state of the art in research on forest-dependent communities.

We have, however, provided the reader with unifying themes that cut across all selections. A sociological perspective on natural resources and a focus on community as a special problem in forested regions focus attention on common approaches and concerns. Hopefully this volume will help set the stage for more rapid advancement of social scientific knowledge about forest-dependent communities. A more complete understanding of the nature and functions of communities is a necessary step toward future policy analysis and prescription.

REFERENCES

Bradley, G.A. (ed.). 1984. *Land Use and Forest Resources in a Changing Environment*. Seattle, WA: University of Washington Press.

Bradshaw, T. and E. Blakely. 1979. *Rural Communities in Advanced Industrial Societies*. New York: Praeger.

Erikson, K.T. 1986. *Wayward Puritans: A Study in the Sociology of Deviance*. New York: McMillan.

Field, D.R. and W.R. Burch, Jr. 1988. *Rural Sociology and the Environment*. New York: Greenwood Press.

Herbers, J. 1986. *The New Heartland*. New York: Times Books.

Hillery, G.A. 1955. "Definition of a Community—Areas of Agreement." *Rural Sociology* 20 (Jan.):11-23.

Kaufman, H. 1939. "Social Factors in the Reforestation of the Missouri Ozarks." M.A. Thesis, University of Missouri, Columbia.

Landis, P. 1938. *Three Iron Mining Towns: A Study in Cultural Change*. Ann Arbor, Michigan: Edwards Brothers.

Machlis, G.E. and J.E. Force. 1988. "Community Stability and Timber-Dependent Communities." *Rural Sociology* 53 (2):220-234.

Salazar, D.J., C.H. Schallau, and R.G. Lee. 1986. *The Growing Importance of Retirement Income in Timber-Dependent Areas*. Portland, OR: USDA Forest Service PNW 359.

Schallau, C.H. and R.M. Alston. 1987. "The Commitment to Community Stability: A Policy or Shibboleth?" *Environmental Law* 17: 429-481.

2

Some Contributions of Sociology to the Study of Natural Resources

Walter Firey
Professor Emeritus
University of Texas

Some continuities in research appear only in retrospect. Even then, our perception of them may indicate little more than a wish to see present achievements "anticipated" in the past. Yet such after-the-fact continuity may serve a purpose. As a source of intellectual identity it can figure in the motivation of scientific researchers. It may, in this way, fulfill itself as a genuine continuity; issuing in a cumulative fund of scientific knowledge it can serve as a polestar for research endeavors (Merton, 1957: Introduction).

A case in point is the sociology of natural resources. This is an area of research in which a number of substantial scientific contributions have been recorded; yet it is an area that remains notably devoid of self-conscious continuity. In the present paper it is proposed, first, to survey some of the contributions sociologists have made to the study of natural resources; second, to try to determine why sociologists have not been more self-conscious about these contributions; and finally, to suggest a frame of reference within which sociologists can study natural resources more conscious of and confident in the continuity of their research.

THE CONTEXT OF REGIONAL ANALYSIS

The first explicit interest in natural resources as an area of sociological research seems to have arisen in the context of regional analysis—an association that has continued to the present time. In 1926 Radhakamal Mukerjee published *Regional Sociology*, where he develops the proposition that "the role of man on the surface of the earth is placed in the organic setting of great harmonic vegetable or animal aggregations which have arrived at a more or less stable equilibrium" (Mukerjee, 1926:vi). The holistic viewpoint Mukerjee formulates has since come to pervade nearly all the work sociologists have done on natural resources. From this perspective natural resources can be recognized as components of an "entire circle of man's life and well-being" (p. 231). Human adaptations include control, increased utilization, and extension of the environment. This "entire circle," for its part, is predicated upon "securing a more or less stable equilibrium of the whole living world" (p. 33).

In a noteworthy series of subsequent investigations Mukerjee extended his holistic perspective into both practical and theoretical directions. In *The Changing Face of Bengal*, published in 1938, he notes that "Cooperation in the conservation of land, in the use of water, in forest management, in the training and management of rivers, and, finally, in the reciprocal relations of village and city must be the keynote of the future" (Mukerjee, 1938a:17). In another volume, *Food Planning for Four Hundred Millions*, published in the same year, Mukerjee addresses himself to the specific problem of food supply within an evolving context of "Malthusian checks," "food standards and food values," "crop planning and nutrition," "industrial crops and rural industrialization," and "new social attitudes" (Mukerjee, 1938b:xvii). *Man and His Habitation*, first published in 1938, continues Mukerjee's emphasis on "the total situation standpoint in which man's conscious strivings, aspirations, and ideals mingle silently with the ecological forces and processes" (Mukerjee, 1968:preface). More recently, in *The Dimensions of Human Evolution*, published in 1963, Mukerjee observes that "The notions of wholeness, solidarity or symbiosis as applied to the vast harmonious ecological communities have, indeed, great practical significance for the stability and continuity of human civilization" (Mukerjee, 1963:295).

At the same time that Mukerjee was initiating his regionally-oriented studies of natural resources, Rupert Vance published in 1929 *Human Factors in Cotton Culture*, giving it the subtitle "A Study in the Social Geography of the American South." The parallel in viewpoints between the two sociologists, writing in the contexts of two different cultural traditions, is noteworthy. Speaking of "the cotton culture complex," Vance characterizes it as a "whole that is so closely interconnected that no one can suggest any place at which it may be attacked" (Vance, 1929:295). This whole possesses "a kind of natural harmony" (p. 295) which partakes, not only of the soil, the seasons, the sunshine and rain, but of mules, supply merchants, tenant farmers, and spinners. Associated with it, too, are some characteristic attitudes—a speculative outlook, an irrational commitment to the single crop, a thriftlessness, and a lack of feeling for the land.

THE HOLISTIC VIEW OF NATURAL RESOURCES

The holistic viewpoint, independently formulated by Mukerjee and Vance, according to which natural resources can be seen, not only as attributes of the physical environment, but as attributes of the social and cultural order as well, has been characteristic of the approach sociologists have since developed in their study of natural resources. And yet this viewpoint has all too often remained an implicit rather than an explicit one, an *ad hoc* rather than a generalized concept. For this very reason it has failed to exhibit the continuity that sociological research on natural resources must have if it is to develop a cumulative character.

Vance's continued interest in natural resources is apparent in much of his subsequent work. In *All These People*, published in 1945, he reiterates his conception of the dual origin of natural resources, according to which resources partake of both physical and cultural attributes. He argues that, "what people want and need thus determine what portions of their physical environment they will develop and what they will leave untouched" (Vance, 1945:480). He asserts too that *laissez-faire* and conservation are incompatible objectives—that public policy must figure in the planned use of natural resources (p. 482-486). Vance's colleague and mentor, Howard T. Odum, developed a very similar conception of natural resources. Speaking of the different types of "wealth" in the American South, Odum notes that that region excels in some resources but is deficient in others. This faulty "balance," as he puts it, (Odum, 1936:51) should be the focus of regional planning endeavors, inasmuch as "the measure of the region's ultimate wealth must be found in a working balance between nature's endowment and its use " (p. 23).

The dynamic implications of a holistic conception of natural resources were early seen by Carle C. Zimmerman, and they comprise one of the many seminal themes that have characterized his series of investigations on community and regional organization. As early as 1936, in *Consumption and Standards of Living*, Zimmerman notes that a people's standard of living is not solely a function of their physical resources or their industrial techniques but is a function too of their mode of family life. He then makes the observation that "Man is a vain and careless animal, and often tends to create the very structures which destroy him " (Zimmerman, 1936:212). The full import of this insight for our understanding of the dynamics of resource practices was to become evident in Zimmerman's later studies.

In *The Changing Community*, published in 1938, Zimmerman develops the thesis that different communities may have different "personalities" or "life organizations" (Zimmerman, 1938:1-2) and that these "immanent" characteristics can determine the responses which communities will make to external or "transient" circumstances. Thus the decline of whaling in one New England community is related to the atrophy of traditional Quaker values in the face of economic affluence, and to an attendant inability on the part of the community to meet new competitive developments " (p. 382 ff). The implications of this holistic perspective are further developed in the proposition that only "realistic" (contra "nominalistic") communities are capable of the "longer-time perspective," which is presupposed in planning over long periods of time" (p. 154).

In *Outline of Cultural Rural Sociology*, published in 1948, Zimmerman applies to the national and supranational level the holistic perspective that had been so fruitful in his community studies. Here he traces a dialectical succession, following the American Civil War, from a "system of international capitalism in agrarian food products," (Zimmerman, 1948:27-28) to a politically grounded, monopolistic, and bureaucratized agrarian system (p. 34-37). During the course of this dialectical succession, Zimmerman notes, there has been a widespread dislocation in the "balance of nature" attended by soil erosion, forest depletion, and an impoverishment of the rural population (p. 37). Looking to the future, Zimmerman suggests, in an idiom that is reminiscent of his early 1936 warning, that "Unless we perish from this earth a conservation system will be the next step " (p. 39).

Meanwhile, the same holistic point of view was being applied to the regional level of analysis, first in *Outline of American Regional Sociology*, published in 1947, and then, in collaboration with Richard E. DuWors, in *Graphic Regional Sociology*, published in 1952. In the latter work regions are conceived as real "geosocial entities," each comprised of a distinctive character that is at once geographic and psychosocial (Zimmerman and DuWors, 1952:138-139). Zimmerman and DuWors see submarginality, for instance, not as an inherent attribute of particular geographic areas, but rather as evidence of a mismatching between actual and potential resource uses (p. 11).

PERSPECTIVES ON THE SOCIOLOGY OF NATURAL RESOURCES

Another early sociological study of natural resources is Paul H. Landis' *Three Iron Mining Towns*, published in 1938. Landis' focus is the rise and fall of a population and its institutions as a corollary to the development and depletion of iron resources in northern Minnesota. The similarity of Landis' viewpoint to that of Mukerjee, Vance, and Zimmerman is apparent in his statement, "The various natural resources of the Mesabi have taken on meaning to resident groups only as their culture patterns have been able to utilize them " (Landis, 1938:17). But Landis also finds it helpful to take resources, once they have been constituted by the culture pattern, as a given—as an independent variable, so to speak. Much of his study is devoted to an analysis of synchronous cycles in the rise and fall of a mining area. Population growth, vital rates, folkways and mores, institutional structure, and organizational characteristics are all taken as dependent variables with respect to successive stages in the development and depletion of iron resources. Landis' study is valuable in showing the methodological legitimacy of varying dependent and independent variables, as between the physical environment and the culture pattern, according to the purposes of a given analysis.

In 1944, J. L. Hypes published his paper, "The Social Implications of Social Erosion." Its theme is stated in these words: "soil erosion and human erosion are so closely associated that neither can be studied adequately without the other," (p. 375) and "each, if extended, tends to produce the other " (p.364). Hypes proceeds to show the complex causal relationships between soil erosion, on the one hand, and taxation policy, land settlement policy, farm credit, land ownership, attitudes of farmers toward the land, and living standards on the other hand (p. 365). Hypes' treatment, while more descriptive than analytical, does emphasize the fact that a workable program of soil conservation must include human as well as physical factors.

Another perspective on natural resources is afforded by the work of Harold F. Kaufman, first in his monograph *Toward the Stabilization and Enrichment of a Forest Community* (Kaufman and Kaufman, 1946) and then in his paper, "Sociology of Forestry (Kaufman, 1953). Kaufman takes as his main reference point the norm of "stability," defining it as a process of orderly change. He goes on to consider some of the positive and negative factors which condition this hypothetical state of affairs in an area of depleted timber resources. Kaufman, like Mukerjee, Vance, and Zimmerman, seeks to identify what the uniquely sociological contribution might be to such research. He finds it in the study of "the processes by which social order is developed and maintained " (p. 113). Concepts such as "group," "social organization," "social control," "values" and "culture" are prominent in his analysis. For example, says Kaufman, to a sociologist "The forest economy is seen as a part of the total culture " (p. 114).

In 1947, Howard W. Beers and Catharine P. Heflin published *People and Resources in Eastern Kentucky*. In this study the authors address themselves to the task of determining some of the sociological factors involved in the use of resources in an isolated, submarginal agricultural area. They pose this question: "Could improved agriculture or revived forestry become effective means of economic restoration? What, if any, are the sociological foundations of conservation in the area (p. 5)? They then proceed to investigate "folkways in the use of land, ... and the climate of local opinion concerning the utilization of resources " (p. 6). On the basis of responses to a schedule administered to a sample of households in one county, Beers and Heflin find a prevailing "complacency" in people's attitudes toward their declining resource base, combined with a pessimism concerning the future of the area, an uncertainty in personal plans for the future, and a lack of effective local leadership (pp. 36-48). They conclude that tradition, the pressure of subsistence, and the lack of experience in planning, all stand in the way of the adoption of better resource practices (p. 55).

A somewhat more abstract approach to the sociology of natural resources is found in a paper by Nathan L. Whetten (1948), entitled "Sociology and the Conservation of Renewable Natural Resources." Whetten begins by observing that "Many conservation practices do not benefit the individual owners of renewable resources, yet are of vital importance to society as a whole" (p. 313). How, then, are such practices, which are so contrary to private self-interest, ever to be built into the social order? According to Whetten, the problem is one of social control. "The task is one of getting conservation beliefs and practices incorporated into the folkways and mores so that legislation and governmental policies will be reinforced by the more or less automatic controls of the local communities" (p. 312). Once conservation becomes a part of the mores of a population, "The whole range of persuasive social controls—reward, blame, derision, suggestion, praise, recognition, imitation and response—will be brought to bear on the recalcitrant individual. The power of this kind of social pressure is not to be underestimated" (pp. 313-314). For Whetten, then, conservation is a type of resource use which can only be understood by reference to some normative attributes of the social order.

That conservation practices can indeed conflict with the self-interest of resource users and may require social control for their implementation is evidenced in the findings of Edward O. Moe (1952), as reported in his monograph *New York Farmers' Opinions on Agricultural Policies and Programs*, and those of John C. Frey (1952), as reported in his study, *Some Obstacles to Soil Erosion Control in Western Iowa*. Moe finds, in a sample survey of New York farmers, that while nearly four-fifths of his respondents favored conservation planning, less than two-fifths of them practiced it. Frey, too, notes a wide discrepancy between belief in soil conservation and erosion control among west Iowa farmers and actual participation by those farmers in recommended erosion control measures.

The use of natural resources, of course, is related to their ownership, as well as to collateral economic rights and duties involved in their exploitation. In a 1948 study of the fisheries industry of the North Atlantic, entitled "Custom and Contract: A Functional Analysis of the Wage System in the Atlantic Fisheries," Richard E. DuWors examined the ambiguities that attach to ownership of fish both before they are caught and, more particularly, after they have been brought on board the fishing boat. Does ownership vest in the fisherman, in the captain of the boat, or in the owners of the boat? In an analysis of the complex kinship, employment, and property norms governing the Atlantic fisheries, DuWors observes that: "These fisheries...may serve as focal points to study existing and defunct value systems—codes, definitions of rights and duties, roles and statuses, etc." (DuWors, 1948:55). Resources, then, constitute a strategic point of departure for the study of "the rights and duties which 'inhere' in a functional analysis of roles related to the ends of economic activity" (p. 55).

A practical perspective on the sociology of natural resources is afforded by Charles E. Lively and Jack J. Preiss, in their book, *Conservation Education in American Colleges*, published in 1957. Lively and Preiss emphasize that an effective program of conservation "must become an integral part of the acquired personality pattern, a characteristic of the fundamental culture" (p.29). This is true because resources are "a joint function of the environment and of the sociocultural level of the people " (p. 227). Lively and Priess do not view conservation as a type of resource use in which only minimum inventories are maintained against depletion or until scientific discoveries produce a substitute. Rather, they take a dynamic view of resource conservation, in which the definitions of what constitutes a resource may change over time in response to technological advancement and emerging values.

In a number of earlier papers Lively emphasized the difficulties placed in the way of conservation by the existing social order. He finds these difficulties to stem, above all, from "a sociocultural environment that is at best neutral, and at its worst openly antagonistic to the idea of saving resources" (Lively, 1953:5). In another paper, "Some Social Aspects of Forest Conservation," Lively elaborates this thesis with respect to forest resources. He begins by noting that forestry involves a "a series of problems in human relations" (Lively, 1951:1). Forest fires, for example, are "...part of [a] historic cultural complex and cannot be fully understood apart from it" (p. 4). Because forestry practices so intricately implicate the whole social order, it is necessary that remedial measures go beyond simple police methods, particularly where such methods run counter to the mores of a population (pp. 4-5). Two of Lively's most interesting suggestions are that (1) on the research side, sociologists should develop a typology of population subgroups that will classify groups according to the degree of their involvement with a given natural resource, such as forests (p. 6), and (2) on the action side, conservation agencies ought to adopt some of "the methods of group and community organization in working with their constituent publics" (p. 12).

The usefulness for practical conservation programs of joining together systematic sociological theory with sophisticated research methodology is evident in recent studies (Jones, Taylor, and Bertrand, 1965; South, Hansbrough, and Bertrand 1965; and Folkman n.d.). Jones, Taylor, and Bertrand inquire into the "personal-social characteristics" of residents of a national forest in America, relating these to educational endeavors of the U. S. Forest Service, on the one hand, and to an "open range" cultural pattern, on the other hand. They find that, despite the open range ideology, according to which "anyone has customary 'rights' to range or graze livestock that is not fenced" (p. 9), including the right to set fire in order to obtain good grass, there has been, over a period of twenty years, a marked improvement in forest residents' attitudes and practices regarding forest management (pp. 27-28). Attitudes supportive of the U.S. Forest Service were found to be associated with people's educational status, their knowledge of the forestry program, their knowledge of the consequences of human-caused forest fires, and their estimate of the status of the forest ranger. South, Hansbrough, and Bertrand find a significant difference in forest woodland owners between "adopters" and "nonadopters" of recommended forest practices, relating this difference to certain familial, educational, occupational, and status characteristics. Folkman, too, is able to identify distinct "groups of people representing different degrees of risk from a fire prevention standpoint" (p. 1), and relates these differences to a number of socioeconomic variables, including adequacy of knowledge of, and attitudes toward, the use and abuse of fire in woodland areas.

In recent years the proposal has been advanced that natural resources be made a central focus of human ecology. Jack P. Gibbs and Walter T. Martin (1958) in their paper, "Urbanization and Natural Resources," observe that the "organization of effort to convert natural resources into objects of consumption is a critically important part of organized human effort, and, as such, is a legitimate and important area of sociological analysis" (p. 267). Ecology, according to Gibbs and Martin, can profitably be viewed as "the study of sustenance organization" (p. 267). In their analysis Gibbs and Martin find it useful to take the distribution of natural resources as an independent variable and to see how the size and location of cities vary with respect to the dispersal or concentration of natural resources (p. 270). On the basis of appropriate measures of independent and dependent variables they are able to confirm an important theory concerning the role of cities in a population's sustenance organization.

THE CONTRIBUTIONS OF SOCIOLOGY

In a survey of the contributions sociologists have made to the study of natural resources three facts are striking: (1) the very substantial magnitude of these contributions, considered both from a theoretical and practical point of view; (2) the apparent lack of self-consciousness on the part of sociologists of the true magnitude of their own contributions; and (3) the merely *ex post facto* continuity, which these contributions seem to possess. It is reasonable to suppose that sociological research on natural resources will achieve a fuller recognition when it acquires more self-consciousness and more genuine continuity in its research efforts.

Continuity, of course, presupposes that the findings of different studies have some kind of unity. It requires that similar facts be given similar names. All this, of course, is a matter of conceptual formulation. It would appear that there is a consistent conceptual formulation implicit in the studies reported above. It is a formulation that needs only to be made explicit. At its center is the sociological view of natural resources as a whole, which partakes of both the physical and the cultural. When Mukerjee speaks of the "entire circle of man's life and well-being," he is placing into a single system such diverse factors as social organization, flora, fauna, fertility, climate, and topography. When Vance refers to "the cotton system" he has in mind "a complex whole" partaking of certain attributes of the physical environment—chemical, climatic, and genetic—and of certain attributes of the sociocultural order—structural, attitudinal, and organizational. When Odum speaks of "balance," Zimmerman of "*real* communities," Landis of "patterns," Kaufman of "stability," and Gibbs and Martin of "sustenance organization," there is implied some reference to a *system* whose components are not exclusively physical nor exclusively social or cultural. In these expressions there is a dual reference to two orders of phenomena, both of which have been articulated into a single conceptual construct.

This concept of a resource system has two features which should particularly recommend it as a point of departure for further sociological research on natural resources. First, it is congruent with a great deal of important work that is being done in systematic sociological theory, centering around the concept of "social system." Second, it is noncommittal as to the mode of formulating causal relationships among the variables that enter into a resource system. In other words, either physical or sociocultural variables can be taken as independent, so that, with appropriate measures of both, a wide variety of hypotheses can be formulated and tested.

With interest in natural resources presently on the rise, particularly in the self-transforming countries of the world, it should be a singularly appropriate time for sociologists to become conscious of their own past achievements in this field and, by reaching some agreement on basic terms, to reap the benefits that will come with a continuity of research.

ACKNOWLEDGEMENTS

Adapted from a paper by the same title in M. Barnabas, S. K. Hulbe, and P. S. Jacob (eds.). 1978. *Challenges to Societies in Transition.* Delhi, India: Macmillan Company.

REFERENCES

Beers, H. W. and C. P. Heflin. 1947. *People and Resources in Eastern Kentucky.* Kentucky Agricultural Experiment Station Bulletin 500.

DuWors, R. E. 1948. "Custom and Contract: A Functional Analysis of the Wage System in the Atlantic Fisheries." *American Sociological Review* 13:55-61.

Folkman, W. S. [n.d.]. *Residents of Butte County, California: Their Knowledge and Attitudes Regarding Forest Fire Prevention.* Berkeley, CA: Pacific Southwest Forest and Range Experiment Station. USDA Forest Service Research Paper PSW-25.

Frey, J. C. 1952. *Some Obstacles to Soil Erosion Control in Western Iowa.* Iowa Agricultural Experiment Station Research Bulletin 391.

Gibbs, J. P. and W. T. Martin. 1958. "Urbanization and Natural Resources." *American Sociological Review* 23 (June):266-277.

Hypes, J. L. 1944. "The Social Implications of Soil Erosion." *Rural Sociology* 9:364-376.

Jones, A. R., M. L. Taylor, and A. L. Bertrand. 1965. *Some Human Factors in Woods Burning.* Louisiana Agricultural Experiment Station Bulletin 601.

Kaufman, H. F. 1953. "Sociology of Forestry". In W. A. Duerr and H. J. Vaux (eds.), *Research in the Economics of Forestry.* Washington, DC: The Charles Lathrop Pack Forest Foundation.

Kaufman, H. F. and L. C. Kaufman. 1946. *Toward the Stabilization and Enrichment of a Forest Community.* Missoula, MT.

Landis, P. H. 1938. *Three Iron Mining Towns: A Study in Cultural Change.* Ann Arbor, MI: Edwards Bros.

Lively, C. E. 1951. "Some Social Aspects of Forest Conservation". Missouri Agricultural Experiment Station Circular 359.

——. 1953. "Some Reflections on the Conservation Movement". Washington, DC: Offprint of address before the Eighteenth North American Wildlife Conference and Related Meetings, 9 March.

Lively, C. E. and J. J. Preiss. 1957. *Conservation Education in American Colleges.* New York: Ronald Press Co.

Merton, R. K. 1957. *Social Theory and Social Structure,* Revised Edition. New York: The Free Press.

Moe, E. O. 1952. *New York Farmers' Opinion on Agricultural Policies*. Cornell Agricultural Experiment Station Extension Bulletin 864.

Mukerjee, R. 1926. *Regional Sociology*. New York: The Century Co.

———. 1938a. *The Changing Face of Bengal*. Calcutta: University of Calcutta.

———. 1938b. *Food Planning for Four Hundred Millions*. London: Macmillan.

———. 1963. *The Dimensions of Human Evolution*. London: Macmillan.

———. 1968. *Man and His Habitation*, Second Edition. Bombay: Prakashan.

Odum, H. T. 1936. *Southern Regions of the United States*. Chapel Hill, NC: University of North Carolina Press.

South, D. R., T. Hansbrough, and A. L. Bertrand. 1965. *Factors Related to the Adoption of Woodland Management Practices*. Louisiana Agricultural Experiment Station Bulletin 603.

Vance, R. B. 1929. *Human Factors in Cotton Culture*. Chapel Hill, NC: University of North Carolina Press.

———. 1945. *All These People*. Chapel Hill, NC: University of North Carolina Press.

Whetten, N. L. 1948. "Sociology and the Conservation of Renewable Natural Resources." *Proceedings of the Inter-American Conference on Conservation of Renewable Natural Resources*. Washington, DC: U.S. Department of State, Publication 3382.

Zimmerman, C. C. 1936. *Consumption and Standards of Living*. New York: D. Van Nostrand Co., Inc.

———. 1938. *The Changing Community*. New York: Harper and Bros.

———. 1948. *Outline of Cultural Rural Sociology*. Cambridge: Phillips Book Store.

Zimmerman, C. C. and R. E. DuWors. 1952. *Graphic Regional Sociology*. Cambridge: Phillips Book Store.

3

Toward the Stabilization and Enrichment of a Forest Community

Harold F. Kaufman
Professor Emeritus
Mississippi State University

Lois C. Kaufman

EDITOR'S PREFACE

This chapter is a condensed version of a report with the same title prepared for the Montana Study in 1946. The Montana Study was an effort by the University of Montana to better understand rural communities so that their persistence and development could be facilitated. It was directed by Baker Brownell, Professor of Philosophy at Northwestern University on leave at the University of Montana. Brownell hired Harold and Lois Kaufman to study two adjacent timber-dependent communities in Montana: Libby and Troy. The best introduction to their report is an exchange of letters between A.G. Lindh, Assistant Regional Forester and Brownell.

These letters only hint at the sensitive nature of a study that examines the actions of a resource management agency. What the letters do not reveal is the extent to which the report sacrificed independent scholarship to the interests of maintaining a spirit of cooperation with the U.S. Forest Service. Many issues identified in the report could have been examined in greater depth had the report been done under different auspicies.

The contraints land management agencies place on research are as much a concern today as they were in the 1940s. Organizational prerogatives and myths are still threatened by facts—especially by facts that limit policy options for expressing the core values of an organization. Primary emphasis on wood production has long been the central concern of the U.S. Forest Service, with issues of community stability or development secondary to "getting the wood out." The timber-orientation of the U.S. Forest Service has been evident in the lack of subsequent interest in any empirical sociological studies of forest-dependent communities; there has been no follow-up to the Kaufmans' study. Moreover, examination of communities has been discouraged in many regions—especially on the Tongass National Forest in Southeast Alaska where Congressionally mandated acceleration of timber harvesting was adopted to maintain "community stability."

For these reasons, sociologists studying natural resource systems are as interested in formal land management organizations as they are in communities that depend on lands managed by these agencies. To implement the holistic framework for sociological study identified by Firey in Chapter 2, investigations must look at how communities depend on large formal organizations as much, or more, than they depend on land based resources. The Kaufmans only hint at this important implication. Yet it deserves emphasis as an additional theme cutting across the papers in this volume.

EXCHANGE OF LETTERS BETWEEN LINDH AND BROWNELL

August 30, 1946

Dear Mr. Brownell:

After many delays, we have finished mimeographing the report by Dr. Harold F. Kaufman and Dr. Lois C. Kaufman, entitled, "Toward the Stabilization and Enrichment of a Forest Community." I am delivering an advance copy of the report to you with this letter.

In looking back over the 2 years during which we have jointly considered first, the problem of having the study made, the second, the job of getting the report out, it appears that the Forest Service owes you a large debt of gratitude for your leadership and patient counsel. Please accept the sincere appreciation of the Forest Service group which has responsibility for developing the forest management plan for the Lincoln County area.

I have one major criticism of the report by Dr. Kaufman. It is not intended to be a criticism of his work since I think he ably and honestly carried out the plan which was agreed upon. The criticism is this: By implication and by occasional statements throughout the report, it appears that the Forest Service has conducted its planning and the management of its timber in the Lincoln County area without due regard for the people of the several local communities. I believe that I am correct in interpreting the instructions and Nation-wide policies guiding the work of the Forest Service when I say that the human and community dependency side of timber management planning is receiving and will receive its full share of attention. Actually, in the past, the timber of the national forests of this region was not very much needed in the local and national economy since most of the timber was being harvested from private lands. Under those conditions, the Forest Service was grateful to have a few customers for ripe and overripe timber and the social and economic effect of national forest timber policy was small. Suddenly the timber of the national forests is needed since there is a shortage of timber in private ownership in many parts of the west as well as most of the east and south. With the growth of pressure on the national forests for maximum use of all sorts of timber and with the increased feeling of community dependency on dwindling timber being felt in most parts of the country, the job of planning the timber management and disposal policy on the national forests has become much more important, more difficult, and more fraught with conflicts between social objectives and economic obstacles. Under these new conditions, it may be considered that national forest timber management and disposal planning is in its infancy. It was with a realization of this that the Forest Service welcomed the cooperation of the Montana Study in opening up this opportunity to examine the human side of the timber planning job.

I could go through the report page by page and state the current Forest Service position. Some of this would involve criticism of our own past positions and in some instances it would involve criticism of Dr. Kaufman's conclusions from the existing facts. However, it appears that locally, within the immediate area concerned, more good will come from the study of the problems presented here prior to the publication of the details of the proposed timber management plan for the unit.

Frankly, the forest planners are still engaged in the basic job of shaping the forest management and timber disposal plans and have a number of unsolved major problems. Perhaps study of the Kaufman report by community and group leaders will result in the development of community plans and programs which will help solve some of the forest problems.

I would appreciate it if you would transmit a copy of this letter with a copy of the report to each of those whom The Montana Study makes its distribution.

Very sincerely yours,

A.G. Lindh
Assistant Regional Forester
Division of Timber Management

August 31, 1946

Dear Mr. Lindh:

I have received your letter of August 30 along with the advance copy of the Kaufman report. I am glad to include a copy of your letter with the reports which we shall send out.

As I look over the final assembly of the report upon which so many of us have worked to a greater or less degree for many months, it seems to me nothing less than thrilling that the results of this pioneer work should shape up so well in the final form. May I congratulate you, particularly, and the Forest Service upon the magnificant cooperation which you have given us and upon your willingness to have us make an objective, critical report, let the chips fall where they may.

I have long known that the Forest Service, ever since its early days under Gifford Pinchot and Theodore Roosevelt, has been one of the most progressive and public-minded agencies in the United States. After my two years of close contact with the Forest Service in Montana during my work with the Montana Study, I am more than ever convinced that the Forest Service is motivated by a high interest in public welfare and in efficient management of timber resources in the United States, for the benefit both of the people of the country as a whole and of the communities located in the forest region. In fact, our project itself, in which you encouraged another and independent agency, the Montana Study, to make an objective, critical report of the Lincoln County situation, is proof enough that the Forest Service is concerned primarily in the truth and public service.

In the work of this report, our directives to Dr. Kaufman were to record what he saw and heard in Lincoln County and to make his own, individual conclusions and recommendation as a thoughtful, public-minded individual concerned in the sociological and community problems of the region. By the nature of his report, he was limited to the interpretation of local conditions. If he found that the Forest Service policies and practices were believed to be bad by local people, it was his business to report it. Where this the case, it is evident that either the policies and practices of the Forest Service were not understood or that the local application of them had not expressed the social attitude for which the Forest Service as a whole has long been known.

At best, the situation is a difficult one with the inevitable conflict between mangerial efficiency and general public welfare. Even the wisest direction when confronted by concrete problems in the field is bound to make compromises or other types of decision which will not fully carry out these two important objectives. In the long (sic) and at long range I believe that these two objectives, efficiency and public welfare, will be identical but I realize that in the immediate problem it is often extremely difficult to decide to which one priority should be given without ruining the entire project by that decision.

It comes down eventually to a statement in your letter of the 30th, namely, that timber management policy, which must make use of the full national forest resources, is essentially a new problem. The pressure for maximum use of timber from the national forests is new. There are no basic precedents for handling this problem, particularly in relation to social and community adjustments. The Forest Service has had a fine record in this respect in regard to grazing lands, land tenure, recreation and the like. I am confident that a similar record will be made in this newer field of use of national forest resources.

Meanwhile, it is inevitable that all parties to a sustained yield program, with the present undeveloped policies and traditions in this field, will be subject to criticism. Some of that criticism probably is justified but I, for one, am confident that the Forest Service is the kind of agency that welcomes criticism and profits by it.

Sincerely,

Baker Brownell
Director, The Montana Study
Professor of Philosophy (on leave)
Northwestern University

INTRODUCTION

The stabilization and enrichment of life in a forest community are broad social objectives. A pertinent question to ask is why stability is declared the objective of planning in a forest community. What is the meaning and what are the implications of this term? What specific projects and programs might be initiated in the community studied by which this objective might be realized? A discussion of these and related questions is the purpose of this report.

Of desirable community characteristics probably the one most conspicuous by its absence in forest areas has been that of stability. The exploitative timber industry has been a migrant one, having within a century and a half moved from one coast to the other. Consequently, the communities built around this industry have been noted for their instability; they have been either boom towns or ghost towns.

The boom town is characterized by a rapid increase in population, in employment, and in apparent wealth; by shortages of goods and services; and by social maladjustments. Social change rather than being orderly and planned is sporadic and haphazard. In the boom communities which are booming because of rapid liquidation of the forest resource, ghosts foretelling an unhappy future frequently lurk. These are the ghosts of an exhausted resource, of unemployment, of a declining population, and of empty and decaying buildings. With such a future in view, the incentive is lacking for building permanent houses and stores, and stable institutions and organizations. Rather the philosophy, "eat, drink, and be merry for tomorrow we may die," is more appropriate.

The Libby-Troy community is not only in an area in which the traditionally unstable forest industry is the dominant one, but this community is also in a state which during its history has known much instability. The Montana booms and depressions in mining, in livestock raising, and in dry farming are well known. Consequently, the question is pertinent as to whether a stable forest community in Montana can be realized.

COMMUNITY STABILITY—WHAT IT IS AND WHAT IT IS NOT

The term community stability, as used here, does not imply a static condition, the absence of change, or the necessity of maintaining the status quo. The basic implication is orderly change rather than a fixed condition. Synonyms of stable are lasting, permanent, and durable. But for an institution to be lasting, especially in the modern world, it must gradually change to meet new conditions. For this reason the most stable type of community in the present day would probably be one in which there was orderly change toward given goals; those goals embracing "the good life" in whatever way that might be defined.

Community stability as the term is used here is a broad social objective. It is impossible to know all the principal answers, even for one small community. No blueprint is possible. Furthermore, in a democracy it should be the task of the people in the local community to determine finally their goals and procedures. All that is attempted in this short report is to suggest tentatively some approaches that should be considered and to indicate some problems that require solution if reasonable stability is to be gained in the Libby-Troy community.

As a community is made up of people living and working in a physical environment, there are of necessity several types of approaches to stabilizing the community. A three-fold classification is made here. (1) *The land use approach.* A rural community's survival is dependent on the conservation and wise use of its natural resources. (2) *The industrial and employment approach.* For the highest standard of living a community must have, among other things, efficient industries and it must provide adequate services. (3) *The social welfare and organizational approach.* From this point of view the satisfactions and interests of people and the organizations and institutions necessary for meeting their needs are considered. In order to see the community as a whole, all of the above approaches are needed.

This report begins with a short description of the Libby-Troy community, and then considers possibilities for more efficient organization and expansion of industries, trades, and services.

It is significant that some of the major problems and trends in the Libby-Troy community are of nationwide importance. Chief of these are the conservation of natural resources, labor-management relationships, and the centralization of economic control.

THE FOREST COMMUNITY

A community is composed of many elements, among them, the people, their material possessions, and the natural resources of the area. Attention is focused here on the relationships of people with each other and on their adjustment to their physical environment—the two-way relationship of people and natural resources.

Place and People

The Libby-Troy community is located in the west and south portions of Lincoln County, Montana. Lincoln County is in the extreme northwest corner of the state, and is bordered on the west by Idaho and on the north by British Columbia. The county has an area of approximately 3,750 square miles; the Libby-Troy community may be regarded as covering from two-thirds to three-fourths of the total area of the county. Ninety-seven percent of the land area in the county is in forest. This makes Lincoln County the first forest county in the state in terms of volume of timber.

In 1940 over 5,000 people lived in the Libby-Troy community; over 1,800 in the county-seat town of Libby and nearly 800 in the town of Troy. Five-sixths of the total population resided either in or relatively near these two centers.

Possibly two-thirds or more of the basic income of the area comes from the forest. The forest furnishes a livelihood for workers in sawmills and wood remanufacturing plants, in logging, and in the Forest Service. Other major sources of employment, but far below the forest in importance, are agriculture, the Great Northern Railroad, and mining. Agriculture in the area is limited because of soil, climate, and topography. Sale of beef cattle is the major source of cash income for farmers.

Indications of both stability and instability are found in the community. Signs of stability are found in the civic organizations, schools, and churches, all with a long history; in the attractive and well-built courthouse and city hall located in Libby; and in some substantial and attractive homes. Indices of instability are the temporary business structures, unkept streets and sidewalks, and the many rather hastily constructed dwellings. This sense of impermanence is expressed by residents when they say, "You can't expect too much from a sawmill town."

Libby shows greater economic prosperity than Troy, largely because it has the two largest and most stable industries in the community—the Libby Mill and the Zonolite mining operation. The former employs approximately 500 to 600 workers at full capacity and the latter approximately 50 to 60. The population of Libby along with its economic activity has continued to increase over the years. Each decennial census beginning with 1910 shows a definite population increase in Libby and vicinity. On the other hand, Troy reached its zenith of industrial activity in the late 1920s when it was a division point on the railroad, had a medium-sized sawmill, and had some mining. Since then, these sources of employment have either markedly declined or disappeared entirely.

STABILIZING THE COMMUNITY

Although many forces and activities in the area are contributing to a more stable community, many real problems remain to be faced and solved. There is a need for trained leadership with vision, for widespread participation on the part of all groups, and for cooperative action toward common ends. The possible projects and programs that might be considered as promoting community stability are manifold. Attention is focused here, however, on ten strategic areas of the physical, economic, and social life of the community. These are:

(1) Developing a stable timber industry with the greatest possible remanufacturing.
(2) Practicing sustained yield forestry on timber lands and wise use of other natural resources.
(3) Promoting greater public participation in determining forest policy.
(4) Creating a more diversified and balanced economy.
(5) Securing adequate leadership in community affairs.
(6) Providing greater assistance to youth, especially with reference to vocation guidance and training in citizenship.
(7) Strengthening the rural home.
(8) Creating a more community-centered religious emphasis.
(9) Developing a forest-centered tradition.
(10) Organizing for united action of the greater Libby-Troy community.

Community Projects

The chief problems facing agricultural producers in the community are efficient production, better integration of part-time agriculture and outside employment, diversification of crops, and enlargement in the size of farms, As possibilities for profitable expansion in agriculture are decidedly limited, emphasis should be placed on improving the condition of those now farming rather than on increasing the number of farmers. Courses of action include a reconnaissance study that would classify agricultural land and determine profitable types of production; and long-term educational and technical assistance programs. Resources available for the study include the State Agricultural College, the Forest Service, county government, and the farm organizations; while soil conservation district technical advisors, home agents, or a local agriculture committee could assist with educational programs and assistance.

Wise recreational planning is necessary for maximum economic returns from the tourist trade and for the greatest satisfaction to local residents. Such planning includes consideration of tourist facilities, roads, advertising, game and fish management, preservation of scenic beauties, and promoting community attractiveness. Civic organizations, like the Libby Chamber of Commerce and the Troy Development Association, might take the lead in working out a recreational program but many other groups, such as the Forest Service, providers of tourist accommodations, and groups interested in game and fish management and regional beautification, would also be involved.

Considerable study concerning the development of water resources in the area is being carried on by various federal agencies, with a possibility of action in the future. Thus, one or more civic organizations should assume responsibility (along with the local newspaper) of keeping the community informed on developments and encouraging public discussion so that when specific action is considered the community will be ready to take an intelligent stand with respect to it. As part of the larger problem of the use of water resources, the desirability of public ownership of the water and electricity utilities in the community might well be considered.

In order to identify additional employment opportunities in trades, services, and industries and to provide information for planning the vocational program in the schools, a survey should be conducted jointly by the schools and civic organizations.

Farm and labor groups, among others, might well consider the formation of cooperative organizations to supply one or more types of services—e.g., groceries, petroleum products, farm supplies, credit (credit union), and electricity (REA).

Attention should focus on reducing the cost of public services in isolated areas. To this end a state zoning law is needed, but in the absence of such a law, local regulation of settlement in isolated areas can help.

A clean-up, paint-up, and build-up program for town and conuntryside might be initiated. This would include the removing of debris from vacant lots, demolition of unsafe and rundown buildings, the improvement of streets and sidewalks, and the beautification of homes. Civic organizations should take the leadership in such a campaign.

The building of a new, modern hospital would be an important step in improving health and medical care. There is also a real need in the Libby-Troy area for more extensive health education and more comprehensive medical care. Prepayment plans, an increase in the number of physicians, and the coordination of services in a hospital could play a part in improving the health of the community.

The citizenship training and vocational guidance and training functions of the school should be strengthened. The use of the school as a community center should be encouraged.

The county should cooperate with the Extension Service in bringing a home agent to the county. Leadership is badly needed in the field of homemaking and family life.

Cooperative endeavors of the churches in the area should be encouraged, as should the application of ethical principles and leadership to community problems.

A council representing the major organized groups in the greater Libby-Troy community should be established. The principal function of such a council would be to coordinate various programs and projects of community-wide concern.

THE FOREST PROGRAM

Major features of the forest utilization policy that have been evolving during the last ten years are (1) that the Libby-Troy area be operated as one sustained yield management unit and (2) that the Libby Mill be the major manufacturer of sawlogs and be sustained at a given level. Forest products not utilized by the Libby Mill have been available to other operators but there is no assurance as to the amounts. Planning for raw materials has been done for only one operator. During World War II, sawmills, at least those of any size, were discouraged from coming into the area, although operators were referred to other locations.

The present forest policy was well expressed in the "gentlemen's agreement" made in 1942 between the Forest Service and the Libby Mill. Under this arrangement the Libby Mill agreed to selective cutting on their own lands and in return the Forest Service would permit the mill to cut up to fifty-five million feet from the national forest.

An enabling act, Public Law 273, passed by Congress in 1944, makes it possible to give present forest policy legal status. This Act enables timber lands under the jurisdiction of the Secretary of Agriculture or of the Interior to be combined with reasonably large private holdings into one sustained yield management unit. In return for following desirable forestry practices the private cooperator is to be sold public timber without competitive bidding. The primary objective of the cooperative enterprises set up "under the Act is to obtain the community stability and other public benefits which flow from uninterrupted operations under a sustained yield management plan" (U.S. Forest Service, 1944).

Under this agreement the national forest and the forest land of the Libby Mill in the Troy and Libby working circles would be combined in one management unit. It is to be proposed that of the eighty million feet estimated allowable cut the Libby Mill utilizes seventy million feet. Two-thirds of the latter amount will come from the national forest and one-third from the forests owned by the Libby Mill. National forest timber may be purchased by the Libby Mill at appraised value and without competition.

One function of this survey has been to sample community opinion with respect to the forest policy outlined in part above. Interviews of some length (up to several hours) were conducted with nearly 100 representative persons who had definite interest in forest policy. In addition, questionnaires on the forest program were filled out by nearly 450 individuals. In all, some expression of opinion on forest policy was obtained from probably one-sixth or one-seventh of the adult population. Business people in Libby were on the whole most favorable to the present forest program while the small timber operators (actual and potential) and Troy leaders were most unfavorable.

The public appeared to support overwhelmingly the principle of sustained yield in forest management, was less certain that it would be followed, and was deeply divided as to how national forest timber should be utilized. The chief merits of the present forest program as described by those interviewed were: (1) nearly nine-tenths of the timber in the area to be placed on sustained yield management basis; (2) the stabilizing of an efficient and community-minded operator (3) resulting in an industry which has the advantage of size; and (4) other administrative advantages. Major limitations and disadvantages were: (1) inordinate power in the timber industry to be given the private cooperator (in the agreement under Public Law 273); (2) undue social and political influence resulting from such a monopolistic position; (3) labor is disadvantaged; and (4) the stability of one community created at the expense of others.

It is most significant that arguments favoring present forest policy stress efficiency—industrial and administrative—while unfavorable arguments emphasize discrimination resulting from too much power given one group. Thus, the basic issue is not rapid liquidation of the forest resource versus sustained production but rather concerns the problem of protecting the public interest and distributing equitably the rewards from the forest. The analysis of community opinion suggests the two basic questions raised by this report. First, what type of industry, in terms of type of product, size, and number of operators, is most likely to survive in the area and to supply continuous and full employment? Second, with a given type of industrial organization, what controls are necessary to insure that the public interest is best served and that the welfare of the whole community is promoted?

Specific suggestions or recommendations as to forest policy include the following. Community stability is accepted as the long-term social goal. This broad aim comprises three elements or objectives with respect to forest policy: (1)

the forest objective—the timber lands should be so managed that a continuous supply of forest products is available to the industries dependent upon them, (2) the industrial objective—the maximum of manufacturing possible within the limitations of raw materials, costs of production, and markets should be promoted so as to offer the highest possible employment in the area, (3) the social objective—forest policy (in its nontechnical aspects) should be democratically determined so that the best interests of all major groups in the community are served and the rewards from the forest are equitably distributed among those dependent on it. These three objectives must be integrated and no one of them sacrificed to the others if community stability is to be realized. It is suggested that forest programs be evaluated in terms of these objectives.

A more comprehensive plan of forest management and utilization is needed than has been proposed thus far. The need is to plan for the stability of the whole community; this is much broader than assuring one plant of the necessary raw materials. Therefore, it is recommended that no attempt be made to put the proposed cooperative agreement between the Libby Mill and the Forest Service into effect until the industrial and social aspects of the forest program as described herein are worked out in much more detail.

Many assumptions and inferences have been made with respect to the type of industrial organization that would be most desirable in the community. What is needed, however, are specific proposals buttressed with all the available facts. Thus, it is recommended that a study be made of the industrial pattern or patterns most likely to survive in the area, and that this information be made available to the public before any decision is made concerning a cooperative unit, a federal unit, or the volume of national forest timber allocated to the Libby Mill. It is assumed, of course, that the Libby Mill is an essential part of any industrial pattern likely to survive in the area.

After this industrial study is completed and if the economic facts indicate that a stable timber industry in Troy should be created, planning to this end should be initiated. In working out a forest program no community should be overlooked in the planning and none should be allowed to decline, unless such a policy has been established to be in the greatest public interest in the long run, both locally and nationally.

If the best interests of all major groups in the community are to be served, the public must have a voice in determining forest policy. This is especially true if competitive bidding is ruled out in the sale of national forest timber. Heretofore, all major decisions have been made, chiefly or entirely, by the Forest Service and the one large operator. Therefore, ways in which the public can participate more extensively in forming forest policy should be studied. A committee with strong Forest Service support should be formed to advise on the public aspect of the management and utilization of the timber area. This committee might consist of representatives from the public, labor, timber operators, owners of timber land, and the Forest Service. Such a committee would not only represent a cross-section of community opinion in determining forest policy but it would also have the important educational function of keeping the public informed on forest programs. The study groups now in session in the community considering forest programs and policies might well take up the question of the composition of this committee, its method of selection, and its various functions.

The Forest Service has the key position in any program of timber management and utilization which has community stabilization as its major social objective. Traditionally, the major function of the Forest Service has been to manage federally owned timber lands. But another and important role (as implied in Public Law 273) has been thrust upon this organization—that of leadership in forming public policies relating to the forest. In carrying out this function the Forest Service at various times must assume the roles of leader, expert, educator, arbiter, and protector of the public interest. Thus, it is recommended that increased attention be paid to the role of the Forest Service in planning for community stability and in related public service functions associated with the management of the forest. This implies study of specific techniques and procedures to use in carrying out this role and the training (both academic and in-service) of personnel who are to perform this function.

CONCLUSION

The forest situation in south Lincoln County presents real problems, but also great opportunities. The community has a relatively large acreage of forest land which, if managed properly, would provide continuous crops of timber. The public is, however, greatly divided as to how this raw material should be utilized. Thus, this report closes with the same question with which the discussion on forest policy was opened: Can the public, labor, industry, and government plan together for the common welfare? The writers have high hopes that the Libby-Troy community will answer this question in the affirmative. If they do they will set a precedent which may have nationwide significance. It will demonstrate the success of democratic planning in conserving the forest resource and in the promotion of community well-being.

REFERENCES

USDA Forest Service. 1944. "Policy and Instructions Governing the Establishment of Sustained Yield Units under the Provisions of Public Law 273." Unpublished mimeograph.

4

Human Choice in the Great Lakes Wildlands

Samuel P. Hays
Department of History
University of Pittsburgh

Environmental policies regarding the Great Lakes forest stem primarily from the factor of human choice. Alternative policies arise from differences in the perception and meaning of forests to different people and the values they place upon forested areas. Environmental and conservation controversies turn on disputes over such matters. Because the nature and meaning of a forest to people today is vastly different from what it was a century ago, so must the knowledge about the forest be different, as well as human interaction with the forest. Our biggest problems lie not so much in our knowledge about the way in which the forest has evolved but in our understanding of the evolution of the human choices that have been made with respect to the forest environment.

Through this perspective, this chapter analyzes changing human choices about the forested wildlands—that area of sparse or no habitation beyond the city and the countryside—in the Great Lakes region between about 1840 and the present. This evolution has had three distinct stages: 1850 to 1910, when wood production predominated; 1910 to 1945, when out-migration took place and real-estate values declined drastically, and when these "lands that nobody wanted" were rescued by public ownership and management; and 1945 to the present, a time of a revival of intense interest in the forest. The revolution in forest-related human values that has taken place since 1945 has been so fundamental that a historical approach must inevitably stress change rather than continuity. Such an approach emphasizes not so much the impact of the forest on people as the impact of people on the forest.

The analysis is organized around three phenomena: changes in the way in which people perceived the Great Lakes forest and their relationship to it; the evolution and development of management perspectives; and the changing role of local communities as the specific context in which choices about the forest are made.

CHANGING PUBLIC ATTITUDES

The most important long-term change has been the way in which people valued forested wildlands. How were forests perceived? What role did people wish forests to play in their personal lives, and in the the life of their community, region, and nation? At the start, we can make a simple distinction between the image of the forbidding forest of the nineteenth century and the attractive one of the twentieth century, a source of pleasure, relaxation, and inspiration. Although "wilderness" historically had a negative connotation, today it has a markedly positive one (Opinion Research Corporation, 1977). A dramatic reversal of values has taken place.

These new values do not represent a desire to return to some primitive, prescientific, pretechnological society. On the contrary, they represent an integral part of the standard of living of an advanced industrial society. There is a reciprocal relationship between the desire to enjoy the material commodities of the world of conveniences and the desire to enjoy intangible experiences in the world of amenities. Consumption in the United States has changed over the years from an emphasis on necessities to one on conveniences, and later, to an emphasis on amenities; each earlier stage has been retained firmly as each later one evolved. Modern technology has made it possible to live in or near wildland areas while enjoying most modern conveniences. It has also produced a vast array of sports and leisure-oriented products with which people can experience and enjoy wildlands more readily and with greater safety and comfort.

We know much about these changing values in the years after World War II because they have been examined in detail. There are studies of those who use wildlands for recreation, most of them undertaken because managers wanted to know who the users are and what they prefer. There are also studies of the values of people who purchase land in wildland areas for homes and recreation, a phenomenon in which professional foresters have long been interested. Why, they have asked, do such owners not wish to produce wood on their properties for commercial sale? In state after state, including states in the Great Lakes area, studies have shown that owners value these lands for the natural setting of forest and microclimate, with its cleaner water and air and less-cluttered landscape. Watson (1975) examined real estate advertisements in papers in Philadelphia, Harrisburg, and Pittsburgh for properties in Potter County, Pennsylvania, in the north central highlands of the state. To attract buyers, such descriptive phrases as "at the end of a forest road," "by a sparkling stream," "lies along the boundary of a state forest," and "in a secluded woodland," were used. To clear-cut such areas would destroy the very values for which they were purchased—that is, the environmental quality under the forest canopy, which even some form of selective cutting might markedly degrade.

Sparse evidence for earlier years makes it difficult to chart stages in the evolution of these values and perceptions. The main value of the forest in the nineteenth century lay in its wood and the resulting cleared land which could be farmed. Permanent habitation provided little conceptual space for the permanent role of the canopied forest, let alone sustained and continuous wood production. The struggle over tax-delinquent and tax-reverted lands between 1900 and 1930 involved intense controversies over the agricultural possibilities of the formerly forested land; the hope that it could sustain a high level of farming and support farm communities died hard. In Michigan, where the lands reverted to the state, local communities exercised considerable pressure to put them back on the market so that farming could be tried again (Schmaltz, 1972). Out of this agonizing debate slowly emerged the view that the forest provided the only potential for a sustained economy, that stability in the long-run flow of wood production provided relief from the uncertainties of marginal agriculture.

Over the decades there were vast changes in the significance of these wildlands to the people who experienced them. In the nineteenth century they were a raw material for extraction, as people looked beyond the forest to the agricultural lands they hoped would provide permanent homes. In the decades from 1910 to 1945 they came to be "lands nobody wanted," retained in public ownership, protected, and regenerated by public agencies because of their rapid decline in value to the private economy. But other meanings and uses were being implanted even in those years, and they emerged in the decades after World War II. The "lands that nobody wanted" became the "lands many people wanted." The value of wood production fell. Real estate values tell the tale—if land competed both for wood production and for environmental amenities such as a vacation home, the latter brought a far higher price. The shift in market values, as contrasted with private values, from the 1920s to the 1970s is a measure of the depth of the transformation in perceptions that began a century and a half ago.

EVOLUTION OF MANAGEMENT PERSPECTIVES

Shifting our focus from the evolution of public values with respect to wildlands to those who manage the forest, it is apparent that human choice is still very much a factor—choices made by business entrepreneurs and corporate managers, and by administrators in private and public forest agencies. Central to such management are the managers themselves, but there is an increasing number of technical and professional experts upon whom managers rely for needed skills—scientists, economists, and planners. Forest managerial systems today bring together these skills under single centers of control.

It was not always this way. In the nineteenth century, when extraction of raw materials was the dominant story, individual entrepreneurs made their mark in the Great Lakes states. There are numerous examples of enterprising people who saw a good thing, invested, built mills, and shipped lumber; some established manufacturing plants to utilize the raw material (Maybee, 1960). The cost of timber was low and the investment small relative to the size of the operation. All this enterprise was short-term, for long-term management was a concept of the future. Entrepreneurial control, over both wood production and the communities dependent on it, was not part of a long-term, continuously evolving process. The entrepreneurs did not want the land, only the timber; they were experts in extraction, not land management. This resulted in temporary institutions and little cumulative acquisition of capital and skills. One can speak of the rise and fall of individual entrepreneurs, but, even more important, of the rise and fall of private exploitation as a phase in the long course of Great Lakes forest history.

A few enterprises became the beginnings of more intensive and permanent wood-production management systems. But, unlike iron and copper mining, there was little continuity in wood production. The private wood-production institutions declined and into this vacuum came other, more permanent, public wildlands management. Private entrepreneurs, for the most part, abdicated, and when they returned with greater long-run purpose in the mid-twentieth century they had to come on different terms. These new public forest-management systems—county, state, and federal—came first as protectors of a resource that had been depleted in dramatic fashion and then left as orphan land. Unattended, it became a great fire hazard. Reforestation and protection against fire came to be the major themes of management; slowly but surely a depleted resource was restored. A breed of caretakers grew up who were distinctive for their time and place, whose training was in the woods, and whose accumulated personal experience gave them an authoritative wisdom about how to protect what they personally knew. They did not exactly welcome the new stage of more technical and complex management that was to come.

After World War II, came the era of intensive forest management; both the drive for wood production and the public demand for more forest uses grew rapidly. Management shifted from a protective and custodial approach to greater investments of money and skills to achieve ever more intensive outputs. Private timber companies preferred a limited set of objectives dominated almost exclusively by wood production, with little room for other uses such as wildlife, recreation, and environmental amenities. Hence they extended their corporate holdings and geared up for continuous and ever more intensive high yield fiber growth. The management of public lands involved more varied objectives and uses, which increased rapidly over the years from beginnings early in the century, through the expansion of access to the countryside which the automobile stimulated in the 1920s, to the flood of users who came with the rising leisure and fast-speed highways after World War II. In response, public forest managers adopted a more intensive approach to wildlands resources. They were inventoried and described more precisely; systems of land classification became more intricate, with such elaborations as water-influence and travel-influence zones, natural areas, and wilderness. Specific uses were confined to specific lands.

One imperative became uppermost—to grow trees and harvest wood (Bultena and Hendee, 1972). For many years the elementary systems of gathering and classifying information about the forest had been based on that objective. Wildlands were described in terms not of the interaction of species in an ecosystem, but of the standing timber they contained. Despite the growing demands from other types of forest users, the fundamental way in which the forest was thought of, described, and classified remained heavily influenced by a traditional, dominant concern for wood production.

The management system that evolved after World War II was even-age or area management. This approach grew out of the need to develop a simplified method of regulating the flow of products within the forest. Each area was considered as a single unit, one data point, with a volume figure attached to it; it was measured to determine growth, cut as a unit, and regenerated as a unit. The product flow from start to finish was vastly simplified for managers. Area management could be carried out with skills that did not require experience in the woods but used forest accountants who could quantify the output, computerize the data, and program the resulting manipulations. Inventory description by aerial photography was developed as a time-saving alternative to on-the-ground measurement.

At the same time, however, the values of the public regarding the meaning and use of forests were changing rapidly. This change in values took place in a realm that was, for the most part, beyond the immediate experience of forest managers; its intensity caught them by surprise. Trained in older ways and accustomed to more traditional objectives and values, public and private managers grew apprehensive as aesthetic and recreational demands on the nations' wildlands increased. Forest managers opposed an expanded national park system, wilderness designations, and wild and scenic rivers, all of which threatened to make inroads into the uses of forestlands for wood production. Frequently, their opposition was ideological, based more on a perceived threat to their values than on an actual decrease in wood production.

The different perspectives of manager and environmental user, one shaped by the efficient manipulation of a resource for wood production and the other shaped by the aesthetic appreciation of wildlands experiences, have continually come into conflict since World War II. One result has been an increase in the variety of skills required for public forest management. No longer do professionals come overwhelmingly from the field of wood production, although these are still the majority.

There has also been a marked increase in the contribution of scientific and technical information to forest planning and management. For years the transfer of new forest planning policies into management decisions was often slow, especially if it challenged established policy. From the very start of public involvement in management decisions in the 1950s, one of the most significant citizen strategies was to absorb the ideas in publications of forestry experiment stations, the literature in professional journals, and the research of forestry schools, and to bring them to bear on management decisions. In numerous hearings, information meetings, and environmental-impact analyses, forest managers were forced to confront new knowledge. They were faced with a science information transfer vigorously conducted by citizens and facilitated by the new group of professionals in management itself, who were younger, fresh from forestry school, and more eager than their elders to bring the latest in forest science to their tasks.

Despite these changes, the professional public forest manager still considers the bottom line to be the periodic removal of mature trees for wood production. This view is not shared by those who view the forest as an environmental amenity and who seek a different mix in forest values. From this viewpoint, regeneration might preferably take place through the decay of mature trees and the constant re-creation of smaller openings, leading to a more varied forest. The environmental view gives rise to different systems of measurement and classification of the wildlands resource, to different concepts as to what the flow regulated by management should be, and to different management skills and plans. Site indexes might be shaped by the ability of given tracts of land to produce varied and diverse biological species, most of which might be plants other than commercial trees. Small area, group-selection type cuts of one-third to one acre might be preferred to forty-acre uniform cuts, and small-scale logging machinery to massive field wood chippers. All this seems incomprehensible in the perspective of large-scale modern management. The difference in view is not a minor one; it goes to the root of the description, measurement, classification, and organization of a forest by those who use it.

COMMUNITY CHOICES

There is a third set of choices we should examine, coming from an altogether different vantage point—the local community. Debate over wildlands policies often involves people far beyond the local community—business corporations whose headquarters and stockholders are far away, public lands managers located at distant state and national capitals, and wildland users, both direct and vicarious, who live most often in the major metropolitan centers remote from forestlands. But ultimately these debates deal with specific uses of specific lands in specific communities. Located amid the wildlands, these communities have their own perceptions, their own values, and their own choices with respect to the forests around them. What have those choices been?

In the raw-material extraction phase of the history of the Great Lakes forest, these communities were almost wholly an adjunct to the extractive economy. They provided its labor and they serviced it. They came and went as the entrepreneurs and their timber came and went. Lumber and mill towns were spread throughout the north country, rising and falling with the fortunes of the economic firms on which they depended. A review of this phase of community history finds a sense of fatalism in that era, a realization that the raw material in the woods would not last forever. At the same time, however, there was an intense preoccupation with the moment of economic glory, without much looking ahead. Perhaps a farming economy would follow, but there was no clear plan of action. When the mills collapsed, it was seen as the natural order of things. One did not expect permanent communities to endure in the rush to provide the raw material needs of the burgeoning cities to the south.

The years from 1910 to 1945 were equally insecure for communities throughout the north country. There was a constant attempt to build communities on the basis of agriculture, and although poor soils led to failure, attempts were made again and again. In the nineteenth century, one could become resigned to the fact that timber would disappear as the foundation for sustained community growth, but it was difficult to believe that the soil provided no firmer foundation. When agriculture collapsed with a vengence in the 1920s, local communities opted for permanent state and federal ownership of tax-reverted land.

As the lumber economy had provided a vigorous but temporary period of prosperity, so also the limited agrarian economy provided short-lived hope during the prosperous farming years before 1920. No wonder that the cutover lands of the Great Lakes states was one of the severest political problem areas of the 1920s and the New Deal—a legacy of the first century of development, from the 1840s to the 1940s, when the forest rarely served as a basis for building sustained communities.

The years after World War II were vastly different. The forestlands became an integral part of the new economy of the Great Lakes region. In a few communities, wood production provided an important base; but in many more the main asset of the forest lay in its role as an environment for home, work, and play in the new economy of recreation, leisure, travel, and tourism. One is struck by the degree to which specific forest landmarks such as Hartwick Pines or the jack-pine home of the Kirtland warbler have become distinctive objects of identification for their nearby communities, or the way in which such areas have become vital to agencies that promote travel and tourism. Of equal importance with tourism and recreation is the attractiveness of forest areas to young people seeking a pleasant environment for home and livelihood and older people seeking amenities for retirement. The environmental quality of forest areas, relatively unspoiled and undeveloped, seems to have been the major reason for their recent settlement, and it has given rise to demands that the forest be managed to enhance those amenities rather than to compromise them.

A number of environmental issues arise repeatedly in these regions. Recently, the most dramatic one has been the reaction to aerial spraying of pesticides to control forest insects and herbicides to control competing vegetation. Containing the drift from spraying, and avoiding human settlements with their vegetable gardens and water supplies, has been difficult if not impossible. The widespread concern over the use of 2,4,5-T and Silvex is most intense. Monoculture and clearcutting are concerns of people who have chosen to make their permanent home in forested areas and who wish to maintain the canopied forest as an environmental asset. Several pockets of new support for wilderness arise from such areas, for example, Trinity County, California, where local environmental groups and businesses cooperated on RARE II, which included far more wilderness acreage than the U.S. Forest Service would agree to. In cases such as these, the central factor is the role of the forest in the life of the human settlement that it surrounds. Without such settlements management practices in these forests would be more remote in their human impact. With them, the adverse effects are direct and immediate.

Environmental issues often result in clear differences of opinion in a community. Several studies have indicated a marked difference within communities between the attitudes of political and economic leaders on the one hand and the general public on the other. The former are more interested in rising levels of population, jobs, real estate values, and taxes. The latter are far more concerned with environmental quality. A study of Niagara County, New York (Milbrath, 1977) indicated that the general public is more concerned about water quality than are leaders, and that leaders are more interested in jobs and population growth. Studies like this help us to understand the internal dynamics of competing values within the forest region.[1]

There is also competition among external forces as institutions in the nation at large concerned with economic development vie with those who seek growth in environmental amenities. Some local groups have reached out to establish close ties with the U.S. Economic Development Administration, represented in the Great Lakes states by the Upper Great Lakes Regional Commission. The commission vigorously promoted the national lakeshores in Michigan and Wisconsin, touting their ability to draw vast numbers of tourists to bolster the local economy. It has also promoted industrial parks, vocational training institutions, and a wide range of activities associated far more with economic growth than with growth in environmental amenities. Joining this external involvement with the region are private corporations, some concerned with mining and wood production, others with more commercial enterprises such as retail franchises, and still others with light industry.

In the competition between environmental and developmental forces to shape decisions about forested wildlands, there is considerable emphasis on the relative political jurisdiction of community, state and federal authority. For the most part, local communities seek to protect the quality of their environment by means of local zoning actions implemented in order to ward off the adverse effects of development. This is supplemented by action against specific large-scale projects, usually initiated from outside the community or the state, such as nuclear or coal-fired electric generating plants, and waste-disposal sites or incinerators. In previous decades such development went forward with little opposition. Now it is seriously questioned, a reflection of the changed value and meaning of forested areas to the general public. Those advocating large-scale development seek to shift the location of decision-making upward to the state and federal levels to override this opposition from local communities and the states that often speak for them. Large-scale private enterprise has steadily advocated more federal power and authority in such matters to overcome objections from communities concerned with their own quality of life.

The relationship between local communities and external groups concerned with environmental quality is more mixed. Environmental groups often seek state and federal creation of programs such as federal wilderness and wild and scenic rivers to protect wildlands from more intensive development. Often this leads to local opposition when it appears that these programs will create an influx of recreationists who will interfere with local patterns of life and degrade the environment with litter, noise, and crowds, or when such actions reduce local property-tax revenues. Yet the common interest of both groups in maintaining high levels of environmental quality often leads to effective cooperation after initial suspicions are overcome. Environmentalists from outside the community defend local authority in the wildlands, depending in pragmatic fashion upon the degree to which environmental quality objectives can be met.

These relationships are a product of the years after World War II. In earlier times less complex demands came from local communities as they simply called upon state governments to aid them in their economic distress, to acquire and manage forestlands, and to put an economic floor under their communities. We are now in a period of history when these lands are highly desired, their use is subject to intense competition, and the competitive pressures represent different values. One can find enormous variations among communities in the north country on this score. Some seek rapid economic development and population growth; others emphasize environmental amenities. Within the same community one can find similar divergent tendencies. The context has changed from an emphasis on relationships between dominant and dependent regions to one on conflict between political forces within the north country itself.

CONCLUSION

The history of human choices in the Great Lakes forest has gone through several distinct stages. Changes have been especially dramatic since World War II, as an advanced industrial society has taken shape in the United States. New perceptions regarding the role and meaning of forests have arisen that emphasize forests as an environment for home, work, and play rather than as a source of commodities. Yet management systems, with strong and deep roots in the earlier commitments of scientific and professional foresters to wood production, have responded to these changing values slowly and often with strong and bitter resistance. At the same time, the forest community has changed markedly, absorbing many of the new environmental values and expressing them in community quality vis-a-vis many adverse influences from both within and without. These are the current conditions highlighted by historical analysis and upon which future policy must be firmly based. If there is historical guidance to our current task of formulating forest policy, it can be found not in the remote past but in the massive changes in human perceptions of the forest that have taken place during the past thirty years.

ACKNOWLEDGMENTS

Adapted from a chapter by Samuel P. Hays with the same title, in S.L. Flader (ed.). 1983. *The Great Lakes Forest*: Copyright © 1983 by the University of Minnesota. Reprinted by permission of the Publishers.

NOTES

1. The gap between leaders and the general public appears in several recent surveys. The Opinion Research Corporation (1977) Survey for AFI, for example, indicated that 62 percent of those questioned felt that the Forest Service should "continue to preserve these trees in their natural state" rather than "try to increase the yield and sales of timber from our National Forests." The ORC also surveyed the attitudes of "thought leaders" in Washington, D.C., which indicated that only 38 percent of these thought that forests should be "preserved in their natural state." The ORC advised the AFI: "We do not find sufficient support among the American people to warrant a mass communications program to increase public support for

greater timber harvesting on public lands. Instead, since this issue is perceived more rationally and with greater expertise among Washington thought leaders, we recommend that your persuasive efforts be directed toward this target audience among others" (American Forest Institute, 1977). Another survey was conducted for AFI two years later which indicated that although government officials thought timber production was the most important function of the National Forest System, 80 percent of the general public felt that protecting wildlife habitat was the main purpose and that too much timber harvesting was taking place (Sierra Club, 1980). In the Niagara County study (Milbrath, 1977), which ranked various community factors in terms of importance, leaders ranked daily work second and job opportunities ninth, and the general public ranked them ninth and thirteenth. The public ranked clean air sixth; the leaders ranked it thirteenth.

REFERENCES

American Forest Institute. 1977. *Research Recap #10*. Washington, DC.

Bultena, G.L. and J.C. Hendee. 1972. "Foresters' Views of Interest Group Positions on Forest Policy." *Journal of Forestry* 60:337-342.

Maybee, R.H. 1960. *Michigan's White Pine Era, 1840-1900*. Lansing, MI: Michigan Historical Commission.

Milbrath, L.W. 1977. "An Extra Dimension of Representation in Water Quality Planning: A Survey Study of Erie and Niagara Counties, New York, 1976." Buffalo: SUNY, interim report.

Opinion Research Corporation. 1977. *The Public's Participation in Outdoor Activities and Attitudes Toward National Wilderness Areas*. Princeton, NJ.

Schmaltz, N.J. 1972. "Cutover Land Crusade: The Michigan Forest Conservation Movement, 1899-1931." Ph.D. dissertation, University of Michigan.

Sierra Club. 1980. *National News Report, March 7*. San Francisco, CA.

Watson, M.K. 1975. "Behavior and Environmental Aspects of Recreational Land Sales." Ph.D. dissertation, Pennsylvania State University.

II

Wood Products Industry and Community

5

Sustained Yield and Community Stability in American Forestry

Johannes H. Drielsma
Forestry Commission, New South Wales

Joseph A. Miller
School of Forestry and Environmental Studies
Yale University

William R. Burch, Jr.
School of Forestry and Environmental Studies
Yale University

"Sustained yield" is a concept as old as forestry itself and is virtually synonymous with its professional application. A quick survey of the literature will confirm the central importance of sustained yield in forest management (Drielsma, 1984:3). In America, the practice of forestry on public lands has generally been guided by one or another legislative version of sustained yield. Foresters who secured the legislation and implemented it hoped that sustained yield would provide for stable, forest-dependent industries leading to stable, prosperous, even "happy" rural communities.

This paper examines the historical relationship between sustained yield wood production and community stability. It presents a summary history of sustained yield, with particular emphasis on the ideas of foresters, and compares those idealized constructs with the social reality of present-day forest-dependent communities.

ORIGIN AND U.S. BEGINNINGS

Though superficially a simple concept, sustained yield is quite complex and capable of many definitions and interpretations. The range of those interpretations may be seen in the recently published *History of Sustained Yield Forestry: A Symposium* (Steen, 1984). There are two categories of definitions: in the narrower, forest management sense, sustained yield is a technique for rationalizing production to generate a continuous flow of raw material within a time period, over a specific area or management unit. The second category embraces broader philosophic, political, or symbolic ideas of continued flow of materials to meet society's needs, or policies that perpetuate forest productivity. In either case, meanings of sustained yield vary widely, with significant consequences, as this brief history will show.

Sustained yield wood production was first developed in Germany between the thirteenth and sixteenth centuries. Forest clearance and increased population throughout this period led to diminishing supplies, expanded demands, and a fear of wood famine. By the end of the eighteenth and early nineteenth centuries, the systematic organization of forest management, dominated by a highly controlled sustained yield principle, had been introduced in most German state forests. Characteristic of this organization was a pervasive state control of forest cutting which extended over all classes of ownership. Self-sufficiency, rationing, and control characterized the economic and cultural milieu from which sustained yield forestry emerged (Drielsma, 1984).

The ideological origins of sustained yield are of more than academic interest. The "scientific forestry" that reached the United States through Bernard Fernow and the German-influenced Gifford Pinchot was based on the conception of a "normal" even-aged forest and a closely calculated, sustained annual yield of timber (Winters, 1974). It is difficult to overestimate the influence of German forestry on American foresters. In addition to the influence of Pinchot and Fernow, it was standard practice for American foresters to spend some time studying or visiting Europe, particularly Germany. Visitors to the Black Forest were overcome with admiration for the small, stable communities that drew their livelihood from the regular and sustained outputs of the forests.

The contrast between stable German forest communities and the American forest communities at that time could not have been more striking. The beginnings of forestry in America during 1900 to 1920 coincide with the end of commercial lumbering in the Lake States forests. The pine forests of the Northeast and Lake States had largely disappeared, to be followed by ghost towns and fires (Fries, 1951). Railroad logging in the South and Pacific Northwest were creating new scenes of forest destruction. The process seemed out of control.

Forest management on federal lands, the object of the forestry movement at the turn of the century, began in 1905, when the forest reserves in the Department of the Interior were transferred to the Department of Agriculture and renamed national forests. Sustained or continued yield of these resources for the benefit of local communities was stated as an objective in the Reports of the Chief of the Forest Service in 1908 and 1910 and became a regulation in 1914; the regulation was expanded in the 1920s (Parry, Vaux, and Dennis, 1983:151-152). Sustained yield was defined until the 1920s as harvests within the allowable cut, which, in the absence of inventory information had been arbitrarily set on the basis of timber sales in 1907 (Clary, 1986).

On private lands, forest management was merely an interesting experiment, given the enormous amounts of available timber and the economic situation confronting the forest products industry. In the early 1900s, lumber production and prices of timberland in America had reached record heights. After the financial panic of 1907, "Consumption and production began to decline, stumpage prices stabilized, and carrying charges mounted" (Zivnuska, 1952:57ff).

The industry, perceived by many reformers as evil and all-powerful during the period of Progressive conservation, was also desperate. The Forest Service, in a series of studies just before 1920 (Greeley, 1917, 1951), gradually came to recognize the industry's economic problems and their implications for dependent communities. Kirkland (1917) stated the problems as: excessive timber holdings leading to overcutting and overproduction, overinvestment in mills and logging camps leading to excess capacity, and destructive competition.

Kirkland's suggested solutions to these industrial problems anticipated later developments: consolidation of ownership into efficient production units; physical organization so as to provide annual returns from each forest unit; stable ownership policies; and lower interest rates. But his main objective was community stability:

> Whenever we desire to put our forest industry on a stable basis where each forest will yield continuously and each will be a permanent institution, we can introduce the permanent town, the school, the church, family and community life (Kirkland, 1917:61).

This statement marked the beginning of a brief period of interest (1917-1921) by foresters in the effects of uncontrolled lumbering on dependent communities and labor unrest. Dana (1917, 1918) chronicled the experience of Cross Forks in Pennsylvania, from high prosperity in 1906 to oblivion in 1913—the abandonment of towns, farms, and railroads, and the lowering of living standards. Chandler (1920) pointed to the "physical, mental and moral bankruptcy" incurred by "destructive lumbering." To this bankruptcy, foresters also ascribed the "problem of the lumberjack" (MacKaye, 1918) characterized by labor strife in the Pacific

Northwest during the World War and the rise of the International Workers of the World (IWW) thereafter (Todes, 1931; Jensen, 1945; Clark, 1970).

Concern for community, both urban and rural, marked the reformers of the Progressive era. Progressives saw both city and country endangered by explosive social situations arising from immigration and industrialization. President Theodore Roosevelt's Country Life Commission had revealed how bad rural conditions were in a nation whose symbol had been the yeoman farmer. Farm and city migration was increasing. The need to stabilize rural communities was a recognized problem.

SUSTAINED YIELD BECOMES POLICY

The forestry profession's concern for community stability reached a climax in the years after 1919 when national forest policy was being debated. Some in the forestry profession, led by Gifford Pinchot, wanted the federal government to regulate the use of private forest lands. The effect of such a forest policy on community stability is made explicit in this passage from a report by the Pinchot faction to the Society of American Foresters.

> When the owner of a forest is prohibited from devastating it, when he is required to make one crop of timber follow another, then, and only then, can the lumber camp and lumber town become permanent, and only then can forest labor be assured of a chance at those living conditions to which every worker is justly entitled, a chance at a real home. (Committee on Forest Policy, 1919).

Meanwhile, on the national forests sustained yield was assumed to be practiced and the interests of communities safeguarded. But in the 1920s the policy of restricting annual cut to annual growth changed as foresters sought to remedy the imbalance between old and young growth by accelerating the cut. "Operationally, sustained yield management now focused on regulating of the growing stock rather than regulating the yield" (Parry, Vaux, and Dennis, 1983:152). Moreover, the Forest Service was selling more timber. As Clary has recently shown, the welfare of local communities and their stability was not always consistent with timber sales policy. Then too, federal foresters were preoccupied with forest fires, timber taxation, reforestation, and land acquisition—the policy agenda of the Clark-Mc-Nary Act of 1924. From these would come long-term forest productivity and attendant community stability (Clary, 1986:76 ff).

Sustained yield was explicitly linked to community stability in the 1920s by

David T. Mason and his associates. Mason was a forester, forestry consultant, and after 1928 Executive Secretary of the Western Pine Association. He argued that sustained yield, a textbook forestry maxim, was the way out of a national forestry situation untenable for business and government. Forest conservation and management were impossible for private owners in the short term, given business conditions, but were absolutely necessary over the long term. A sustained yield policy, as he envisioned it, would unite short- and long-term interests, making timber ownership more valuable, reducing chronic overproduction, stabilizing forest-dependent communities, and providing for the nation's future timber supply (Mason, 1927, 1969; Loehr, 1952).

A major obstacle to sustained yield as Mason presented it were the thousands of small logging and sawmill operations whose fierce competition made the forest products industry inherently unstable. In Mason's view, community stability was bound up with the continuous productive capacity of large, efficient firms (Mason, 1927:645; Parry, Vaux, and Dennis 1983). His ideas were adopted in the final report of the Timber Conservation Board (1930) and later by New Deal administrators in the National Recovery Administration (NRA). Each industry was bound by sets of rules or codes that were enforced by its trade association. The Lumber Code was drawn up by Mason and a handful of industry leaders, and Mason became the Lumber Code Administrator (Loehr, 1952; Conkin, 1971).

Article X of the Lumber Code contained a series of forest practice rules covering protection, reproduction, logging, and sustained yield. After the Supreme Court declared the NRA unconstitutional in 1935, Mason and industry leaders maintained an informal cooperative relationship through the Article X Committee. The committee's primary objective was to reduce the flow of federal timber into the market, particularly from the Oregon and California revested lands managed by the Department of the Interior. In 1937, partly as a result of their pressure, the Oregon and California Railroad Lands Act was passed. It provided that:

> ... permanent forest production, and the timber thereon shall be sold, cut, and removed in conformity with the principal (sic) of sustained yield for...providing a permanent source of timber supply, protecting watersheds, regulating stream flow and contributing to the economic stability of local communities, and providing recreation facilities (sic) (Act of August 28, 1937, 50 Stat. 874).

There was also in the 1930s a reawakened sense of forestry's role in the social welfare of communities, and a revitalization of the German-European approach. The social welfare orientation of New Deal conservation could be seen in such projects as the CCC, TVA, Great Plains Shelterbelt, and the Resettlement Administration. The Forest Service had ambitions plans for contributing to economic recovery through a massive program of land purchases and reforestation (USDA Forest Service, 1939; U.S. Congress, 1933; Zon, 1939). Foster (1941) wrote of "our national debt to forest communities" and specified that forest management "must be related in a positive way to the needs of the community through planning." The social impulse also expressed itself in a renewed but unsuccessful attempt to achieve public regulation of private forest lands (1938-1941) (Hamilton, 1965).

The Sustained Yield Forest Management Act of 1944 realized many of the community stability ideas of the 1920s and 1930s, and owed its passage principally to the work of David T. Mason (Loehr, 1952). The purpose of the Act was to: (1) stabilize communities, forest industries, employment, and taxable forest wealth; (2) assure continuous and ample supplies of forest products; and (3) secure the benefit of forest influences on streamflow, erosion, climate, and wildlife conditions (Granger, 1944).

The Act authorized the Secretaries of Agriculture and Interior to establish cooperative sustained yield units consisting of federal and private forest lands, or federal sustained yield units consisting only of federal lands, when the maintenance of stable communities was primarily dependent upon federal stumpage and when such maintenance could not be secured through usual timber sales procedures. It bound federal agencies to supply timber at appraised values to one or a few mills within the dependent communities (Hoover, 1978).

By August 1944, forty to fifty proposals for sustained yield units had been received in the Pacific Northwest region (Hoover, 1978), but only one was approved: the Shelton Cooperative Sustained Yield Unit, involving the Simpson Logging Company and the communities of Shelton and McCleary in the Olympic Peninsula region of Washington. Subsequent efforts (Quincy, California and Missoula, Montana) were blocked by the vigorous opposition of smaller operators and labor groups. Similar efforts under Oregon and California land legislation also failed because of strong local opposition (Loehr, 1952; Clary, 1986).

POST WORLD WAR II QUESTIONING OF POLICY

The cooperative sustained yield policy was running against national economic and political currents. By the 1950s, the postwar boom had raised demand and prices for lumber, logs, and timber to an all-time high. Western national forests had become major timber suppliers, rising from 2.86 billion board feet in 1952 to 8.3 billion board feet in 1959 (Parry, Vaux, and Dennis, 1983:153). The economic realities within which the sustained yield legislation had been worked out no longer existed (Loehr, 1952; Schallau, 1974).

The rules, procedures, and formulas used to determine annual yield of timber and nontimber resources came under increasing scrutiny by those most vitally affected. Who got what, how, and when became matters of debate more important than broad principles of sustained yield and community stability. Those had become institutionalized—in legislation, Forest Service policy, and the subconscious of the forestry profession (Amidon, 1953; Harkin, 1969).

Opposition to well-intentioned resources management was strikingly apparent in the unhappy experience of the Forest Service in promoting the Vallecitos Sustained-Yield Unit on the Carson National Forest, New Mexico. Established in 1947, the unit was terminated in 1977 after failing dismally to manage the forest the way the local communities, composed of poor Hispanic ranchers, wanted it managed. The Flagstaff Unit, a federal sustained yield project established on the Coconino National Forest in 1949, worked mainly to the benefit of Southwest Forest Industries. Its continuation was stubbornly supported by the Forest Service until 1980 (Clary, 1986:126-146).

Yet the hold of the sustained yield idea never weakened. In the Multiple Use-Sustained Yield Act of 1960, it was broadened to include all the renewable resources of national forests. Significantly, however, the Act made no mention of the role of forests in ensuring continuity of employment and stable communities.

Ideas of economists rather than foresters began to define the concept of sustained yield. According to some, sustained yield was not a sufficient, nor even a necessary condition for economic community stability. Researchers began to look at the regional effects of forest regulation policies on employment and income, usually in aggregate terms (Josephson, 1955; Wood, 1955; Dickerman and Butzer, 1975).

Zivnuska (1949) pointed to the fact that general economic business cycles were perhaps more important elements affecting industries and communities. Duerr (1966) advocated abandonment of the sustained yield concept in favor of modulated yield, such that yields could be adjusted to general economic conditions and objectives. Noting that the vast majority of foresters accepted the sustained yield article of faith, Zivnuska (1949:99) replied:

> The sustaining of the yield, it is said, is an aspect of sustaining life itself, of sustaining employment, income, and indeed, the economic affairs of the community. To this line of reasoning comes the reply—communities may in years gone by have wished to be sustained. Surely, in the fatalistic, even-tenored traditional society of Western Europe in the sixteenth and seventeenth centuries, where sustained yield doctrine originated, the principle was beautifully appropriate. But now that many communities have experienced industrial revolution,

to be sustained is no longer their aim. They want to develop, and
they recognize that this means some steady change, some fluctuations, and the appearance of new income sources as the old
decline.

There was growing criticism by some economists of the Forest Service's
interpretation of sustained yield, which had become institutionalized as the
policies of "even-flow" (Duerr, 1966) and "non-declining even-flow" (Newport
1973). Both policies were based explicitly on the objective of maintaining stable
communities and opportunities for employment by constant or slowly increasing
annual yields (Newport, 1973; Clawson and Sedjo, 1984).

Schallau (1974) did not think "sustained yield, regardless of how it is defined
(even-flow or modulated), necessarily fosters economic stability." But the door
was left open for "localized situations in the West" where some form of "sustained
yield policy designed to foster orderly adjustment to reduced timber supplies
should be an acceptable strategy" (Schallau, 1974).

The passage of the National Forest Management Act in 1976 added further to
the revival of interest in these ideas by focusing on timber regulation and sales
procedures. After reviewing the literature, Waggener (1977) concluded that traditional definitions of stability, community, and dependency were vague and the
relationship between timber flow and stability was largely conjectural. He stressed
"the need for logical and systematic interpretation of stability as an economic
concept which unfortunately is largely incompatible with traditional forestry
connotations." Byron (1978) has also argued for an economic interpretation of
stability.

Moreover, analyses of future timber supplies have predicted declines in harvests from nonfederal lands. Forest economists have pointed out that strict adherence to even-flow under these conditions would deny managers an opportunity
to coordinate harvests on a regional basis, so as to avoid the projected decline with
its implications for economic stability (Schallau, 1974; Zivnuska, 1977; Beuter
and Schallau, 1978). In many ways these ideas seem to hark back to the cooperative
sustained yield legislation of 1944.

In this renewed interest, however, the social reformist zeal of earlier decades
is lacking. Waggener (1977) recognized that "many local concerns expressed with
regard to resource policies are fundamentally income redistribution issues," and
suggested that if redistribution among individuals and regions is a goal of forest
policy, then it ought to be made explicit. Krutilla and Haigh (1978) bluntly
concluded that:

> ...The Forest Service is neither suitable in most respects, nor cost
> effective in others, for an active role in achieving distributive

justice. The Forest Service nevertheless should be aware of the impact that prospective changes in its policies or practices may have on the welfare of groups greatly dependent on an existing state of affairs.

The involvement of the Forest Service in community stability in the 1980s through RPA is another story, beyond the scope of this paper.

CONCLUSION

What does this brief historical excursion into sustained yield ideas and community stability reveal? From the historical viewpoint, the writings of foresters and forest economists seem to support many interpretations. Drielsma (1984) sees a cycle of interest by foresters in community development; Schallau (1974) says that community stability was not an objective of sustained yield initially and has not really been a factor of importance since the 1940s; Lee (1984) thinks that sustained yield in its several manifestations has been a powerful symbol for the long term social benefits of forestry. Those who doubt Lee's conclusion are invited to look over the papers in Steen (1984) or the literature cited in Drielsma (1984).

Much of the social meaning of forestry is embodied in the phrase "community stability." Despite a seeming lack of interest by the Forest Service in community stability since the 1940s—and a definite lack of interest by the forest products industry (Robbins, 1987)—concern for communities and community stability, expressed as sustained yield, remains a significant force in forest policy decisions.

It is appropriate, then, to have some true sense, aside from gross economic performance, of what rural communities are really like and how they are and would be affected by forest management policies. As Schallau (1974) observes, communities are not created alike. But that sense is missing from discussions of community stability. Most twentieth century foresters came from rural communities, and their notions of life in those communities became more idealized as time passed—happy families, healthy children, schools, churches, well-kept houses (Shirley, 1952).

To what extent do present-day forest communities measure up to the ideals defined in the rhetoric of the forestry profession? They are among the least prosperous of all rural communities, with high seasonal unemployment, low wages, and high rates of population turnover. Standards of health and happiness appear to be lower than average. While the status of the family remains high, divorce rates are also high. Housing, public services, and amenities are poor. Outside forces seem to predominate over community institutions that might provide an integrated and cohesive community life. Perhaps the only characteristics of forest communities in accord with ideology are the somewhat lower crime rates and the smaller scale of industrial activity, which provides opportunities for independent, entrepreneurial activity.

While communities with well-developed pulp and paper processing industries do, in fact, tend to be more prosperous than other forest communities (they may have, for example, a higher quality of housing and public services and lower rates of population turnover), they are still among the least prosperous of rural communities. In addition, the more highly industrialized communities remain relatively unhealthy, with higher death rates from suicide and alcoholism; statistically they rank among the lowest levels of social integration and, perhaps, "happiness" of any communities, rural or urban (Drielsma, 1984).

It is of more than passing interest that the gains in economic stability and community prosperity have largely been achieved in the context of large-scale industry, in direct contrast to the "small man" myth that has formed part of professional rhetoric. Stability is associated with an industrial pattern of wage and salaried workers employed in large firms, which are themselves a part of large, multifirm corporations controlled by centers far removed from the forest. While the early forester sought in sustained yield a solution to the labor problem, this pattern of industry has permitted the development of a far stronger and more effective union organization than has been possible in smaller logging and saw-milling firms where labor is fragmented. This suggests that the quest for community stability, to the extent that it has been achieved through the development of large-scale forest industry, is achieved at the cost of those very qualities of individualism and independence so highly prized at both individual and community levels. Whereas professional rhetoric has long joined these two qualities, they may in fact be incompatible. It was just this incompatibility that undermined the effective implementation of the Sustained Yield Forest Management Act of 1944.

As a study in the sociology of knowledge, the sustained yield idea of forestry is a valuable case. It is a further confirmation that ideas directed to the benefit of lower social strata are most often controlled by upper social strata. Further, the rise and fall of such ideas are best predicted by understanding patterns in the circulation of elites, rather than the increasing or decreasing misery of particular dependent populations and ecosystems.

ACKNOWLEDGMENTS

The paper is based on research done at the Yale School of Forestry and Environmental Studies by the senior author, with revisions and additions by the coauthors.

REFERENCES

Amidon, G.B. 1953. "Planning for Sustained Yield Operations." *Journal of Forestry* 51:720-725.

Beuter, J.H. and C. Schallau. 1978. "Forests in Transition: Relationship to Economic and Social Stability." Paper presented at Eighth World Forestry Congress, Jakarta, Indonesia.

Byron, R.N. 1978. "Community Stability and Forest Policy in British Columbia." *Canadian Journal of Forest Research* 8:61-66.

Chandler, B.A. 1920. "Financial Loss to the Community Due to Forest Lands Becoming Wastes." *Journal of Forestry* 18:31-3.

Clark, N.H. 1970. *Milltown*. Seattle, WA: University of Washington Press.

Clary, D.A. 1986. *Timber and the Forest Service*. Lawrence, KS: University Press of Kansas.

Clawson, M. and R. Sedjo. 1984. "History of Sustained-Yield Concept and Its Application to Developing Countries." In H.K. Steen (ed.), *History of Sustained Yield Forestry: A Symposium*. Santa Cruz, CA: Forest History Society.

Committee on Forest Policy. 1919. "Forest Devastation: A National Danger and a Plan to Meet It." *Journal of Forestry* 17:911-945.

Conkin, P. 1971. "The Conservative Welfare State." In O.L. Graham, Jr., (ed.), *The New Deal: The Critical Issues*. Boston, MA: Little, Brown.

Dana, S.T. 1917. "A Forest Tragedy: The Rise and Fall of a Lumber Town." *Munsey's Magazine* 60:353-363.

——. 1918. *Forestry and Community Development*. USDA Bulletin No. 638.

Dickerman, A.R. and S. Butzer. 1975. "The Potential of Timber Management to Affect Regional Growth and Stability." *Journal of Forestry* 73:268-269.

Drielsma, J.H. 1984. "The Influence of Forest-Based Industries on Rural Communities." Ph.D. dissertation, Yale University.

Duerr, W.A. 1966. "The Allowable Cut of Timber, Policy Issues and Alternatives." In *Proceedings of Society of American Foresters*. Seattle, WA, pp. 95-99.

Foster, E. 1941. "A Plan to Help Stabilize Rural Economy by the Wise Use of Forest Resources." *Journal of Forestry* 39:793-799.

Fries, R.F. 1951. *Empire in Pine: The Story of Lumbering in Wisconsin, 1830-1900*. Madison, WI: State Historical Society of Wisconsin.

Granger, C.M. 1944. "The Cooperative Sustained Yield Act." *Journal of Forestry* 42:558-559.

Greeley, W.B. 1917. *Some Public and Economic Aspects of the Lumber Industry*. USDA Report No. 114.

———. 1951. *Forests and Men*. Garden City, NY: Doubleday.

Hamilton, L.S. 1965. "The Forest Regulation Issue: A Recapitulation." *Forest History* 9(1):2-11.

Harkin, D.A. 1969. "Defining Sustained Yield Under Law: A Wisconsin Case." *Journal of Forestry* 67:154-157.

Hoover, R.D. 1978. "Public Law 273 Comes to Shelton: Implementing the Sustained Yield Forest Management Act of 1944." *Journal of Forest History* 22:86-101.

Jensen, V.H. 1945. *Lumber and Labor*. New York: Farrar and Rinehart.

Josephson, H.R. 1955. "Forest Resources in the Pacific Coast Economy." *Proceedings of Society of American Foresters*. Portland, OR, pp. 173-177.

Kirkland, B.P. 1917. "Continuous Forest Production of Privately Owned Timberlands as a Solution of the Economic Difficulties of the Lumber Industry." *Journal of Forestry* 15:15-64.

Krutilla, J.V. and J.A. Haigh. 1978. "An Integrated Approach to National Forest Management." *Environmental Law* 8:382-383.

Lee, R.G. 1984. "Sustained Yield and Social Order." In H.K. Steen (ed.), *History of Sustained Yield Forestry: A Symposium*. Santa Cruz, CA: Forest History Society.

Loehr, R.C. 1952. *Forests for the Future: The Story of Sustained Yield in the Diaries and Papers of David T. Mason*. St. Paul, MN: Minnesota Historical Society.

MacKaye, B. 1918. "Some Social Aspects of Forest Management." *Journal of Forestry* 16:210-224.

Mason, D.T. 1927. "Sustained Yield and American Forest Problems." *Journal of Forestry* 25:625-658.

———. 1969. "Memoirs of a Forester, Part II." *Forest History*. 13(1/2):28-39.

Newport, C. 1973. "The Availability of Timber Resources from the National Forests and Other Federal Lands." In *Report of the President's Advisory Panel on Timber and the Environment*. Washington, DC: Government Printing Office, pp. 158-217.

Parry, B.T., H.J. Vaux, and N. Dennis. 1983. "Changing Conceptions of Sustained Yield Policy on the National Forests." *Journal of Forestry* 81:150-154.

Robbins, W.G. 1987. "Lumber Production and Community Stability: A View from the Pacific Northwest." *Journal of Forest History* 31(4):187-196.

Schallau, C.H. 1974. "Can Regulation Contribute to Community Stability?" *Journal of Forestry* 72:214-216.

Shirley, H.L. 1952. *Forestry and its Career Opportunities*. New York: McGraw-Hill.

Steen, H.K. (ed.). 1984. *History of Sustained Yield Forestry: A Symposium*. Santa Cruz, CA: Forest History Society.

Todes, C. 1931. *Labor and Lumber*. New York: International Publishers.

U.S. Congress. 1933. National Plan for American Forestry. 73rd Cong., 1st sess. Washington, DC: Government Printing Office. Senate Document No. 12.

———. 1937. Oregon and California Railroad Lands Act. 50 Stat. 874.

USDA Forest Service. 1939. A National Forest Economy: One Means to Social and Economic Rehabilitation. Washington, DC. Waggener, T.R. 1977. "Community Stability as a Forest Management Objective." *Journal of Forestry* 75:710-714.

Waggener, T.R. 1977. "Community Stability as a Forest Management Objective."
  Journal of Forestry 75(11):710-714.

Winters, R.K. 1974. *The Forest and Man.* New York: Vantage Press.

Wood, G. B. 1955. "The Role of Public Forests in the Economic Development of
  the Pacific Coast Region." In *Proceedings of Society of American Foresters.*
  Portland, OR, pp. 187-189.

Zivnuska, J.A. 1949. "Commercial Forestry in an Unstable Economy." *Journal of
  Forestry* 47:4-13.

———. 1952. *Business Cycles, Building Cycles and Commercial Forestry.* New
  York: Institute of Public Administration.

———. 1977. "Section 13—Unlucky for Even Flow." *Journal of Forestry* 75:783-
  785.

Zon, R. 1939. "The Human Side of Land Use." *Journal of Forestry* 37:735-737.

6

Community Stability: Issues, Institutions, and Instruments

Con H. Schallau
USDA Forest Service
Pacific Northwest Research Station

> Society refuses to turn itself into a giant vending machine that
> delivers anything and everything in return for the proper number
> of coins. When members of my profession sometimes lose sight
> of this principle, they invite the nastiest definition of an
> economist: the person who knows the price of everything and
> the value of nothing. (Arthur M. Okun, 1975)

Not everyone benefits from economic growth. This fact is apparent from statistics on the nation's robust recovery from the 1980 recession—the deepest since World War II. Despite increasing total employment and declining unemployment, millions are receiving little direct gain. So what? Given our capitalistic system of rewards and penalties, some are bound to lose. To the extent that our "efficient" system encourages effort and channels it into socially desirable activities, there is no apparent need for intervening with market exchange. As Okun (1975) points out, however, "the pursuit of efficiency necessarily creates inequalities. And hence society faces a tradeoff between equality and efficiency."[1] Most mainstream economists recognize the merits of equal opportunity, but few argue, as Okun has, for equality of output (i.e., income distribution). The tradeoff between equity (i.e., fairness) and efficiency, however, is a commonly debated topic.

Public debate regarding the management of the nation's forest lands often focuses on the relative merits of efficiency and equity. For example, much of the concern that led to the establishment of a system of forest reserves in 1891 was provoked by fears that the nation eventually would run out of timber. Presumably, future generations would be unfairly penalized if an efficient, unfettered timber industry was allowed to cut and run. The prospect of intergenerational inequities was not the only concern that fostered the public's role in forestry. The specter of more destitute communities—like those stranded in the Great Lakes states as the lumber barons moved to the South and West—gave rise to a fundamental tenet of public forest management in the West; namely, the need to achieve community stability.

Despite common usage, there is no consensus regarding the meaning of community stability. Consequently, there is no consensus regarding the ability of current forest management policy, namely sustained yield, to achieve community stability. Resolving this problem is beyond the scope of this paper. The purpose of this paper is rather to identify some of the impediments to consensus by (1) examining some of the forest management policy issues and related legislation that have a bearing on community stability and (2) providing a brief overview of economic literature related to community stability.

COMMUNITY STABILITY NOT CONSIDERED BY EARLY LEGISLATION

Although the demise of stranded communities in cutover areas of the Great Lakes states attracted considerable attention (for example, Sparhawk and Brush, 1929), Congress did not enact any explicit direction to assure community stability until nearly fifty years after the national forest system was established. Because of abundant timber on private lands, demand for public stumpage was practically nonexistent until after World War II. Custodial management—fire protection and road and trail construction—characterized early forest management directives. Although forest resource policies were intended to prevent a "timber famine," timber management per se had yet to gain a foothold.

Although community stability was not an early policy issue, sustained yield was. During the 1920s, private authorities were concerned that premature harvesting on national forest lands would disrupt the market for their stumpage. Strangely enough, it was the oversupply of private timber, not the need for maintaining community stability, that led to sustained-yield management of public forests in the West.

The late David T. Mason is generally regarded as the granddaddy of sustained yield in the United States. Although Mason spoke of community problems, his main concern reflected the once popular theme, "Keep your public timber off my private market" (Popovich, 1976). Mason (1927) envisioned sustained-yield management as a means of discouraging small, undisciplined operators (mainly in the South) from moving to the West. He wanted to change the lumber market from a buyer's market to a seller's market, and believed that a sustained-yield policy for public forest lands would help by withholding "from cutting a moderate quantity below what the market would readily absorb."

The Great Depression postponed official adoption of the sustained-yield concept. Although the Secretary of the Interior was authorized in 1937 to establish sustained-yield units for the support of dependent communities and local industries, no action was taken until after World War II. The Sustained Yield Forest Management Act of 1944 (53 Stat. 132) authorized the Secretaries of Agriculture and Interior to establish either (1) cooperative sustained-yield units involving both public and private forest land or (2) federal sustained-yield units consisting only of federal land, in order to "promote the stability of forest industries, of employment, of communities and taxable forest wealth, through continuous supplies of timber." This Act led to the establishment of the cooperative unit on the Olympic National Forest and five federal units elsewhere in the West. Of the latter, only the Lakeview (in Oregon) and the Grays Harbor (in Washington) remain active.

No cooperative or federal sustained-yield units were established by the Department of the Interior. In 1946 and 1947, however, the Secretary established twelve marketing areas "the product of which should logically go to a definite marketing area" (Dana 1956). Although this primary processing requirement was initially strictly enforced, the marketing areas were eventually abolished in April 1959.

The establishment of the marketing areas and the cooperative and federal sustained-yield units comprised of national forest lands represent the high-water mark where community stability policies are concerned. During the ensuing twenty to twenty-five years, concern for community stability waned. For example, the Forest Service shifted its rationale for sustained yield from community stability to "conservation of resources to help meet the wants of future generations" (Josephson, 1976). Thus, the focus of national forest management had come full circle—from a fundamental concern for timber supply (1891) to community stability (1944) and back to a need for guaranteed timber supplies for the future.

As Waggener (1977) predicted, the enactment of the National Forest Management Act (NFMA) of 1976 (88 Stat. 476) sparked renewed interest in community stability. Pursuant to this Act, the U.S. Department of Agriculture (1979) issued regulations stipulating that community stability be considered in regional forest planning objectives. Furthermore, departures from nondeclining even-flow[2] could be considered when "Implementation [of nondeclining even-flow] . . . would cause a substantial adverse impact upon a community in the economic area in which the forest is located."

Congress continues to reaffirm the obligation of the Forest Service to maintain community stability. For instance, the Senate Appropriations Committee Report on H.R. 3011 (1985) stated:

The Committee, and the Congress in numerous statutes, has
expressed its commitment to the support of state and local
governments and dependent communities, and recognizes the
importance of Forest Service timber sales, and the related road
program, to the economic stability of such communities and
states.

RESPONSIBILITY FOR COMMUNITY STABILITY AMBIGUOUS

Despite frequent reaffirmations of congressional intent, the proper role of the
Forest Service regarding community stability remains ambiguous. A recent
opinion by James P. Perry, Deputy Assistant General Counsel, United States
Department of Agriculture, did little to clarify matters. He stated, "There is no
specific statutory authority generally applicable to the National Forest System for
maintenance of community stability in the management of National Forest system
lands."[3] Furthermore, about the NFMA regulations, he states, "Although 36 C.F.R.
sec. 221 (a)(3) only requires management plans 'so far as feasible' to ensure an
even flow of timber to protect community stability, there is no direct statutory
basis even for such a limited requirement."

INFORMATION REQUIRED TO ASSESS COMMUNITY STABILITY POLICY

Most of the decision regarding community stability must be resolved in the
political arena. I believe, however, that economists and other social scientists have
an important role in helping to resolve some fundamental definitional and theoretical questions. For example: "What is a community?" "What does economic
stability mean?" "How should we determine whether community stability has been
achieved?" Until we have a consensus about the answers to such questions, I do
not believe the public's role in helping achieve community stability can be
properly delineated. The following review of some relevant literature provides a
glimpse of the kinds of theories and studies pertaining to the unanswered questions
about the community stability issue.[4]

The term community is nebulous. Declining business activity in one locality,
provided it is not too abrupt, can contribute as much to national economic stability
as can a vibrant growth area; that is, resources employed in a declining area can
be committed to achieving growth elsewhere. For this reason, public forest
management policies cannot be expected to assure economic stability for all towns

and cities, so municipal boundaries are of little help in delineating a functional economic community. It is unlikely, for example, that the departure of a wood-based industry can be justified simply because the population of a small municipality in Oregon is declining. A departure might be rationalized, however, if a multicounty area encompassing this community is experiencing long-term economic difficulty.

Geographically, a community is a dynamic concept; so attempts to define boundaries may be chasing a will-o'-the-wisp. But geographical limits to dependent communities must be delineated for community stability policies to be meaningful. Fox and Kumar's (1965) functional economic area (FEA) concept is a place to begin. An FEA is defined using quantifiable economic activity; for example, within an FEA, the proportion of resident workers commuting to a central city would exceed the proportion commuting to an alternative central city in a contiguous area. Furthermore, most of the residents' shopping and service needs would be provided by establishments within the FEA.

SUSTAINED-YIELD AND COMMUNITY STABILITY

Generally speaking, administrative edits and other published commentaries about forestry policy assume the reader knows what community stability means. I agree with Waggener (1977) that maintaining the status quo is the most generally accepted definition. Furthermore, sustained yield is often equated with community stability.

In former times, perhaps, one could safely assume that a sustained-yield policy would help achieve community stability. Von Thunen's closed, steady-state economy, however, is not an appropriate model for today's world of dynamic change. Consequently, the achievement of a biophysical optimum (that is, sustained yield of timber products) does not assure the achievement of a socioeconomic optimum (that is, community stability). Waggener (1969) has shown that "Stability of output within the sustained yield sector is achieved only at the cost of greater instability of both price and output in the price-responsive sector." That is, rigid adherence to sustained yield will exacerbate short-term fluctuations in prices for stumpage.

Historically, there are few, if any precedents for equating sustained yield and community stability. Mason (1927) viewed sustained yield not as a means of achieving community stability but as a means of restricting entry into the forest products industry in the West. The management plan for the Shelton (Washington) cooperative sustained-yield unit incorporates a "departure" harvesting schedule for a 100-year period; that is, Forest Service timber within the unit is being harvested much more rapidly than timber on adjacent national forest lands.

Furthermore, the Forest Service can consider departures from the base harvest schedule if necessary to stabilize a community by providing wood supply to compensate for a drop in harvest from private lands (USDA Forest Service, 1979).

Schallau and others (1969) examined the future employment and population changes in the Douglas-fir region associated with and without an increase in timber harvesting. Our analysis demonstrated the difficulty in rationalizing sustained yield (the biophysical concept) in terms of community stability (the socioeconomic concept). To remain competitive, the forest products industry must constantly seek ways to reduce labor costs per unit of output. Even with a nondeclining supply of timber, employment in the forest products industry will gradually decrease. In fact, without new export-producing industries to compensate for declining employment requirements of the forest products industry, we estimated that some nonmetropolitan areas would experience eventual decline in employment and population in spite of a 20 percent increase in harvesting.

Population trends in Oregon provide additional evidence that a sustained yield policy cannot assure economic growth and development. During the 1981-1982 recession, Oregon experienced an unprecedented decline in population. Much of this loss was concentrated in the heavily timber-dependent areas of southwest Oregon. Coos County, for example, had an estimated net out-migration of 1,300; Douglas County, 2,500; Klamath County, 1,100, and Lane County, 3,300.[5]

If sustained yield is not a means to achieve stability, what then does community stability mean? Kaufman (1953) had this to say:

> The term community stability, as used here, implies orderly change rather than a fixed condition. For an institution to be lasting, especially in the modern world, it must gradually change to meet new conditions. For this reason the most stable type of community in the present day is probably one in which there is orderly change toward given goals: those goals embracing "the good life" in whatever way it is defined.

In a similar vein, USDA Forest Service (1982) guidelines define community stability as "the rate of change with which people can cope without exceeding their capacity to deal with it." The concepts of orderly change and coping both recognize change as inevitable, but an objective measure based on either concept might be difficult to devise.

Gilmore's (1976) definition has analytical possibilities. He was confronted with the need to define community stability while analyzing the boomtown phenomenon associated with strip mining in the Rocky Mountain West. Stability, according to Gilmore, is achieved when a community's "basic sector [firms producing for markets outside the area] and public services sectors are more or less in balance." In adapting Gilmore's notions to the forestry situation, Beuter and Schallau (1978) hypothesized that maintaining a balance between basic and residentiary (trade and services) sectors is important whether a community is experiencing growth, is mature, or is declining. It is the manner of change (orderly versus traumatic) and not its direction or magnitude that counts.

VARIABLE ECONOMIC CHARACTER OF COMMUNITIES

Because any two timber-dependent communities are unlikely to be at the same stage of development, a uniform policy could provoke a wide range of response. It is doubtful that the nondeclining even-flow policy will assure community stability for every timber-dependent community. A more realistic policy would allow forest managers to customize forest management planning to the particular needs of each timber-dependent community. But how can the analyst distinguish the needs of communities?

One fairly straightforward way is in terms of community reliance on the forest products industry. Reliance can best be expressed in terms of a community's economic base (Maki et al., 1986); for example, a community in which the forest products industry accounts for 40 percent of economic base earnings is more dependent on timber policies than is a community in which the forest products industry accounts for only 10 percent.

Sometimes the relevance of community stability can be judged on the basis of timber dependency and economic diversification. The issue of community stability arose in conjunction with the controversy over the appropriateness of selling timber from the national forests at a price below the government's cost of making the timber available to the forest products industry. By classifying study areas on the basis of timber dependency and diversification,[6] analysis found that the Forest Service's concern for community stability was not moot in most areas where below-cost sales were frequent, the areas' economies were quite diversified and not very dependent on timber processing.

The growing importance of retirement income could contribute to the diversification of forest resource-based economies in rural areas. Connaughton (1979) found that transfer payments were the fastest growing component of the economic base sectors of timber-dependent communities in northern California. Subsequently, Schallau and Polzin (1983) and Salazar, Schallau, and Lee (1986) also found this to be true for case study areas in Montana, Oregon, and Washington.

STAGES-OF-GROWTH THEORY

Leven (1966) describes how economic strategies might change, depending on an area's stage of development. He delineated five stages: insular, colonization, diversification, industrialization, and maturity. Leven suggests that at early stages of development "society might appear almost indifferent to instability as a cost of achieving higher incomes." Presumably, this would not be the case during the latter stages.

Using loan-to-deposit ratios for commercial banks as an indicator, Schallau (1980) found evidence of a protracted outflow of funds from two multicounty areas—Medford and Roseburg—of western Oregon. Meanwhile other areas in western Oregon were attracting funds. Since generally, funds are thought to move from more advanced, slower-growing areas to faster-growing areas, he concluded that policies designed to achieve economic stability elsewhere in western Oregon may not be appropriate for the Medford and Roseburg areas.

Butler (1980) describes an evolutionary model for tourist areas that involves six stages: (1) exploration, (2) involvement, (3) development, (4) consolidation, (5) stagnation, and (6) decline/rejuvenation. As Stough and Haynes (1986) observe, the cycle model "has gained support . . . largely on the strength of conceptual argument on the one hand and casual observation on the other." They conducted linear and logistic regression analyses of time-series data for hotel and lodging employment for eight sample recreation-oriented counties and found support for Butler's evolutionary model. They foresee, however, the need for additional methodological and empirical studies before this model can be used for assessing alternative development strategies.

MEASURING ECONOMIC IMPACTS

Forest resource planning is not neutral with respect to community stability. Some management policies will have a greater impact on the economic vitality of a dependent community than others. Consequently, policy analysts must be able for forecast the economic impacts of alternative plans. Several types of analytical procedures can be used to determine the long-term economic impacts of alternative resource management strategies on community stability. The simple economic base model provides multipliers for examining interareal and intertemporal changes. This model can be used to estimate the numbers of basic jobs that are necessary to reach target levels of total area employment (Bendavid, 1974). The USDA Forest Service has adopted IMPLAN (Interindustry Model for Planning) as its official model for assessing economic impacts (Palmer, Siverts, and Sullivan,

1985). This input-output (I/O) model is a sophisticated variant of the economic base model.

Although very useful, the static economic base and input-output models do not account for time. Furthermore, static models do not have a way to trace the impacts of changes in investment, in- and out-migration, and occupation. A dynamic interactive policy analysis simulation system (IPASS) developed for use in Alaska (Maki, Olson, and Schallau, 1985) overcomes some of the deficiencies of the static I/O model. This model has been used to demonstrate, for example, how different income-earning units might be affected by changing resource use. A hypothetical $105 million increase in final demand for goods and services provided by the tourism industry would eventually—after five years—compensate for the loss of employment and earnings resulting from a hypothetical closure of Alaska's two pulpmills. This change, however, would not be neutral with respect to community stability since most of the loss of employment would be confined to full-time, higher-paying technical jobs in two remote areas in southeastern Alaska, whereas most of the increase would involve seasonal, lower-paying service-oriented jobs located elsewhere in Alaska.

SUMMARY AND CONCLUSION

Community stability is an important part of the forestry folklore. In the United States it has become a favorite shibboleth as well as a basic tenet of public forest management. Nevertheless, the term remains nebulous from a policy standpoint. Consequently, managers find it hard to determine whether their policies will achieve community stability. Much of the uncertainty could be overcome if a consensus were reached on the meaning of economic stability. Furthermore, economic analysis has an important role in evaluating public policies designed to achieve community stability.

NOTES

1. For example, Stevens (1978) found that younger employees in the forest products industry are more likely to be laid off when mills curtail operation sand are less likely to be rehired as soon as older workers.

2. The nondeclining even-flow policy represents the U.S. Forest Service's interpretation of sustained yield. This policy specifies that "For the base sale schedules, the planned sale for any future decade shall be equal to, or greater than, the planned sale for the preceding decade, provided that the planned sale is not

greater than the long-term sustained-yield capacity consistent with the management objectives of the alternative" (Federal Register, 1982, 47 (190):43047).

3. Memorandum to Christopher Risbrudt, Director, Policy Analysis, USDA Forest Service, August 14, 1985.

4. This review is not exhaustive. Rather, its purpose is to highlight specific unresolved issues and questions that could be productively researched.

5. Data are from unpublished records maintained by the Center for Population Research and Census. Portland State University, Portland, Oregon.

6. Kort's (1979) entropy index was used to measure diversification of fourteen multicounty areas where below-cost sales were prevalent. For a thorough discussion of an application of the entropy index to a forest resource situation, see Schallau and Polzin (1983). The excess employment technique was used to measure how dependent an area's economic base is on the forest products industry. Maki et al. (1986) describe how to measure timber dependency.

REFERENCES

Bendavid, A. 1974. *Regional Economic analysis for Practitioners: An Introduction to Common Descriptive Methods*. New York: Praeger Publishers.

Beuter, J. H. and C. H. Schallau. 1978. "Forests in Transition: Relationship to Economic and Social Stability." Paper presented at Eighth World Forestry Congress, Jakarta, Indonesia.

Butler, R. 1980. "The Concept of a Tourist Area Cycle of Evolution: Implications for Management of Resources." *Canadian Geographer* 24:5-12.

Connaughton, K. P. 1979. *Income and Employment Multipliers for Gaging the Economic Impact of Alternative Levels of Forest Service Timber Harvest in Northern California*. Berkeley, CA: University of California.

Dana, S. T. 1956. *Forest and Range Policy: Its Development in the United States*. New York: McGraw-Hill Book Company.

Fox, K. A. and T. K. Kumar. 1965. "The Functional Economic Area: Delineation and Implications for Economic Analysis and Policy." *The Regional Science Association Papers* 15:57-85.

Gilmore, J. S. 1976. "Boom Towns May Hinder Energy Resource Development." *Science* 191:535-540.

Josephson, H. R. 1976. "Economics and National Forest Timber Harvests." *Journal of Forestry* 74:605-608.

Kaufman, H. F. 1953. "Sociology of Forestry." In W. A. Duerr and H. J. Vaux (eds.), *Research in the Economics of Forestry*. Washington, DC: Pack Forest Foundation.

Kort, J. R. 1979. *The Theory of Regional Economic Stability Differentials: Analysis, Reformulation, and Empirical Evidence*. Knoxville, TN: University of Tennessee.

Leven, C. L. 1966. "The Economic Base and Regional Growth." In W. R. Maki and B. J. L. Berry (eds.), *Research and Education for Regional and Area Development*. Ames, IA: Iowa State University Press.

Maki, W. R., D. Olson and C. H. Schallau. 1985. *A Dynamic Simulation Model for Analyzing the Importance of Forest Resources in Alaska*. Portland, OR: USDA Forest Service, Research Note PNW-432.

Maki, W. R., C. H. Schallau, B. B. Foster and C. H. Redmond. 1986. *Alabama's Forest Products Industry: Performance and Contribution to the State's Economy, 1970 to 1980*. Portland, OR: USDA Forest Service, Research Paper PNW-361.

Mason, D. T. 1927. "Sustained Yield and American Forest Problems." *Journal of Forestry* 25:625-658.

Okun, A. M. 1975. *Equality and Efficiency: The Big Tradeoff*. Washington, DC: The Brookings Institution.

Palmer, C., E. Siverts and J. Sullivan. 1985. *IMPLAN Version 1.1: Analysis Guide*. Fort Collins, CO: USDA Forest Service, Land Management Planning Section.

Popovich, L. 1976. "Harvest Schedules—The Road to Regulation." *Journal of Forestry* 74:695-697.

Salazar, D. J., C. H. Schallau and R. G. Lee. 1986. *The Growing Importance of Retirement Income in Timber-Dependent Areas*. Portland, OR: USDA Forest Service, Research Paper PNW-359.

Schallau, C. H. 1980. *Stages of Growth Theory and Money Flows From Com-*

mercial Banks in Timber-Dependent Communities. Portland, OR: USDA Forest Service, Research Paper PNW-279.

Schallau, C. H. 1986. "Sloshing Around in the Headwaters Without a Map." In *Proceedings of "Below-cost Timber Sales: A Conference on the Economics of National Forest Timber Sales."* Spokane, WA (February 17-19).

Schallau, C. H., W. R. Maki and J. H. Beuter. 1969. "Economic Impact Projections for Alternative Levels of Timber Production in the Douglas-fir Region." *Annals of Regional Science* 3(1):96-106.

Schallau, C. H. and P. E. Polzin. 1983. *Considering Departures From Current Timber Harvesting Policies. Case Studies of Four Economies in the Pacific Northwest.* Portland, OR: USDA Forest Service, Research Paper PNW-306.

Sparhawk, W. N. and W. D. Brush. 1929. *The Economic Aspects of Forest Destruction in Northern Michigan.* Washington, DC: USDA Technical Bulletin 92.

Stevens, J. B. 1978. *The Oregon Wood Products Labor Force: Job Rationing and Worker Adaptations in a Declining Economy.* Corvallis, OR: Oregon State University, Agricultural Experiment Station, Special Report 529.

Stough, R. and K. Haynes. 1986. "The Implications of Development Cycles for Tourism and Regional Economic Development." Paper presented at the 25th annual meeting, Western Regional Science Association, Laguna Beach, CA (February).

U.S. Congress. 1944. Sustained Yield Forest Management Act. 53 Stat. 132.

——. 1976. National Forest Management Act. 88 Stat. 476.

U.S. Senate Appropriations Committee. 1985. Report on H.R. 3011 (September 24), pp. 99-141.

USDA, Forest Service. 1979. "National Forest System Land and Resource Management Planning." *Federal Register* 44(181):53928-53999.

——. 1982. "Guidelines for Economic and Social Analysis of Programs, Resource Plans, and Projects; Final Policy." *Federal Register* 47(80):17940-17954.

Waggener, T. R. 1969. *Some Economic Implications of Sustained Yield as a*

Forest Regulation Model. Seattle, WA: University of Washington Contemporary Forestry Papers, Contribution No. 6.

Waggener, T. R. 1977. "Community Stability as a Forest Management Objective." *Journal of Forestry* 75(11):710-714.

7

Sustained Yield and Social Order

Robert G. Lee
College of Forest Resources
University of Washington

The United States has been the setting for much recent debate over sustained yield forestry practices. Sustained yield has been the subject of two national symposia (Dowdle, 1974; LeMaster, 1982) and numerous articles in the forestry literature (Behan, 1978; Byron, 1978; Gould, 1964; Jackson and Flowers, 1983; Schallau, 1974; Waggener, 1977). Most of the attention has focused on the assumptions underlying sustained-yield policies and the presumed causal linkage between sustained yield and community stability. Forest economists in the United States have been the primary originators of this debate; some have questioned whether sustained yield is an appropriate policy for regulating timber harvests in the industrial economy of the United States and other advanced nations. The first major criticisms of sustained yield emerged at the same time that timber harvesting was accelerating on U.S. national forests following World War II.

By the 1960s, this critique had solidified into widely shared assumptions about the German origins of sustained yield and its inappropriate application to the conditions found in the United States. In short, critics claimed that sustained yield was developed about 1800 to fit stable, self-sufficient communities in Europe, especially in Germany. Some have claimed that sustained yield originated earlier in closed feudal economies that were faced with wood scarcity (Waggener, 1977). Richard Behan (1975:18), an influential spokesman for critics of sustained yield, stated that:

> The technological, political-economic, social and geographic features of Germany in those days were such that sustained-yield was an ingenious and wholly sensible solution to the forestry problems that Germany faced.

Behan (1975) went on to explain that eighteenth century German technology depended heavily on wood for industrial fuel and construction materials, construction of houses, and the construction of military and merchant vessels for shipping. Wood was of both "strategic and comprehensive importance" (p. 18), and there were no technical substitutes for it. Cameralism, a variant of the prevailing mercantilist system, was the form taken by the eighteenth century political economy of Germany. This economic doctrine created a closed economic system dependent on self-sufficiency by discouraging imports and encouraging exports. Also according to Behan, "The social organization of Germany was hierarchical, stratified, and highly structured—this imposed a high degree of stability in society" (p. 18).

Given the prevailing view that eighteenth century Germany had a closely integrated, stable society and a mercantilist economy dependent on wood-based technologies, Behan (1975) concluded: "It made enormously good sense to limit the periodic consumption of wood to the periodic growth of the forest that dealt with the scarcity of the closed system" (p. 18). Behan noted earlier work by Gould (1964) and Raup (1964) to claim that foresters in eighteenth century Germany developed sustained yield to fit a social system typified by wood scarcity, social stability, and planning certainty (Gould, 1962). These three assumptions were attributed not only to early German forestry but also to ideas underlying contemporary forestry practices.

Given these assumptions, it is not difficult to understand why sustained yield was thought to be poorly suited to the United States. Unlike Germany, the United States as a whole has never suffered from serious wood scarcities. It was endowed with an enormous supply of virgin forests and sufficient land to renew these forests when they were harvested. Also unlike this view of Germany, the United States developed a market economy that facilitated rapid social change and economic growth; assumptions of social stability and certainty about the future did not accompany the industrial development of the United States or the exploitation of its vast stock of natural resources. Thus, according to historical inferences drawn by contemporary American critics, sustained yield would indeed appear to be an archaic practice that should have been abandoned when nations entered the modern era of coal and petroleum, material substitutes for wood, cheap transportation, free trade, national and international economic communities, and rapid social change. However, there are reasons to question the validity of this criticism. Some of the problems with the conventional critique will be discussed before turning to an alternative interpretation.

LIMITATIONS TO CONVENTIONAL
CRITIQUE OF SUSTAINED YIELD

There are five primary limitations to what has become conventional wisdom regarding the inappropriate application of sustained yield to wood harvest regulation in modern industrial society. First, the criticism of sustained yield has been based only on its meaning as a technical method for matching periodic harvests to periodic growth. The possibility that sustained-yield practices may embody social as well as technical meanings has been totally ignored. By far the most evident social meaning embodied in such practices is a particular society's commitment to creating a future by perpetuating basic biological conditions that support important sectors of that society (Duerr and Duerr, 1975). Critics of sustained yield have been oblivious to such meanings and their implications for forest policy.

Second, inferences about the historical origin of sustained yield have been drawn from sweeping generalizations about European, especially German, social and economic life in the last three centuries. Such broad interpretations have provided no basis for evaluating the plausibility of inferences. The contemporary critique is based on insufficient evidence of actual situations, since it does not attempt to connect global or societal patterns with particular events, places, persons, and groups. Critics have not adequately grounded historical interpretations in evidence describing when, where, how, and by whom sustained yield was developed or adopted. Arguments against sustained yield will remain conjectural until investigations have adequately documented the social and economic history of this practice.

Third, contemporary critics of sustained yield have not attempted to explain why this practice was developed by German foresters and later adopted by their counterparts in so many different countries. All that has been provided is an argument for why sustained yield is poorly suited to advanced industrial economies. The fact that sustained yield has persisted as a fundamental forestry institution in industrial nations throughout the world, including Germany and the United States, should stimulate the curiosity of social scientists and historians. Why we still have sustained yield remains an unexamined question. An answer to this question is fundamental to a well-grounded critique, as well as to the advancement of historical knowledge.

Fourth, some critics of sustained yield have substituted ideology for evidence in attempting to make their argument more convincing. The "capitalist-democratic" system of the United States is pitted against the "centralized" and "socialistic" (see Behan, 1975) system. Since sustained yield is most often practiced on lands under public ownership and operation, it has been associated with an economic system that is alien to the United States. Government ownership and regulation, including the regulation of harvests, is argued to be inconsistent with an individualistic, capitalist economy. By placing the argument in an ideological context, critics foreclose the opportunity to empirically examine the ideological context in which sustained yield may have been developed or practiced. The fact that many private forest landowners in capitalist economies have adopted sustained yield is thereby ignored (see Loehr, 1952). Minimal requirements for sound empirical social science demand that ideological systems be examined objectively, not used as instruments for persuasion.

Finally, critics of sustained yield generally work with a limited view of society as an aggregate of individuals. The public interest, or general welfare, is presumed to emerge spontaneously from the independent initiatives of individuals. Sustained yield makes little sense when society is viewed only as an aggregate, since the attempt to consciously preserve future options is ignored. The possibility that some interests of the public may be secured by government or private planning does not receive sufficient consideration. A view of society that recognizes the contributions both of individual initiatives and corporate or centralized direction would enable investigators to account for all types of social and economic actors associated with the development of sustained yield—the role of central government, corporations, social elites, communities, interest groups, professional associations, and self-interested individuals.

Any efforts to understand the social and economic history of sustained yield must attempt to overcome these limitations. Various meanings of sustained yield must be identified; general patterns of history must be connected with particular places and events; explanations for the tenacity of sustained yield practices must be offered; policy and ideology must be studied as objects rather than advocated; and a view of society encompassing both corporate, centralized, and individual action must be adopted.

AN APPROACH TO THE SOCIAL HISTORY OF SUSTAINED YIELD

Meanings of Sustained Yield

One of the most interesting features of sustained yield is the complexity associated with its meaning. There is no universal definition of sustained yield. Instead, we find that its meaning varies with time and place in response to prevailing social, economic, and political conditions. The meaning attributed to sustained yield is a product of particular historical circumstances—it acquires meanings that reflect the interests and concerns of individuals, groups, and social institutions. Yet, in the midst of this complexity, there are some themes that persist, although varying in the precise form of their expression.

Technical definitions of sustained yield as a set of scientifically-based rules for balancing harvest with growth have prevailed since about 1800 (Parry, Vaux, and

Dennis, 1983). When referring to sustained yield, most foresters and modern forest economists refer to rules such as "area regulation" or "volume regulation" as means to produce a "normal forest" (Society of American Foresters, 1958). Since rules change with social and economic circumstances, the precise meaning of sustained yield also changes. Changes in meanings attributed to sustained yield since its adoption in the United States about 1900 have culminated in the existing "nondeclining even-flow" policy that guides the regulation of U.S. national forests (Parry, Vaux, and Dennis, 1983).

Functional definitions of sustained yield generally take the form of statements about the influences of a regulated forest on social, economic, or environmental conditions. They specify assertions about the benefits or contributions of managing a forest so that periodic harvest matches growth. The functional meaning of sustained yield is far older than its technical meaning, since scientifically-based rules were developed after forest harvests had been regulated. Schwappach (1904) and Heske (1938) both reported restrictions on the cutting of German forests as early as the thirteenth century. They also noted laws and restrictions for the regulation of fellings in the fourteenth and fifteenth centuries. Hence, recognition of the functions of a regulated forest may have preceded technical definitions of sustained yield by at least 600 years.

Contemporary critics of sustained yield have reacted primarily to the claim that a regulated forest will promote the stability of local communities by providing a continuous supply of wood for local industries (Waggener, 1977). Thus, arguments have centered on the functions sustained yield is supposed to perform. Is it capable of providing stability in an age when fluctuating interest rates, regionalization and globalization of log markets, and economic diversification disrupt local timber based economies? Answers to this question have eluded investigators.

The symbolic meaning of sustained yield is perhaps the oldest, yet the least understood, of its many themes. Although implicit in the history of wood regulation practices, symbolic meanings have gone largely unexamined until recently. Since at least the early nineteenth century, sustained yield appears to have served as a symbol for social continuity. Sustained yield has served as a repository for future-referring values in German and North American cultures (Lee, 1982). People associate sustained yield with the act of creating the future by perpetuating the biological basis for social continuity. William and Jean Duerr (1975:36) characterized sustained yield as an article of faith, noting:

> To fulfill our obligation to our descendants and to stabilize our
> communities, each generation should sustain its resources at a
> high level and hand them along undiminished. The sustained
> yield of timber is an aspect of man's most fundamental need; to
> sustain life itself.

Given the changing character and complexity of its meaning, sustained yield can best be studied as a general concept to which people in various times and places have attributed specific social meanings. Thus, the first task in any sociological investigation of the history of sustained yield must account for the social meanings and practices that have been associated with this term.

Origins of Sustained Yield

The social history of sustained yield is marked by two distinct phases: its original development in Germany, and its subsequent adoption by foresters in other nations.

To date, there has been insufficient historical research on the social and economic origins of sustained yield in Germany. Existing historical accounts of forestry practices do not account for the social and economic events and conditions associated with its development. But the few historical accounts that do exist, together with more comprehensive social histories of Europe, do not support the interpretations put forward by contemporary critics of sustained yield. Germany was not a stable, hierarchical, stratified, and highly structured society. It developed more slowly than its neighbors, and industrialization did not begin to have a major impact until the middle of the nineteenth century. Germany was split within by divisions between Catholics and Protestant princes, as well as by conflicts between Lutheran and Calvinist Protestants. The Thirty Years War (1618-1648) brought devastation to Germany's agricultural base, capital, and population (Fernow, 1913). Rural life in Germany was progressively devastated by the Thirty Years War, wars of the eighteenth century, and bloody peasant rebellions. Even before the Thirty Years War, the feudal institution of the commons (which had protected the forest use rights of the peasants) had been weakened by growing state and individual property ownership. Princes usurped vast areas of common forest land. By 1800 few traditional communities remained, and most were dependent upon forests owned by the state or the nobility (Fernow, 1913). Thus, sustained yield was developed in a turbulent society in which war and social and economic change were commonplace (and have remained commonplace, with three major crises occurring in the first half of the twentieth century). Rather than a product of stability, sustained yield appears to have been a response to uncertainty and instability (Alston, 1983).

It appears that sustained yield has evolved as an instrument for ordering social and economic conditions, as well as for managing the production of wood from forests. Several specific questions need to be answered in order to evaluate this hypothesis. These questions concern ways in which the functions as well as the symbolism of sustained yield may have contributed to the creation and main-tenance of social order. I will suggest five questions and show how each may be used to evaluate this hypothesis.

First, who were the social agents responsible for the development of sustained yield and for whom did they act? The first half of this question has been at least partially answered by Schwappach (1904), Heske (1938), and others. A succession of scientifically inclined foresters, including Hartig, Cotta, Spath, and Konig, originated rules for forest regulation at the end of the eighteenth century and beginning of the nineteenth century. Yet there has been inadequate accounting of the particular landowners and interests for whom these early foresters acted. The social identity of these landowners is important, since it would reveal much about the reasons for adopting sustained yield practices. Much of the present controversy over this practice has concerned the original functions for which it was developed.

The second question is related to the first. Where, when, and by what social agencies was sustained yield developed? Did it originate in the cities where free persons voluntarily cooperated in developing public utility districts and taxing schemes to support these services (Pirenne, n.d.)? Or did it originate on the private estates of the princes? Or did the emerging centralized government of the late eighteenth and early nineteenth centuries promote sustained yield? The functional and symbolic meaning of sustained yield could be expected to vary substantially in these three circumstances, since the benefits to be derived and the type of social organization to be perpetuated would differ for each of these agencies.

The third question further specifies the first two by asking: What social functions were pursued by developing sustained yield? Was it designed only to provide continuity in wood supplies for domestic and industrial consumption? Or did it have other purposes as well? More specifically, was the development of sustained yield also related to the need for a form of management that would sustain a wide variety of local uses—uses guaranteed by the use rights extended to landless, displaced persons? Both Fernow (1913) and Schwappach (1904) refer to the servitudes that were extended to the peasant. Fernow (1913:47) notes that servitudes were

> conferred to propitiate the powerless but dangerous peasantry ...servitudes that grew to such an extent that in almost every forest someone outside the owner had the right to use parts of it, either the pasture, or the litter, or certain classes or sizes of wood.

In short, did sustained yield originate as a means for manipulating forests to produce multiple benefits, or was it adopted solely to regulate wood production, as is often reported?

The fourth question asks about the symbolic meaning of sustained yield. Did sustained yield serve as a symbol for social continuity, and if so, for whom (what agents or groups) did it promise a future? Who was told (and by whom) that sustained yield would provide continuity for particular forms of activity? Foresters of the past, like today's foresters, generally did not reveal whether they gave much thought to what they had to do in order to secure support for their policies. Despite the preoccupation of foresters with the technical aspects of their work, historical records may reveal how future-referring values were embodied in sustained yield policy statements to solicit support from particular groups or interests.

The final question also concerns symbolic meanings. How was sustained yield related to the major intellectual and ideological movements of the period in which it developed? The potential for sustained yield to serve as a repository for social meanings may have been related more to its conformity to the political climate of the time than to any efforts to solicit support. Was sustained yield an expression of early nineteenth century thought advocating a strong state instead of the emerging capitalist order (see Alston, 1983)? Was the organic model of society, in which the individual was merely a necessary part, symbolized by the forest (Vikor, 1964)? This was clearly the view of Heske (1938) when he wrote about sustained yield. Rather than reject or discredit Heske for his political affiliations (Alston, 1983), perhaps we should empirically examine his organic view of a stable society and its roots in the social history of eighteenth and nineteenth century Germany. The works of Thakurdes (1980) and Vikor (1964) warrant careful examination as original attempts to discredit the growing influence of Adam Smith's individualism. Is it possible that sustained yield emerged along with the rationalization of the organic model of society? Did Heske simply represent the most recent expression of the organic model of society and the state?

Adoption of Sustained Yield

Although difficult, the task of explaining the adoption and persistence of sustained yield in the United States is much simpler than answering these questions about German origins of sustained yield. Records are accessible and the events are recent enough to provide relatively unambiguous interpretations. Records show clearly that an emphasis on sustained yield was associated with turbulent periods in recent U.S. history. It was advocated by federal government officials as a means of creating social stability during periods of social unrest among citizens or workers. This occurred during the Progressive Era when rapid industrialization, population growth, and an end to the western frontier had led to fundamental social and economic change. It occurred again at the end of World War I when government officials became concerned with the problems of soldiers returning from Europe (Magnusson, 1919). The lumber industry in the West had just recovered from work stoppages organized by the International Woodworkers of the World— a radical labor movement that identified with the Left. Sustained yield was again emphasized during the Great Depression as a means for creating stability and prosperity in small rural communities (Loehr, 1952). The end of World War II was marked by the passage of the Forest Management Act of 1944—an attempt to answer the question of how small communities could avoid instability in times of rapid economic change and social readjustment following a major war.

Perhaps the most interesting case was the adoption of sustained yield by the timber industry in the Pacific Northwest. The beginning of the twentieth century was also characterized by an abundance of inexpensive timber on the West Coast. The timber industry had migrated west after harvesting the forests of the Great Lakes States. The industry was highly competitive. Overproduction resulted from a large number of investments in mills and logging camps. Antitrust laws prevented companies from entering into agreements to regulate production. Devastating price instability resulted from overcapitalization by independent producers. By 1920 sustained yield was gaining acceptance in industry as a method for voluntarily limiting production (Drielsma, 1979). Sustained yield was adopted by many companies long before they had begun to consider reforesting lands. This action suggests that sustained yield served as an institutional means for bringing order to relationships between companies that had been engaged in mutually destructive competition. A legal means was found for collectively withholding wood from the market.

This brief interpretation of sustained yield's adoption in the United States is obviously insufficient for evaluating the hypothesis that sustained yield serves as an instrument for promoting social order. Regardless, the evidence adds plausibility to the hypothesis and encourages us to look further for additional information. The plausibility of this explanation also encourages its extension to examining the adoption of sustained yield by other societies.

If sustained yield serves as an effective instrument for creating social order because of its multifunctional capabilities and the way it embodies future-referring values, then it seems likely that other societies might have adopted it in attempts to bring order to unstable social and environmental situations. Thus, it is worth asking: Did foresters working for colonial governments established by European nations adopt sustained yield? If so, did its adoption promote social control over rural people who might have otherwise used the forest indiscriminately? Most of the questions asked about the development of sustained yield in Germany could be rephrased and asked in the context of colonial settlements. The same questions could be asked about the governments that have replaced colonial powers.

CONCLUSIONS

Debates over sustained yield policies in the United States have very high stakes. The criticism of sustained yield has led the U.S. Forest Service to consider departing in some situations from its present sustained yield policy (nondeclining even-flow), especially in the Pacific Northwest where there are still vast areas of old-growth forests. Such departures can adversely impact people who depend on forests for water, recreation, wildlife appreciation or consumption, fisheries habitat, scenery, and other multiple benefits. The possibility that sustained yield serves to create or maintain orderly working relationships among people who depend on forests for such multiple benefits has escaped the attention of foresters wedded to the technical meaning of sustained yield. Therefore, a better understanding of the development and adoption of sustained yield is essential for clarifying the choices to be made by foresters, government agents, the public, local communities, and elected officials. This preliminary study of sustained yield as an instrument for creating social order suggests that it may have important unrecognized functions and legitimizing symbols. The history of sustained yield has a direct bearing on a major public policy issue, and is of immediate concern to forest- dependent communities.

We know too little about the history of sustained yield to either accept or reject the claims of critics. What is clear is that these critics have not adequately researched or documented their claims. It is now incumbent upon historians, sociologists, institutional economists, political scientists, and geographers to document the social and economic history of sustained yield so that alternative explanations for its development, adoption, and persistence may be evaluated adequately.

ACKNOWLEDGEMENTS

Adapted from a paper by the same title in H.K. Steen (ed.). 1984. *History of Sustained-Yield Forestry: A Symposium.* Santa Cruz, CA: Forest History Society.

REFERENCES

Alston, R. 1983. *The Individual vs. The Public Interest.* Boulder, CO: Westview Press.

Behan, R.W. 1975. "Forestry and the End of Innocence." *American Forests* 81 (May):16-19, 38-49.

———. 1978. "Political Popularity and Conceptual Nonsense: The Strange Case of Sustained-Yield Forestry." *Environmental Law* 8 (Summer):209-342.

Byron, R.N. 1978. "Community Stability and Forest Policy in British Columbia." *Canadian Journal of Forest Resources* (Aug.):61-66.

Dowdle, B. (ed.). 1974. "The Economics of Sustained Yield Forestry." Unpublished manuscript, University of Washington, College of Forest Resources.

Drielsma, J.H. 1979. "Sustained-Yield and Community Stability: A History of Ideas in American Forestry." Unpublished manuscript, Yale University.

Duerr, W.A. and J.B. Duerr. 1975. "The Role of Faith in Forest Resource Management." In F. Rumsey and W.A. Duerr (eds.), *Social Sciences in Forestry: A Book of Readings*. Philadelphia London Toronto: W.B. Saunders Co.

Fernow, B.E. 1913. *History of Forestry*. Toronto: University Press, and Washington, DC: American Forestry Association.

Gould, E.M., Jr. 1962. *Forestry and Recreation*. Cambridge, MA: Harvard Forest Papers, No. 6.

———. 1964. "The Future of Forests in Society." *Forestry Chronicle* 40 (Winter):431-444.

Heske, F. 1938. *German Forestry*. New Haven, CT: Yale University Press.

Jackson, D.H. and P.J. Flowers. 1983 "The National Forests and Stabilization: A Look at the Factual Record." *Western Wildlands* 8 (Winter):20-27.

Lee, R. G. 1982. "The Sustained-Yield Concept: Content and Philosophical Origins." In D. LeMaster, D.M. Baumgartner, and D. Adams (eds.) *Sustained-Yield*. Pullman, WA: Washington State University, Cooperative Extension.

LeMaster, D., D.M. Baumgartner, and D. Adams (eds.). 1982. *Sustained Yield*. Pullman, WA: Washington State University, Cooperative Extension.

Loehr, R.C. 1952. *Forests for the Future: The Diaries of David T. Mason*. St. Paul, MN: The Forest Products History Foundation and Minnesota Historical Society.

Magnusson, L. 1919. Disposition of the Public Lands in the United States with Particular Reference to Wage-Earning Labor. Washington, DC: U.S. Department of Labor, Office of the Secretary.

Parry, T., H.J. Vaux, and N. Dennis. 1983. "Changing Conceptions of Sustained-Yield Policy on the National Forests." *Journal of Forestry* 81 (March):150-154.

Pirenne, H. n.d. *Economic and Social History of Medieval Europe*. New York: Harcourt, Brace and World.

Raup, H. 1964. "Some Problems in Ecological Theory and Their Relation to Conservation." *Journal of Ecology* 52 (supp.):19-28.

Schallau, C. 1974. "Can Regulation Contribute to Economic Stability?" *Journal of Forestry* 72: 214-216.

Schwappach, A.F. 1904. *Forestry*. London: A.M. Dent and Co.

Society of American Foresters. 1958. *Forest Terminology*. Washington, DC.

Thakurdes, F. 1980. *German Political Idealism*. New Delhi: Radiant Publishers.

Vikor, D. *Economic Romanticism in the Twentieth Century*. New Delhi: New Book Society of India.

Waggener, T.R. 1977. "Community Stability as a Forest Management Objective." *Journal of Forestry* 75 (11):710-714.

8

Forest Industry Towns in British Columbia

Patricia Marchak
Department of Anthropology and Sociology
University of British Columbia

A basic characteristic of single industry towns, including the forest-industry-based towns described in this paper, is their dependence on the labor force requirements of a specific company. The economic survival of such towns can be tied to a company, but the company may have no such ties to the town. If the resource on which the industry is based is depleted, if markets or technologies change, or any number of other criteria dictate the closure of a mine or mill, the town can rapidly decline. There are many ghost towns in Canada that are the victims of such industry decisions.

Towns with a more diversified base, even where the major industry is resource extractive, have greater security and can better withstand economic downturns (see Byron, 1976 for comparative data on B.C. forest-based towns). Canadian governments seem to have assumed that if a mill, mine, or other large project is established, it will eventually spin off all kinds of economic benefits, the population will grow, new industries will be attracted to the region, and the area will become a stable community. Conventional staples theory advanced this as an argument (e.g., Mackintosh, 1923; Lower, 1938), though that variant of the theory advanced in Innis (1930) and extended by Watkins (1963, 1977) questioned the premises, pointing out that investment and trade patterns, especially for a region marginal to central growth regions, would not necessarily fulfill the promise. Some towns in Canada have grown from single industry bases—Ottawa and Vancouver, among them—but the realization of the dream is much rarer than its invocation. After all, investors build company towns not for purposes of creating regional centers, though such growth may occur, but simply to house their labor force while extracting a resource in regions remote from existing population centers. Far from markets, and dependent on either nonrenewable or gradually depleting resources, such towns are not well situated to become larger, more diversified centers.

The forest industry, like other resource industries, has a history of "booms" and "busts." Its products have fluctuating demand on world markets. Recognizing this, governments might reinvest some portion of the wealth extracted from the resource into more diversified industries. One way of doing this is to charge high resource rents during "boom" periods, using the rents to replenish the resource, fund research on new products with higher embedded value, and establish additional and different industries. Another way is to attach conditions for greater value-added manufacturing to harvesting rights. British Columbia governments took neither of these actions (see B.C. Royal Commission Report, 1976, for data on stumpage rates and forest tenures; also Copithorne, 1979, for analysis of stumpage formula; and Debates of the B.C. Legislative Assembly (Hansard), 1978, 3rd Session, 31st Parliament, May 1 to June 23, for extended discussion of government policy).

The post-war "boom" in forestry was prolonged, but it finally came to an end in 1980; with the industry's recession the entire provincial economy went into a severe depression. With half of all export dollars deriving from wood products, the provincial economy had established very few industrial linkages such as pulpmill machinery, logging and sawmill equipment, computer hardware, or the range of consumer products required by resident populations (see B.C., Industry and Small Business Development, annual, for production and export statistics). At the bottom of the recession, in 1982, overall unemployment rates rose as high as 17 percent, with rates of up to 40 percent in some forest-dependent towns (International Woodworkers of America, 1982). As late as 1987, with the North American economy generally much healthier, unemployment in British Columbia was still above 10 percent. Lumber producers have met stiffened competition because of the imposition of U.S. countervailing duties and new export taxes on goods destined for the major U.S. markets, and pulp producers are beset by overcapacity and technological developments that reduce the long-term market prospects for softwood pulp. These developments have had impacts on company and other forest-based towns, but even during the "boom" period, such towns tended to be unstable.

EXAMPLES OF FOREST-BASED TOWNS

Mackenzie, situated in northeastern British Columbia, is one such town. With a population of about 5,000, it strikes the observer as a suburb in search of a town. It emerges suddenly, 30 kilometers from the junction of a highway: a compact, car-oriented area very much like post-war North American suburbs near large cities, though it is, in fact, 190 kilometres from the nearest urban center. Constructed in the mid-1960s as the townsite for a large company mill, the town has a small hospital, a curling rink, and a community recreational center. The land for the townsite was provided by the provincial crown under special legislation. About half of resident families live in houses built by the major company, B.C. Forest Products, and then purchased on affordable terms by millworkers. The other half live in trailers, hotels, or apartments. At the time of my study of this town (1977; see Marchak, 1979; 1983), millworkers and loggers earned hourly wages that were high by standards of similar workers in other parts of Canada and the United States. Though the average income for town residents was high, living costs were also high.[1]

Several theses have studied Mackenzie's quality of life, taking the form of questionnaires using various "satisfaction scales" (Lauder, 1977; Moore, 1976; see also Matthiasson, 1970; Bradbury, 1977; Cornerstone Planning Group, 1977; Veit and Associates, 1978). These studies showed, for example, that residents were dissatisfied with shopping facilities, more satisfied with recreational activities, and somewhat satisfied with medical services except that any specialized medical or dental services could only be obtained by traveling long distances.

These theses describe a population's likes and dislikes in a vacuum and provide no clue about the most significant aspect of the town: a high proportion of residents leave every year, and very few plan to stay there longer than five years. One study found less than 5 percent of respondents intended to remain in the town indefinitely. My own study confirmed this. In the one-month period between selection of the sample and start of interviewing, 20 percent of our sample had moved away. Mackenzie, despite company housing, crescent-shaped suburban streets, and high incomes, failed to sustain many long-term residents. Why, and what does this say about Mackenzie's quality of life?

The reasons for this instability were varied, but most particularly had to do with the nature of the resource industry. Loggers and sawmill workers experience frequent layoffs. Turnover rates are often counted as if all job changes are personal choices of workers (see Cottell, 1974; 1975). In fact, much of the transience of such towns reflects the continuing search for more permanent employment (Marchak, 1983). Pulpmill workers have much greater job security, and their turnover rates, defined as the ratio of leavers to stayers per annum, are much lower (B.C. Research, 1974)[2].

Companies require a flexible labor force in sectors that have variable markets or rapidly changing technologies. Sawmills and logging operations have high labor demand in contrast with pulpmills, but can be closed down without great loss to the company. This is because production is geared to the high marginal costs of labor, energy, and other inputs, and not to the fixed costs of plant or continuous production technologies as is the case for pulpmills. Workers in sawmills can be trained fairly quickly, so that loss of experienced hands is not the problem it is for higher-technology and capital-intensive pulpmills. Workers in logging are more skilled, but there are more available workers than jobs and thus relatively little need to invest in the labor force or in its stability. In short, while companies would prefer to have stable work forces, they also want flexibility and low operating costs. They are more likely to accept greater rigidities and labor costs where high turnover undermines productivity, sustained operation, or maintenance of large investments in plant and equipment, than where turnover has relatively small impact on production[3] (Marchak, 1979; 1983).

The second reason for instability is the geographical isolation of the town and the lack of employment for women. Women coresident with loggers, in particular, are likely to live in trailers with their children while their husbands are at logging camps. Few can find work in these resource-extractive towns; very few employers in resource industries employ women in production lines or logging camps (see Northern British Columbia Women's Task Force Report, 1977; also Marchak, 1983). These women have no social network of kinfolk as they would in a rural community. In Mackenzie, the demographic profile implies this, with virtually the whole adult population under age fifty-five. Women are profoundly isolated, and spoke of this in interviews. A fairly typical negative statement: "There are more marriages here destroyed than anywhere I've been. The people here are not bad. It's the town that stinks. All I can say is I will be glad when we move out of Mackenzie" (reported in Marchak, 1983:317).

A third reason for instability is that no one knows what the future holds: residents do not believe their children will have employment in Mackenzie because they know how impermanent these towns are. They worry about their teenage children's life chances in such towns, so they try to earn enough to buy their way back to urban centers before children leave school. The local school strives to keep children through to graduation, but admits it has difficulty persuading youngsters of the need for education when there are few role-models of "successful" individuals benefiting from it. The children either take employment in sawmills and repeat the pattern of their parents' transient lives, or rush away from the town toward cities in search of something better.

Nearly two-fifths of a 1977 study sample expressed strong interest in moving out of the town to a rural subdivision where they might build a home, garden, and keep animals (Lauder, 1977). That is not an option for residents of Mackenzie because the company has control of surrounding land and has no interest in an expanding rural community. The municipality says that it cannot afford the servicing of such lots. If the intent of provincial government policies in establishing such communities was to create stable living conditions for a resident population, the fact that many people prefer a more rural lifestyle should be significant, and investment in servicing rural lots should take higher priority. But if the intent was simply to create temporary towns to house the labor force engaged in resource extraction, then such investment is unnecessary. What then is the objective of public policy: to create diversified communities or to enable companies to profit from the resource base (see Bradbury, 1977 for more extended discussion)?

In the literature on company towns, much is made of the distinction between formal company control and municipal status. Although it is supposed to be a sign of maturity that a community achieves municipal governance in place of company control (see Veit and Associates,1978, literature review), municipalities have limited power when the economic conditions of the town are controlled by a single company. This is especially true when the single company is owned and controlled from outside the region. This is the case in Mackenzie, and it is the case in almost every single-industry town in Canada. The major decisions affecting these towns are not made in municipal council chambers. They are made in New York, Toronto, Tokyo or wherever the parent company is situated, and they are made without reference to the needs of workers in these communities.

Not all single-industry towns are as bereft of a sense of community as Mackenzie was in 1977. But all have external constraints on their survival capacities. Consider, for example, the case of Ocean Falls.

This pulpmill town was built on the coastal edge of a rainforest in 1949 by Crown Zellerbach. To attract families, the company built a magnificent swimming pool and employed Canada's top coach. During the 1950s, this little town produced several members of Canada's Olympic swimming teams.

But the mill was already becoming obsolete by the late 1950s, when kraft sulphate mills provided superior technology over kraft sulphite mills such as Crown Zellerbach's Ocean Falls plant. Crown Zellerbach had to make a decision typical of resource companies: whether to plan a new mill in the 1960s that would be competitive with other new mills being constructed in British Columbia, or to phase out Ocean Falls. It chose the latter course, and permitted the mill to deteriorate. Crown Zellerbach continued cutting nearby forest and directed surplus wood from the region to a more modern mill situated further south, closer to its American parent company (Hayter, 1973, provides a detailed account).

Formal closure came in the early 1970s. The provincial government responded to the pleas of townsfolk by purchasing the properties and attempting to operate the pulpmill under the management of a crown corporation. But the resource base was depleted, the mill was antiquated, and although in a buoyant market it was kept alive for two years, ultimately the project was abandoned. It is now an abandoned townsite.

Older towns that were first established as railway junctions and farming centers with a mixture of small mills have tended to be more resilient through the booms and busts of the forest industry. One such town is Terrace, in the northwest of

British Columbia. With a population of between 10,000 and 14,000 (fluctuating with economic conditions), some 600 miles north of Vancouver, Terrace is situated at the confluence of three rivers, near the Nass, Kitimat, and Bulkley valleys: a stunningly beautiful setting appreciated by its inhabitants and missed by those who leave to seek a livelihood elsewhere. Several Indian tribes have inhabited the region for many centuries, and non-Indians have settled there for over a century. What distinguishes this region and others like it from towns like Mackenzie and Ocean Falls is that it developed slowly and had roots preceding the establishment of large, externally owned industries. Indian bands and descendents of pioneer families still call it home and are prepared to struggle for their right to live there. This makes it all the more tragic that the resource base has been severely eroded, and that the future of Terrace and many towns like it is bleak.

In the case of Terrace, Columbia Cellulose obtained the harvesting rights to nearby forests in the late 1940s, built saw and pulp mills, and took over small family firms in the region. It harvested the trees but neglected to adequately replenish the resource. As the mills became dated by the introduction of new technologies in the late 1950s and 1960s, the company made essentially the same decision as Crown Zellerbach had in Ocean Falls. It let the mill run down and directed surplus wood to other mills. Then, as in Ocean Falls, the property was sold to the crown. In this case the crown built a large new pulpmill, but the surrounding resource base is inadequate to sustain industrial activity far into the future. The townsfolk know this. In interviews I heard time and again, "the forest has come to an end. The town is dying." Some residents have tried to develop survival techniques by growing their own food by or spending part of the year elsewhere seeking jobs that might provide minimal income for survival in a cash economy (Marchak, 1983).

COMMUNITY PROPOSALS FOR LOCAL CONTROL

In Terrace and nearby communities in the Northwest, and in another forestry region of the Southeast, groups have formed over the past decade to protect their environment and their livelihoods. In one case they have undertaken a detailed study of the resource, the industry, and markets, and have published this together with proposals for reorganizing their economic conditions (Slocan Valley Community Forest Management Feasibility Project, 1975).

They argue for the community as a whole to have the resource harvesting rights and the control of local mills and further investment decisions. Given this, they could harvest the resource judiciously and create an industry that efficiently utilized the resource and manufactured a more finished end product for specialty markets. They could direct profits toward further manufacturing in the region and greater economic diversification. They would pay wages established by community decision, in line with wages elsewhere, but with a view to sustaining the community on a "social wage" rather than sustaining transient individuals on a personal wage. The net benefits would be a resource base that would last longer and be regenerated; the possibility for reinvestment in the region instead of export of surplus to parent companies outside; and a permanent community with collective control over its destiny, a future for its children, and more occupational choice for its residents. This alternative would require a provincial government to invest in such a community, provide it with resource rights, and provide an umbrella marketing agency enabling it to create and sustain its viability. However, there is no certainty that community firms would have access to world markets. Several may already have insufficient resource supplies. It could be very difficult to sustain community-controlled manufacturing plants in an industry beset with both traditionally variable markets and rapidly changing market and technological conditions. But the current situation does not provide obvious long-term solutions, and it may be time for experiments. Such experiments might be viable in regions such as the Northwest, with Terrace at its base, or the Slocan valley in the interior of British Columbia, where a sense of community and a desire for permanent settlement are strongly evident. They might not be viable in regions such as the Northeast, with Mackenzie as its base, where a permanent community has not been established.

Similar proposals have been advanced by other groups, though none so detailed. One group's brief to the government during the 1978 Forest Act debates described its objectives as "a stable community with meaningful work for all and a forest environment that can provide a sustained yield of all resources" (Smithers Forest Advisory Committee, 1978). The common thread running through the briefs and studies of these groups is a demand for local access to resource rights, community control of investment decisions, and a strong commitment of residents to their regions. They are saying, sometimes in these words, "we live here; we love this place; we want our children to have employment here; we want to plan our own futures and have reasonable control over the conditions of our lives." As they point out, they cannot achieve this objective as long as the resource is mass-produced by mills owned outside the region. As phrased by the Slocan group, "Sustained yields can only be guaranteed if the local community is involved in resource-use planning."

CHANGING MARKETS AND TECHNOLOGIES

Resource-use planning is clearly an essential condition for stable communities in the forest industry. But resource dependence is perhaps a more serious problem, especially in view of changes occurring in world markets. Pulpmill technologies have been developed that transform eucalyptus and other species not formerly used into high grade pulp (Hay-Roe's PaperTreeletter, November, 1985). Softwoods are expected to lose markets. This prospect may be part of the reason that several large, American forest companies have sold their properties in British Columbia over the past several years (Crown Zellerbach; International Paper; International Telephone and Telegraph's subsidiary Rayonier; and Mead Corporation among them). In this context, substituting small, community-owned firms for large ones would not solve the problems of dependence on a resource that is both diminishing and facing long-term market reductions. Thus, if small rural communites are to be sustained, resource-use planning must be accompanied by diversification of the economic base.

SUMMARY

This paper has described several forest-based towns in British Columbia, and has argued that towns based on resource extraction and a variable market for their product are economically weak. In some regions, local residents have proposed as a solution greater community participation in resource decision-making and management of forest industries. These proposals, however, do not address the problem of dependence on forest products, and it is suggested that a long-term solution to the problem would involve planning for diversification of the economic base in rural industrial regions.

NOTES

1. Wage settlements in British Columbia are negotiated through regional bargaining between the Forest Industrial Relations Association and the three unions, International Woodworkers of America; Pulp, Paper, and Woodworkers of Canada; and Canadian Paperworkers Union. In 1977, the median income for all men in the labor force in British Columbia was $13,262, and for all men in Canada, $11,740. For loggers in the sample study undertaken that year in Mackenzie, Terrace, and Campbell River, the median was $22,258; for sawmill workers, it was $22,237; for pulpworkers, $22,556. (Canadian and B.C. medians from Statistics Canada, Income Distribution by Size in Canada, 1977, cat 13-206: 12-17). Copithorne (1979:188) argues that the stumpage formula permitted employers to charge some portion of increasing wages to rents, and thereby encouraged escalating wage raises in the negotiations; also that the high wages in forestry, because it is the leading sector of the provincial economy, underlay the

somewhat higher wages throughout B.C. relative to the rest of Canada. However, his argument is not fully borne out by published statistics on average weekly earnings in B.C. industries. Rates have been persistently higher in the construction industry, and about the same in mining as in logging. The manufacturing industries have had lower average earnings, the trades and services sectors much lower. The B.C. rates are higher than in neighbouring United States by an average of U.S.$12 per 1,000 board feet of production, according to the U.S. Senate Investigation on lumber prices (U.S. International Trade Commission, Report to the Senate Committee on Finance on Investigation No. 332-134, under Section 332 of the Tariff Act of 1930, April, 1982).

2. B.C. Research (consultants) was employed by B.C. Forest Products to conduct a study on turnover rates in the sawmills and pulpmills in Mackenzie, and was also employed by a group of employers and unions, The Skeena Manpower Study group, to conduct similar research in Terrace. In the Mackenzie study (B.C. Research, 1974), they found rates of 366 and 589 percent among labor pools in the sawmills, compared to 70 percent for pulpmill utility workers (1974 and follow-up reports). In the Skeena study (B.C. Research, 1978), they found overall rates for forest workers over a four year period from 1973 to 1976 of between 54 and 92 percent, compared to rates of between 5 and 14 percent in government work, 16 and 21 percent in transportation, and 28 and 43 percent in utilities.

3. The following tables indicate the differences in employment durations for workers in the three sections, from sample survey data collected in three towns, 1977-78, as reported in Marchak, *Green Gold*, 1983: Tables 6.2 and 6.3, p. 179.

Table 1. Duration of employment with present employer by forestry sector for men*.

Sector	N = 100%	6 mos. or less	7 mos.- 2 yrs.	25 mos.- 5 yrs.	61 mos.- 10 yrs.	over 10 yrs.
Logging	107	21.5	23.4	26.2	13.1	15.8
Sawmills	90	12.2	31.2	24.5	20.0	12.1
Pulpmills	71	14.1	9.8	16.9	12.7	46.5

*excluding short layoffs

Table 2. Median no. months employed by same employer for men employed in each sector at given dates for two periods of each year 1970-1977. (Interview Sample)*

	Logging Median (N)	Sawmill Median (N)	Pulpmill Median (N)
Interview	30(107)	34(90)	92(71)
J77	36(112)	36(94)	over 120(69)
F77	44(105)	46(80)	over 120(65)
J76	43(110)	53(73)	over 120(65)
F76	49(104)	59(65)	over 120(60)
J74	50(103)	72(56)	over 120(62)
F74	54 (93)	69(57)	over 120(56)
J73	49 (99)	78(55)	over 120(57)
F73	54 (92)	82(53)	over 120(53)
J72	52 (95)	79(54)	over 120(48)
F72	54 (88)	82(51)	over 120(48)
J71	49 (89)	79(47)	over 120(51)
F71	60 (78)	102(44)	over 120(51)
J70	55 (75)	97(40)	over 120(53)
F70	58 (71)	114(35)	over 120(49)

*The coding procedures for duration grouped together all employments lasting longer than 10 years, thus the median for workers in this group cannot be specified.

REFERENCES

British Columbia. 1976. 2 vols. *Royal Commission on Forest Resources*. Peter H. Pearse, Commissioner. Victoria, BC: Queen's Printer.

———. 1978. *Debates of the Legislative Assembly (Hansard)*. 3rd Session, 31st Parliament, May 1 to June 23. Victoria, BC.

———. Ministry of Industry and Small Business Development. Annual. *British Columbia Economic Activity. Review and Outlook*. Victoria, BC.

B.C. Research. 1974 (updates, 1976, 1978). *Labour Turnover at Mackenzie*. Prepared by A. Alexander and D. Bryant for B.C. Forest Products. Vancouver, BC.

———. 1978. *Labour Instability in the Skeena Manpower Area*. Prepared by D. Bryant, C. Hoyt, and B. Painter for the Skeena Manpower Development Committee. Vancouver, BC.

Bradbury, J.H. 1977. "Instant Towns in B.C., 1964-1972." Ph.D. dissertation, Simon Fraser University.

Byron, R.N. 1976. "Community Stability and Economic Development: The Role of Forest Policy in the North Central Interior of British Columbia." M.B.A. thesis, University of British Columbia.

Copithorne, L. 1979. "Natural Resources and Regional Disparities: A Skeptical View." *Canadian Public Policy* 5(2) (Spring):181-194.

Cornerstone Planning Group, Ltd. 1977. *Coal Employment Survey of the North East Region of British Columbia.* Prepared for the Ministry of Economic Development, the Ministry of Labour, and the B.C. Manpower Sub-Committee on Northeast Coal Development. Victoria, BC.

Cottell, P.L. 1974. *Occupational Choice and Employment Stability Among Forest Workers.* New Haven, CT: Yale University.

——. 1975. "Loggers View Instability as Key to Maximum Employment." *British Columbia Logging News* (January):26-38.

Hay-Roe's PaperTreeletter. 1985. Vancouver: PaperTree Economics Ltd. (November).

Hayter, R. 1973. "An Examination of Growth Patterns and Locational Behavior of Multi-Plant Forest Product Corporations in British Columbia." Master's thesis, University of Washington.

Innis, H. (1930) 1954. *The Fur Trade in Canada.* Toronto: University of Toronto Press.

International Woodworkers of America, 1982. *Forest Industry Direct Unemployment in Western Canada as of November 1, 1982.* Vancouver, BC.

Lauder, K.S. 1977. "Planning for Quality of Life in New Resource Communities." Ph.D. dissertation, University of Waterloo, Waterloo, ON.

Lower, A.R M. 1938. *The North American Assault on the Canadian Forest: A History of the Lumber Trade Between Canada and the United States.* Toronto: Ryerson Press.

Mackintosh, W.A. 1923. "Economic Factors in Canadian History." *The Canadian Historical Review 4(1)*:12-25.

Marchak, M.P. 1979. "Labour in a Staples Economy." *Studies in Political Economy* 2 (Autumn):7-36.

———. 1983. *Green Gold: The Forest Industry in British Columbia.* Vancouver, BC: University of British Columbia Press.

Matthiasson, J.S. 1970. *Resident Perceptions of Quality of Life in Resource Frontier Communities.* University of Manitoba, Centre for Settlement Studies, Series 2, No. 2.

Moore, J.P. 1976. "Residents' Perceptions of the Quality of Life in Vanderhoof and Mackenzie, Two Northern British Columbia Resource Communities." M.B.A. thesis, Simon Fraser University.

Northern B.C. Women's Task Force. 1977. *Report on Single Industry Resource Communities.* Vancouver, BC: Women's Research Centre.

Slocan Valley Community Forest Management Feasibility Project on Forestry Utilization Alternatives. 1975. Final Report. Winlow, BC.

Smithers Forest Advisory Committee. 1978. Press release concerning letter and brief to Tom Waterland, Minister of Mines, Forests, and Water Resources, June 7. Smithers, BC.

U.S. International Trade Commission. 1982. *Conditions Relating to the Importation of Softwood Lumber Into the United States.* Report to the Senate Committee on Finance on Investigation No. 332-134, Under Section 332 of the Tariff Act of 1930 (April) (and subsequent debates on the issue of countervailing duties) Washington, DC.

Veit, S. and Associates. 1978. *Labour Turnover and Community Stability.* Report to the Federal-Provincial Manpower Subcommittee on Northeast Coal Development, Project No. 270060-3 (February).

Watkins, M. 1963. "A Staples Theory of Economic Growth." *Canadian Journal of Economics and Political Science* 29(2) (May):141-158.

———. 1977. "The Staples Theory Revisited." *Journal of Canadian Studies* 12(5) (Winter):83-95.

9

The Changing Structure of the Forest Industry in the Pacific Northwest

Andy Brunelle
Special Assistant
Governor's Office, State of Idaho

Vast forests cover nearly one-half of the Pacific Northwest and have played a historic role in the economic development of the region. Even today, the forest industry accounts for approximately one-third of all manufacturing employment throughout the region, from the small communities dependent on a single mill for their primary employment, to the metropolitan areas where many large forest products corporations are headquartered. In fact, there are few areas in the region not affected by the operating level of sawmills and plywood plants.

The solid wood sector of the forest industry (sawmills, plywood plants, and veneer plants) is based primarily in the small towns of Washington, Oregon, Idaho, and Montana. In Oregon alone, there are seventy-nine towns with populations of less than 3,000 that rely on the wood products industry for their economic support. In sixty-two of these communities, more than 80 percent of the total manufacturing work force is employed in wood products firms (Weeks, 1983).

Since many of these small Northwest towns are so dependent on the timber industry, changes in the national economy that affect interest rates, and thus housing demand, can decrease demand for lumber and plywood, in turn leading to mill closures, bankruptcy, and changes in ownership. Because the timber industry is notoriously unstable, "community stability" has been a concern of the U.S. Forest Service and the forest-based industry and communities.

In the current round of the national forest planning process, community stability has been cited as a reason for the Forest Service to maintain or increase its timber harvests. It is commonly accepted that Forest Service policies cannot shield the timber industry from short-run changes in the economy. Instead, the focus of community stability for the Forest Service is long-run stability through a reliable timber supply (Schallau and Alston, 1987).

Another factor important to the stability of forest-based communities, but often overlooked, is the industry structure. Changes in the economy, competition from outside the region, and technology forced most forest products companies to reexamine their operations. Their responses changed the industry's structure over the past ten years. This paper examines the recent structural change in the industry, reflecting both how these companies responded to economic and technological forces and how a reordered industry affected economic stability of forest-dependent communities and the region.

FORCES OF STRUCTURAL CHANGE

The Business Cycle

In the short run, forest-based communities are affected by changes in the economy that affect the industry. In the late 1970s, Northwest timber companies experienced sustained markets and handsome profits. In 1978, lumber production in the four states was at 14.75 billion board feet, and plywood production stood at 11.5 billion square feet. This was followed by the deepest recession in fifty years, hitting the Northwest like a two-by-four over the head. By 1982, lumber production was down one-third from the peak of the late 1970s, and plywood production was off 38 percent. The industry began to recover slowly in 1983, and by the late 1980s industry output was exceeding the palmy days of a decade earlier. Communities dependent on the timber industry rode this roller coaster, whose ups and downs were in most part based on the demand for wood products. The slow recovery from the deep recession had many wondering whether the industry would ever recover.[1]

Competition from Other Regions

For most of this century, the Pacific Northwest has been the "Persian Gulf" of wood products, providing roughly 40 percent of domestically produced lumber, and until the 1960s, nearly all the plywood. But the Northwest's position has been eclipsed by stiff competition from other timber producing regions and from new products. Due to imports of Canadian lumber, the Northwest's share of total U.S. lumber consumption is now less than 30 percent. Canadian lumber producers are aided by government policies that lower transportation costs and keep stumpage prices stable. The exchange rate has been an uncontrollable factor, but one that has worked in Canada's favor.

Competition has also taken its toll on plywood, a product invented in the Northwest. The region's share of plywood production has dropped from 90 percent in 1965 to 40 percent today. Plywood producers in the southeastern United States have become more competitive with cheaper logs and labor, better proximity to markets, and newer plants and processing technologies. Recently developed plywood substitutes like waferboard and oriented-strandboard, both of which cost less, have gained wide acceptance in the construction industry. Plants producing these substitutes are not dependent on high quality trees and are located throughout the country, though in the Northwest there is only one mill each in Idaho and Washington.

Technological Change

Interwoven with changes in the Northwest's competitive position have been recent investments in modernization of mills. Modernization has had a dramatic effect in the Northwest. Its impact has increased the capacity and productivity of some mills, resulted in closure of inefficient mills, and permanently reduced employment. Despite a 30 percent decrease in the number of sawmills since 1970, production capacity of lumber has not decreased, but has shifted toward fewer, larger capacity, and more efficient mills.

Along with competition, forces for modernization have included increased costs of production (from higher wages and log prices), the smaller diameter of logs available for processing (a transition to second growth timber), and increased transportation costs. Efficiency is gained either by decreasing the overall costs of processing a log or by extracting more value from the log (Ehinger, 1983; Polzin and Keegan, 1987).

Modernized mills require substantial investment, which in turn increases fixed costs of running the plant. To realize a return on investment, a new plant must operate at or near capacity. A company with several mills will maximize return on its investment at the expense of its older mills (Weeks, 1983). For example, Potlatch Corporation's $35 million sawmill modernization in Lewiston, Idaho forced the closure of its older mill in Coeur d'Alene. The company decided to expand production from two to three shifts at the Lewiston mill, and to direct logs there for processing.

Modernization has also affected product mix and prices. Automation of mills has resulted in increased production of commodity dimensional lumber and studs, while higher-valued boards and selects make up a smaller share (Polzin and Keegan, 1987). Prices for the lower grade commodity items have fallen because modernized mills can produce larger amounts of these standard products at a lower cost when operating at higher capacity.

The greatest impact from modernization has been in the size of the work force. This has manifested itself in two ways. First, older mills are labor intensive; if a mill is modernized, the work force is affected by gains in efficiency that could decrease employment by as much as 50 percent while producing the same amount of lumber. Total output from a rebuilt mill usually increases, and buffers to some

extent the lost jobs. Investment in modernization can also be incremental, with the
number of jobs trimmed gradually.

Second, the closure of older and less competitive mills in towns like Westfir
and Valsetz, Oregon, and Riggins and Potlatch, Idaho caused major social and
economic upheavals in those communities. Whatever the process, the loss of
timber-related jobs was permanent, creating the impression that the industry was
dying, even though production had returned to the levels of the late 1970s.

THE STRUCTURE OF THE NORTHWEST FOREST INDUSTRY

To understand the role of competition, the business cycle, and modernization
in changing the industry's structure, it is necessary to first develop a baseline. For
this analysis, the hundreds of companies that operate in the Pacific Northwest were
grouped in three major categories: National, Regional, and Local. Companies are
categorized based on the following criteria: (1) location of corporate headquarters;
(2) number of wood products plants and their location; either in the Pacific
Northwest, or elsewhere in the United States or in Canada; (3) variety of products
produced and sold (Local companies usually produce only lumber or plywood
while National firms manufacture both wood products and pulp and paper); (4)
vertical integration of the company, from timberland ownership through manufacturing and marketing of products; and (5) history and background of individual
companies. While this classification is somewhat subjective and inferred from
limited data, it serves well to gauge the effect of size of company and location of
corporate headquarters to performance over the past ten years.[2]

Table 1 lists the firms classified as National or Regional companies and the
location of their corporate headquarters. Most of the National firms are familiar
to the public; many are members of the Fortune 500, others are long-time names
in the forest industry. The National companies, Boise Cascade, Louisiana-Pacific,
and Champion International, operated in each of the four states in 1978. National
companies have the most diverse product mix (many are major paper producers),
own large amounts of standing timber, and are most likely to have organized labor
in their mills.

Regional companies are headquartered in the Pacific Northwest, operating
mills predominantly in the region and Northern California. Most Regional companies are smaller than National companies (measured by sales), but are important
players in the region. Many can trace their origins to a small independent or
family-owned mill in a small town in the Pacific Northwest. Willamette Industries,
Bohemia, and Roseburg Lumber are not far removed from their roots, having
grown from small firms in only the last generation. About half the Regional
companies are independently owned. Firms that are publicly held are owned

Table 1. Firms Classified as National and Regional Companies, 1978

National		Regional	
Company	Headquarters	Company	Headquarters
American Can Co.	Greenwich, CT	Alpine Veneers Inc.	Portland, OR
Boise Cascade Corp.	Boise, ID	Bohemia Inc.	Eugene, OR
Champion Intl.	Stamford, CT	Brans-S Corp.	Corvallis, OR
Crown Zellerbach	San Francisco, CA	Brooks-Scanlon	Bend, OR
Diamond Intl.	New York, NY	Coos Head Timber	Coos Bay, OR
Georgia-Pacific Corp.*	Portland, OR	Dant & Russell	Portland, OR
Hines Lumber Co., Ed	Chicago, IL	Dollar Co., The Robert	San Francisco, CA
International Paper	New York, NY	Evans Products	Portland, OR
ITT Rayonier	New York, NY	Idaho Forest Industries	Coeur d'Alene, ID
Louisiana-Pacific Corp.	Portland, OR	Johnson Lumber Co. DR	Riddle, OR
Potlatch Corp.	San Francisco, CA	Medford Corp.	Medford, OR
Southwest Forest Ind.	Phoenix, AZ	Mountain Fir Lumber	Salem, OR
St. Regis Paper Co.	New York, NY	Murphy Co. The	Portland, OR
U.S. Gypsum	Chicago, IL	Pack River Lumber	Seattle, WA
Weyerhaeuser Co.	Tacoma, WA	Plum Creek Timber	Seattle, WA
		Pope & Talbot	Portland, OR
		Publishers Paper	Los Angeles, CA
		Roseburg Lumber Co.	Roseburg, OR
		Simpson Timber Co.	Seattle, WA
		Stimson Lumber Co.	Forest Grove, OR
		Timber Products Co.	Springfield, OR
		Wickes Forest Products	Dinuba, CA
		Willamette Industries	Portland, OR

*Georgia-Pacific moved their corporate headquarters to Atlanta, GA in 1982.

mostly by Northwest residents. Publishers Paper and Plum Creek Timber are wholly-owned subsidiaries of large corporations (Times Mirror and Burlington Northern respectively), but the forest-based subsidiary head offices and operations are in the Northwest.

The final category of firm is Local companies, firms that are owned and operated locally. A few operate mills in more than one location, but in these cases the plants are within a half day's drive of top management. A listing of the companies (about 400 in 1978) is not practical for this context.

Changes in Industry Structure

To ascertain the shifts that occurred in organization and structure of the forest industry, statistics for the years 1978 and 1985 were used. Data on lumber production and operating plywood capacity were gathered to calculate the share of overall industry production for each company type. Production data by company was easier to obtain than employment or income statistics. Because of mill modernization and productivity improvements in the past few years, production indices more accurately portray the industry's recovery than do employment statistics. The year 1978 represents one of the boom years before the 1980-1982 recession. Data for 1985 represents the latest year of data on the industry at this writing, and was also the third year of recovery from the recession.[3]

Table 2 shows lumber production, plywood capacity, and shares (percentages) of the total by type of company in the Pacific Northwest. The data reveal that the role of Local firms in lumber production is surprisingly large, given the popular impression that National companies control production in the industry. Most noteworthy is a shift in lumber production from National firms toward Regional and Local firms between 1978 and 1985. That small companies are usually assumed to be less stable than larger companies further underscores the significance of this finding. Changes in plywood capacity are more startling than in lumber. Regional and Local firms were able to maintain their production capacity in the industry, but that part accounted for by National firms fell appreciably and is no longer dominant. Plywood capacity is now evenly divided among the three tiers of the industry.

Table 2. Lumber Production, Plywood Capacity, and Shares by Type of Company, 1978 and 1985—The Pacific Northwest

Company Type	Lumber Production (million board feet)		Production Share (by percent)		Plywood Capacity (million sq. ft.)		Production Share (by percent)	
	1978	1985	1978	1985	1978	1985	1978	1985
National	5,141	3,584	34.9%	26.1%	5,911	3,361	45.5%	31.3%
Regional	3,265	3,906	22.1	28.4	3,562	3,732	27.5	34.7
Local	6,347	6,260	43.0	45.5	3,499	3,647	27.0	34.0
Total	14,754	13,750	100.0%	100.0%	12,972	10,740	100.0%	100.0%

A look at the industry state-by-state for the years 1978 and 1985 (Table 3) reveals some interesting contrasts. In Washington and Oregon, approximately one-half of lumber production in 1978 was by Local companies. In Idaho and Montana, with relatively smaller industries (though very important to their states' economies), National companies produced over half of the lumber in 1978. Thus, in the states with greater timber resources a more diverse industry structure was present; the smaller timber base in Idaho and Montana was dominated by National

Table 3. Lumber Production, Plywood Capacity, and Shares by Type of Company, 1978 and 1985

Oregon

Company Type	Lumber Production (million board feet) 1978	1985	Production Share (by percent) 1978	1985	Plywood Capacity (million sq. ft.) 1978	1985	Production Share (by percent) 1978	1985
National	1,777	1,247	24.0%	17.3%	3,905	1,748	43.1%	22.6%
Regional	1,725	2,342	26.4	32.5	2,761	3,350	30.5	43.4
Local	3,914	3,622	49.6	50.2	2,399	2,626	26.5	34.0
Total	7,416	7,211	100.0%	100.0%	9,065	7,724	100.0%	100.0%

Washington

Company Type	Lumber Production (million board feet) 1978	1985	Production Share (by percent) 1978	1985	Plywood Capacity (million sq. ft.) 1978	1985	Production Share (by percent) 1978	1985
National	1,691	1,215	40.8%	35.6%	1,054	670	40.7%	36.6%
Regional	514	675	12.4	19.7	566	152	21.8	8.3
Local	1,945	1,529	46.8	44.7	972	1,010	37.5	55.1
Total	4,150	3,419	100.0%	100.0%	2,592	1,832	100.0%	100.0%

Idaho

Company Type	Lumber Production (million board feet) 1978	1985	Production Share (by percent) 1978	1985	Plywood Capacity (million sq. ft.) 1978	1985	Production Share (by percent) 1978	1985
National	1,045	589	54.1%	35.2%	572	539	98.6%	98.0%
Regional	434	459	22.5	27.4	0	0	0.0	0.0
Local	453	628	23.4	37.6	8	11	1.4	2.0
Total	1,932	1,676	100.0%	100.0%	580	550	100.0%	100.0%

Montana

Company Type	Lumber Production (million board feet) 1978	1985	Production Share (by percent) 1978	1985	Plywood Capacity (million sq. ft.) 1978	1985	Production Share (by percent) 1978	1985
National	628	533	50.0%	36.8%	380	404	51.7%	63.7%
Regional	358	430	28.5	29.8	235	230	32.0	36.3
Local	271	482	21.5	33.4	120	0	16.3	0.0
Total	1,256	1,445	100.0%	100.0%	735	634	100.0%	100.0%

corporations like Boise Cascade, St. Regis Paper, Potlatch, and Champion International.

By 1985, shifts in lumber production had occurred in all four states. National companies in Idaho and Montana reduced their role substantially, while Local firms gained in both production and share of the industry. In Oregon, Regional firms appeared to gain at the expense of National firms, while Local firms held their position.

The plywood sector differs in each state in the region. Control of plywood capacity in Oregon is balanced between industry tiers. In Washington, Regional firms play a subordinate role to the Nationals and Locals. Nationals control nearly all plywood capacity in Idaho and about half in Montana. By 1985, the scene in Oregon had shifted dramatically away from National firms to Regional firms, while Local companies showed modest growth. In Washington, National firms' share was off slightly, and Regional firms fell to a small percentage of the industry total. Local companies increased their actual production capacity by only four percent, but their share of total capacity increased by 20 percent.

It is clear that the industry structure—the position, power, and role of particular types of companies in the industry—changed between 1978 and 1985. Based on the data presented, National companies appear to be most adversely affected by larger economic events. The trend toward industry concentration in a few large corporations, evident since World War II, has shifted unexpectedly to a pattern of mill ownership by regional and local interests. Why this shift happened, and why it was so unexpected based on the conventional wisdom that small companies would be least able to survive hard economic times, should be viewed in the context of the industry's history since World War II.

SHIFTS IN INDUSTRY STRUCTURE

1950 to 1970: Merger and Concentration

Following World War II, when family formation rates soared and a housing boom meant sustained profits for lumber companies, an industry-wide trend was established as some firms began to buy out others to realize the advantages of increased firm size and market share. Between 1950 and 1970 the firms most actively involved in acquisitions in the forest industry became national in scale and the industry leaders (LeMaster, 1977).

Timberland acquisition was seen to be a major motive of mergers. By 1977, six companies—Boise Cascade, Crown Zellerbach, Champion International, Weyerhaeuser, Georgia-Pacific, and International Paper—owned more than 68 percent of all private timberland in Oregon (Young and Newton, 1980). Timberland acquisition reflected a goal of vertical integration for many firms. These companies preferred managerial control of the log market (through ownership) to the vagaries of the marketplace. Timberland ownership allowed for a controlled flow of raw material to the mill through a combination of open market log purchases, government timber contracts, and a corporation's own fee timber. A modern, fully integrated milling complex could enhance the most complete and highest-valued use of the raw material from each log by extracting the optimal mix of lumber, plywood, particleboard, and wood chips (pulp mills were constructed at or near many complexes) (Weeks, 1983).

Development of large integrated milling complexes gave corporations a larger product line, and, coupled with their financial and marketing powers, a competitive advantage over smaller firms with fewer products. A second advantage to large corporations was that an integrated facility was easier to manage from a centralized corporate structure than were many small plants (Youngbar, 1985). Growth of the larger-capacity integrated complex coincided with a precipitous decline in the number of small sawmills and led to a view that small independent producers were endangered. Observers believed this would lead to a situation where only big firms would operate in the industry—much as supermarkets outcompeted corner groceries (Ho, 1964; Bartel, 1985).

1970s: A Stable Structure

By the 1970s, a more stable forest industry structure had evolved. Acquisitions by large firms abated. The focus of mergers shifted from the Pacific Northwest to the South. A resurgent southern timber industry manifested itself as young timber and pulpwood reached commercial size. National firms expanded beyond the Pacific Northwest, acquiring and building plants in the South because they believed dispersed production facilities were important to serve national markets (Youngbar, 1985). Technological developments allowing southern pine to be used for plywood led Georgia-Pacific, Weyerhaeuser and Boise Cascade to invest heavily in southern forests and mills.

Smaller firms in the Northwest also gained an advantage when the Forest Service and the U.S. Small Business Administration implemented a Small Business Set-Aside program. This program set aside a certain percentage of Forest Service timber sales for exclusive bidding by small firms (companies with fewer than 500 employees). Observers of the program believe it helped solidify a timber supply for small firms and created a disincentive for large firms to move into a public timbershed, since other small firms could buy some of the available timber. More evidence of the program's benefit for small companies are the complaints aired by large firms ineligible to bid for the timber (U.S. Senate, 1983).

The end of large company growth in the Northwest was also the end of continued investment and modernization in many mills. As a result, many Northwest mills became marginal producers, in contrast with the southern timber industry, which expanded in the 1970s and suffered fewer dislocations in the 1980-1982 recession than did the Northwest (Youngbar, 1985; Schallau and Maki

1986). While the 1970s were a time of a stable industry structure and good profits, the seeds of future instability were sown.

The 1980s: Two Industry Shake-outs

Inflation in 1979 caused the Federal Reserve to tighten the money supply and interest rates soared. As home construction dried up, lumber and plywood prices tumbled and mills were closed. In 1978 there were 553 sawmills and 113 plywood plants operating in the Pacific Northwest. By 1980, 42 sawmills and 8 plywood plants had closed. In another two years, when the industry bottomed out, an additional 46 sawmills and 22 plywood plant had closed.

Local and National companies accounted for most of these closures. Edward Hines Lumber, Potlatch, and Crown Zellerbach led Nationals with mill closures. Local firms were devastated by a combination of expensive federal timber and no markets for framing lumber. Regional companies closed fewer mills in proportion to their share in the industry, indicating their financial resources could withstand some economic shock (Brunelle, 1986a and 1986b).

As the industry recovered in 1983, the pace of mill closures slowed. The rally in lumber prices was not sustained, however, and increased production soon outstripped demand, forcing prices back to near recession levels until 1986. Although production recovered to roughly 85 percent of the levels of the late 1970s, mill closures surprisingly accelerated in 1984 and 1985, presenting a second shake-out in the Northwest forest industry. Sustained losses, interregional competition, and expensive government timber purchased in the late 1970s, when the industry speculated on continued inflation and restricted supply, combined to cause the second shake-out. This second shake-out affected National companies in particular.

The second shake-out also coincided with a new and different wave of acquisitions. Many mills that had closed were sold and reopened by new firms. In addition, National firms that had closed mills within a manufacturing complex leased these operations to other companies. These reopened mills could be run at lower cost because the new owners were less likely to have organized labor in their mills and did not have large amounts of high-priced timber under contract.

Some Local and Regional companies are today operating mills purchased at a favorable price from National companies. One example of a particularly aggressive firm is WTD Industries. Since 1982, WTD has acquired over a dozen mills in Oregon, Washington, and Montana, most of which were shut down and in bankruptcy. Innovative management policies rewarding employee attendance and productivity, along with policies minimizing resources tied up in log inventories and timber contracts, has proven very profitable for WTD (Parks, 1986).

Other new owners in the industry are workers. Worker-owned plywood plants had been common in the Northwest in the 1950s, but many were subsequently closed or sold. In 1983, Publishers Forest Products closed its Anacortes,

Washington plywood plant. Financing was secured by Publishers' former employees who bought the mill in 1984. A worker buyout of the Champion International mill in Salmon, Idaho in 1985 is another example of local interests' increasingly important role in the industry. As a result, there is a greater chance that profits and capital generated from mills will stay in the local community (Brunelle, 1986b). Hubbird (1987) found much evidence that between 1980 and 1985 locally-owned and, especially, worker-owned plywood plants in Oregon were more stable employers than absentee-owned plywood plants.

During this same period, mergers among National companies and a wave of corporate restructuring affected the industry. Champion International acquired St. Regis Paper and then sold several of its Northwest operations to pay for it. Sir James Goldsmith acquired Diamond International and Crown Zellerbach, mainly to acquire the timberlands, for most of the mills were subsequently sold. Weyerhaeuser largely withdrew from western plywood production, but purchased substantial tracts of timberland owned by Georgia-Pacific in the Willamette Valley. Boise Cascade closed several west coast plants and sold 80,000 acres of timberland in western Washington, but at the same time made large investments in their facilities in the Inland Northwest and solidified their operations in the South. Publishers Paper sold their mills to Smurfit Newsprint, a subsidiary of a large multinational corporation. Within a year, however, the Smurfit mills were sold to two Local companies (Newport, 1987).

The stock market placed low value on timber products corporations as a result of poor market performance. As stumpage and timberland prices decreased through the recession and the mid-1980s, some companies reevaluated their holdings of heavily cut timberlands in the Northwest. A number of transactions involving large amounts of timberland (some mentioned above) resulted from this reevaluation (Newport, 1987). Industrial forest management jobs were especially hard hit by this change.

The large firms also reexamined other components of their businesses. Most large companies shifted to contracting out the logging and trucking end of their business rather than employing their own crews. At the market end, Boise Cascade sold its line of home center retail stores in 1987. Company strategies developed in the 1960s, especially total vertical integration from the timberland to the market, were reassessed by the industry in 1980s.

An important change was the success of National firms in getting unions in their mills to accept wage concessions. Wage increases were granted in 1983 contract negotiations, but subsequent sustained losses forced many National firms to close mills in 1984 and 1985 when they were unprofitable. A dramatic episode came in August 1985 when Potlatch Corporation closed all of its unionized northern Idaho operations. The mills reopened when wage and benefit concessions by the union were tied to a company commitment to modernize the Lewiston mill.

Other large companies were successful in getting the unions to agree to wage concessions in 1986. Weyerhaeuser had to endure a six week strike before workers agreed to wage cuts and a profit sharing plan.

As the industry continued to strengthen in the late 1980s, National companies and unions again fought over wages; workers went on strike in several companies in 1988 to restore wage cuts. Companies argued that immediate, full restoration of wages to their 1986 levels was not possible because the industry had shifted away from a unionized labor force to regionally and locally based companies that generally paid lower wages. To be competitive within the region, wages had to be comparable to the regional standards now being set by these companies.

COMPANY SIZE AND COMPETITIVENESS

Large Company Problems

Why would a segment of the industry that seemed to posses most of the competitive advantages—access to capital for expansion and absorbing losses, ownership and control of vast timber stands, vertical integration allowing managerial control over previously unstable markets, and presumably a more educated and professional management—feel the effects of the recession more adversely than other companies in the industry? One explanation for the shift would be the stage of production at which large companies chose to exit. Having depleted the richest of privately-held stands, the large corporations projected only modest profits for the next few years and chose to shift investments to other timber producing regions, or to diversify investments outside the forest products industry.

Did the large corporations abandon the Pacific Northwest? This view was widely reported in the media (Tapperson and Brewer, 1984). The charge that large companies had resurrected the old practice of "cut and run" first emerged in 1978 when Georgia-Pacific announced its corporate headquarters would move to Atlanta, and crested with the flurry of mill closures in early 1985 by Champion International. One response in the region was support for plant closure legislation, which the Oregon State Legislature came close to enacting in 1981. When Congress finally passed plant closure legislation in 1988, many forest-based communities that had experienced the unstable early 1980s were in agreement.

National companies with operations in one part of the country and offices in another have long been assumed to regard their operations differently than locally-owned enterprises. Critics assume these companies have less commitment than do smaller firms to the regions and communities where they have operations (Young and Newton, 1980; Hubbird, 1987).

The fact that publicly held corporations have to emphasize short term profits to make their stock attractive to investors is another element leading to disposal of operations that do not perform adequately. While a large firm is generally a stable employer with a long-term horizon, it also must act as an investor. If it can find better prospects for profits elsewhere, it will move or change its investment strategy. This assumes that large corporations have the ability to look ahead, projecting economic trends and earnings before choosing an investment strategy. But why would so many National firms act in the same manner? How could they all have projected an era of low profits pointing to an exit from the region in the 1980s, especially when ten years earlier, predictions were that the 1980s would be the "Golden Age" of housing? Evidence suggests that National companies did *not* see the changes coming and were probably too large and cumbersome to respond quickly.

A detailed study of several leading firms in the industry examined the strategic adaptation of the firms to the changing environment of the industry (Falkenberg, 1984). Examining how the firms reacted to the boom of the 1970s and the recession of the 1980s, the study concluded the companies "exhibited little adaptation to changes in the environment." In other words, the major corporations did not see the changes coming to the economy and the industry and reacted slowly. Mill closures in 1984 and 1985, along with wage rollbacks for unionized workers in 1985 and 1986 (countering the increases granted in 1983), are evidence of this slow adjustment.

Statements by industry leaders agreed with the study. For example, George Weyerhaeuser recently stated:

> Through the 1970s we were organized for growth and were producing at a breakneck pace in a seller's market. When the bottom fell out in the '80s, we found ourselves in a buyer's market and some big changes had to be made. We had to regroup, to change our organizational course, structure, and culture—something easier said than done in a large enterprise (Houser, 1988).

Stewart Bledsoe, an industry spokesman in the state of Washington, also agreed with this assessment of the industry.

> Let's be very candid about it, we'd been coasting along, making a lot of money and doing what we thought was a reasonable job of innovative management. When we were really faced with the reality, we found that we had been almost asleep at the switch... we found ourselves trying to start a recovery marathon with a pocket full of rocks. We had over-aged plants, We had the highest forest products wage scales in the world in the Pacific

Northwest with no tie-back to productivity. We had some "yesterday" management attitudes (Bledsoe, 1987).

A broader observation of American industry that seems to apply to the forest products industry is that many large companies in the United States have become bloated and risk-averse "corpocracies." Economist Robert Samuelson recently argued for the existence of a "corporate Peter Principle"; he attributes the problems of big business not to bad managers, but to the fact that companies got so large they could not be effectively managed (Samuelson, 1986).

A Smaller Company Resurgence

Meanwhile, Local and Regional companies have received increased attention because of their growing share of production. A recent study (Lee, 1985) comparing stability in employment in forest industry establishments in Washington and Oregon over the past twenty years found that smaller establishments are more stable employers. Though not directly measured at the company level, the study showed a given local area should experience more stability in employment if an equal number of employees are distributed among several plants rather than employed by one large plant. A small firm per se is not necessarily a more stable employer than a large company, but smaller firms in the aggregate exhibit greater ability.

Evidence indicates that Regional and Local companies in the Northwest may have been among the first to modernize their plants as almost total reliance on more expensive purchased timber forced them to make investments in new processing technologies. National firms' advantage may not have come from greater size and scale, but from ownership of cheaper fee timber. Only in recent years, with the imminent exhaustion of private industrial timber and increased reliance on the log market and government owned timber, did the Nationals modernize (Bartel, 1985). Company strategy involving timberlands may have delayed decisions to modernize (Newport, 1987). Despite the poor condition of the industry in the 1980s, National companies were encouraged to invest in modern plants, partly due to the 1981 tax law changes with accelerated depreciation schedules and options to "lease" tax credits that would otherwise go unused (Weeks, 1983).

The increasingly important role of smaller firms in the industry is significant and reflects a changing orientation. Smaller companies are focused more on recovery of maximum value from each log. Instead of relying on standard commodity products, many independents have taken a more sophisticated approach and are carving out a niche in increasingly specialized and divergent markets. The small owner can use advantages not available to large companies: entrepreneurship, lean management, attention to detail, and ability to convert the logs into the highest-price products.

Because of the unique characteristics of each log that enters a mill for processing, decisions on the most profitable way to cut the log are made by individuals. A firm emphasizing higher value over maximum production needs to have sawyers and millworkers working closely with the marketing end. Mead's (1966) classic study of the wood products industry still holds true: the optimum firm size is not multi-plant, but single-plant, and the optimal mill is a medium sized mill.

Implications for Communities

Structural change in the forest products industry, and the decisions of individual companies have a great effect on the stability of forest-based communities. This is one factor that has often been overlooked, especially in the early 1980s when politicians blamed U.S. Forest Service policies and imports of Canadian lumber for unemployment in the timber industry and the stress experienced by forest-based communities. As this paper shows, there is much evidence that different types of companies responded differently to the changing atmosphere of the industry, and that workers felt the impacts.

The future stability of forest-based communities will continue to depend on the strategies and behavior of individual firms. Attention should focus not only on the traditional issues of long-term timber supply and national forest policies, but also on industry trends and company responses. While much evidence shows the small mill may have fared better than the large company, this does not always mean that a community with a locally-owned mill is less at risk than a community with a mill owned by a National corporation. Each type of ownership has inherent advantages. Community leaders need to be aware of the factors that could affect the future operations of a mill and the potential impacts on their community.

NOTES

1. The industry-wide trend toward mechanization came during the recession and the impacts it had on employment in the forest industry were initially difficult to assess. For example, a series of articles published by Gannett News Service in 1984 concluded in the Northwest forest products industry was dying. While the journalistic report, "God's Country Under the Ax," was comprehensive in its coverage of the issues regarding the industry, its assessment was flawed with gloomy predictions that market losses to Canada and the South would worsen, that the dislocated workers' plight would be a persistent burden on the economy of the region, and that "the worst is yet to come." A similar project, "Northwest Timber: After the Fall," published by the Eugene, Oregon *Register-Guard* in the fall of 1985 was less pessimistic in its findings.

2. A few studies have examined the forest industry's structure and organization in the Northwest. These studies have examined forest products firms and factors

that influence their operations in the areas of mergers and acquisitions, public affairs, timberland ownership, strategic adaptation, and performance. Among the best works are: Mead (1966), LeMaster (1977), and O'Laughlin and Ellefson (1984).

3. Data on lumber and plywood production for 1978 came from *Forest Industries*, April 1979, May 1979, and May 1980; also the 1979 and 1980 editions of the *Directory of the Forest Products Industry*, San Francisco: Miller Freeman Publications. For data on lumber and plywood production in 1985 the following sources were used: *Forest Industries*, April 1986, July 1986; the *1986 Directory of the Forest Products Industry*, San Francisco: Miller Freeman Publications; and *Random Lengths' 1987 Buyers and Sellers Guide of the Forest Products Industry*, Eugene, Oregon: Random Lengths, 1987.

4. The number of mill closures was arrived at by subtraction of operating sawmills and plywood plants from one year to another. Sawmill statistics of Steve Adams, Western Wood Products Association, Portland, Oregon; plywood statistics courtesy of Terry Lamp, American Plywood Association, Tacoma, Washington. The quarterly *Mill Closure Report*, published in 1985 and 1986 by Paul Ehinger and Associates, a Eugene, Oregon consulting firm, included more detailed information on mill operations and transitions in ownership.

REFERENCES

Bartel, D. 1985. "Labor and Technology Key for Mills." *Random Lengths* (November 15):3-4.

Bledsoe, S. 1987. "Industry and Community Stability." Paper presented at National Conference on Community Stability in Forest-Based Economies, November 18, 1987, Portland, OR.

Brunelle, A. 1986a. *Structural Change in the Oregon Wood Products Industry*. Eugene, OR: University of Oregon, Department of Planning, Public Policy and Management.

———. 1986b. "Wood Products: An Idaho Industry in Transition." *Idaho's Economy (Fall):3-5*.

Ehinger, P. 1983. "Plant Modernization and Its Impact on the Structure of the Woods Products Industry." In *Plant Modernization and Community Economic Stability: Managing the Transition*. Presentation at the Policy Roundtable Discussion on Community Economic Stability, University of Oregon, July 10, 1982, Eugene, OR: Oregon Bureau of Governmental Research and Service.

Falkenberg, J.S. 1984. "Environmental Influences on Strategic Adaptation." Unpublished dissertation, University of Oregon.

Ho, F.Y.H. 1964. *Small Lumber Companies in Western Oregon.* Portland, OR: University of Portland.

Houser, D.G. 1988. "Profile: George H. Weyerhaeuser." *Sky* (August):28.

Hubbird, J. 1987. *Absentee, Local and Employee Ownership: Impacts on Community Stability.* Eugene, OR: University of Oregon, Department of Planning, Public Policy and Management.

Lee, R.G. 1985. "Comparative Analysis of Stability in Forest-Dependent Communities of Japan and the Pacific Northwest United States." Prepared for presentation at the annual meeting of the Rural Sociological Society, August 24, 1985, Blacksburg, VA.

LeMaster, D.C. 1977. *Mergers Among the Largest Forest Products Firms, 1950-1970.* Pullman, WA: Washington State University, Bulletin 854.

Mead, W.J. 1966. *Competition and Oligopsony in the Douglas-fir Lumber Industry.* Los Angeles: University of California Press.

Newport, C.A. 1987. "Change in Ownership of Private Timberlands as a Factor in Community Stability." Paper presented at National Conference on Community Stability in Forest-Based Economies, November 18, 1987, Portland, OR.

O'Laughlin, J. and P. Ellefson. 1984. *Wood Based Industry: Industrial Organization and Performance.* New York: Praeger.

Parks, M.J. 1986. "Going Public: Fast in Lumber." *Marples Business Newsletter* (July):2.

Polzin, P.E. and Keegan, C.A. III. 1987. "Trends in the Wood and Paper Products Industry and their Impact on the Economy of the Pacific Northwest." In *Montana Business Quarterly* 25(4):2-7. Missoula, MT: University of Montana Bureau of Business and Economic Research.

Samuelson, R.J. 1986. "How Companies Grow Stale." *Newsweek* (September):45.

Schallau, C.H. and R.M. Alston. 1987. "The Commitment to Community Stability: A Policy or Shibboleth?" *Environmental Journal* 17:429-481.

Schallau, C.H. and W.R. Maki. 1986. *Economic Impacts of Interregional Competition in the Forest Products Industry During the 1970s: the South and the Pacific Northwest.* Portland, OR: USDA Forest Service, Research Paper PNW-350.

Tapperson, T. and N. Brewer. 1984. "Northwest Timber Industry Staggers Under Multiple Blows; Full Recovery is in Doubt." In *God's Country Under the Ax.* Washington, DC: Gannett News Service.

U.S. Senate Committee on Small Businesses. 1983. *Economic Problems Facing Small and Independent Businesses in the Forest Products Industry.* Washington, DC: Government Printing Office.

Weeks, E.C. 1983. "Plant Modernization and Community Economic Stability: Managing the Transition." Background paper presented at the Policy Roundtable Discussion on Community Economic Stability, University of Oregon, July 10, 1982, Eugene, OR: Oregon Bureau of Governmental Research and Service.

Young, J.A. and J.M. Newton. 1980 *Capitalism and Human Obsolescence.* Totowa, NJ: Allanheld, Osmun & Co.

Youngbar, L.B. 1985. "Structural Change in the Forest Products Industry and the Regional Shift in Production Between the Pacific Northwest and the Southern U.S." Unpublished paper, Massachusetts Institute of Technology.

10

Mill Closures in the Pacific Northwest: The Consequences of Economic Decline in Rural Industrial Communities

Edward C. Weeks
Department of Planning, Public Policy and Management
University of Oregon

This chapter examines the impact of economic change on the social ecology of a region. Specifically, it seeks to trace the manner in which structural change within the wood products industry has altered the social and economic landscape of Oregon. The aim here is to assemble a larger, more complete picture from the findings of a number of studies completed over the past several years.[1] This mosaic, it is hoped, will serve to show the often convoluted paths between economic events and their social consequences.

The chapter begins with an overview of Oregon's wood products industry and describes the process by which technological innovation and plant modernization is transforming it. The immediate economic consequences of this transformation for individuals and communities is then reviewed. Finally, the chapter describes how the direct economic impact is altering the demographic characteristics of Oregon, as well as the economic and social vitality of many of Oregon's rural communities.

OREGON'S WOOD PRODUCTS INDUSTRY

In 1968, the lumber and wood products industry accounted for 10 percent of Oregon's civilian employment and 42 percent of total manufacturing employment (U.S. Department of Commerce, Bureau of the Census, 1970). The two key components of this industry are softwood dimensional lumber, and plywood and veneer. In 1968, the dimensional lumber industry employed about 23,700 workers in 300 sawmills; the plywood and veneer industry employed about 24,200 workers in 138 mills. Wage rates in the wood products industry are among the highest in the state. For example, in 1984, average hourly earnings in this industry were $11.56 or 30 percent higher than the average hourly earning of $8.86 for all manufacturing except wood products (U.S. Bureau of Labor Statistics, 1984).

Size alone would make the wood products industry crucial to the economic health of the state. As important as size, however, is the geographic distribution of this industry in the state. Mills operate in thirty-four of the thirty-six counties in the state and are the leading manufacturing employer in twenty-four counties (Howard and Hiserote, 1978). In seventeen counties, the wood products sector accounts for more than 50 percent of total manufacturing employment. Thus, unlike the industrial base of some states, Oregon's industrial base is distributed throughout the state—providing relatively high wage employment for a significant portion of the work force over a broad geographic area.

The geographic decentralization of the wood products industry extends to the level of individual communities. The historic cost advantage of being located close to the source of raw logs has led to the location of many mills in otherwise remote areas of the state. In turn, small towns have grown up around many of these mills. Today there are seventy-nine towns with populations of less than 3,000 that rely on the wood products industry for their economic support. In sixty-two of these communities, more than 80 percent of the total manufacturing work force is employed in wood products firms.[2]

STRUCTURAL CHANGE IN THE
WOOD PRODUCTS INDUSTRY

Since 1970, Oregon has experienced a substantial decline in the number of mills operating in the state and in the level of employment offered by the wood products industry. Compared to 1968, employment in sawmills has declined by 30 percent and the number of sawmills declined by 46 percent. Also compared to 1968, employment in the plywood and veneer sector declined by 50 percent with a 30 percent decline in the number of mills (Howard and Hiserote, 1984; Ehinger and Associates, 1986). Each mill closure has its own unique history. There are, however, a broad set of forces that can be isolated and discussed separately (Weeks, 1983).

In the Pacific Northwest, the depletion of large, "old-growth" timber plays a major role in mill closures. Old-growth timber offers several advantages over younger-growth timber. First, logging operations are less expensive when harvesting old growth timber: fewer acres need to be harvested to produce similar volume, and there are lower costs for measurement, yarding, and transportation. More importantly, greater value can be extracted (per volume) from larger old-growth logs than from second growth logs, which are smaller in diameter (Lane, Henley, and Plank, 1973a; 1973b).

However, the supply of old-growth timber available for harvesting during any given year is decreasing. While the harvest of large diameter trees under public ownership will remain relatively constant under the present sustained-yield management regimen, the inventory of old-growth in private holdings is rapidly being depleted (Tedder, 1979). Private timber holdings provide about 45 percent of the timber consumed in milling operations. By 1976, young growth logs accounted for 31 percent of total log consumption (Howard and Hiserote, 1978).

The increasing dependence on second growth logs places a premium on equipment that allows the maximum extraction of value from each log. Reinforcing the pressure for modernization are relatively high wages for millworkers and tax laws that favor capital investment for "reindustrialization." One consequence of capital modernization is decreased labor requirements for operating mills. Young and Newton (1980), for example, cite Weyerhaeuser's investment of $400 million to modernize its mills in Everett, Washington, and the subsequent reduction of its work force from 900 to 500 employees.

The employment impacts of increasingly capital-intensive mills go well beyond the immediate work force reduction resulting from more efficient production technology. The cost of new equipment greatly increases a plant's fixed operating costs. Most of the more modern mills are owned by corporations that own several mills. During periods of low demand for wood products, the corporation is faced with the problem of where to reduce capacity. At the corporate level the economically rational decision is to curtail operations at those mills that are most labor-intensive and thus have proportionately the largest variable cost. In most instances, the curtailments are intermittent: management resumes and curtails operations to fine-tune its production to match the fluctuating market. By 1980, however, corporations increasingly chose to close their less efficient mills permanently. The annual reports of some major corporations describe this process:

> Crown Zellerbach's carefully developed strategic plan—backed by a $2.1 billion commitment to capital investment and guided by a strong management team—is proceeding on

schedule to modernize and restructure the company for maximum productivity and cost-effectiveness in its most profitable markets. Our program of consolidation of operations, disinvestment, and the monetization of assets continues (Crown Zellerbach, 1981).

Since 1979 [International Paper] has bought a containerboard mill and added over 260,000 tons of paper and paperboard capacity at our most efficient mills, Gardiner, Vicksburg, and Androscoggin, while phasing out several less efficient ones (International Paper, 1981).

The impact of inflation on the high cost of capital, is accelerating the retirement of obsolete and marginally-economic production capacity. [Weyerhaeuser] will be installing new capacity in our Western operations, both to replace older mills and to increase our production through better utilization of raw material. And we will be removing obsolescence, through modernization, replacement, and in a few cases, through closure (Weyerhaeuser, 1981).

There is another way in which newer, larger, and more capital-intensive mills are causing employment losses. The capital-intensive mills have high productive capacities. In addition, their production cost advantage is best realized when the mill is running near capacity. These two factors require that the mill have an assured supply of large quantities of raw logs. Their lower cost of production (at near full capacity) permits them to outbid the more labor-intensive mills for timber contracts. Thus, starved for an affordable supply of raw materials, the more labor-intensive mills are forced to curtail operations.

The situation described so far is a story of technological innovation and plant modernization leading to greater productive efficiency leading to a market "shakeout" of less competitive operations—the laws of natural selection operating through the marketplace. What has not been described is the impact of these adjustments on the social and economic landscape of the state and, especially, on mill-dependent rural communities.

THE ECONOMIC IMPACT OF STRUCTURAL CHANGE IN OREGON'S WOOD PRODUCTS INDUSTRY

One consequence of the decline of the wood products industry is the concentration of economic activity in the metropolitan areas of the state. Although mill closures have occurred throughout the state, rural counties are less able to absorb the excess labor force than are their metropolitan counterparts. Where rural and metropolitan counties once had shared approximately equal unemployment rates, since 1980 rural unemployment has increased significantly beyond that of the metropolitan counties (Oregon Department of Human Resources, Employment Division, 1976 through 1986).

Given the geographic distribution of the wood products industry, many mill closures involve mills located in small communities. For example, since 1980, 41 percent of closures have occurred in communities with populations less than 3,000 and 57 percent have occurred in communities with populations less than 5,000. Small, mill-dependent communities are highly vulnerable to plant closures. Other than government transfer payments, the mill operations are the community's only meaningful export base. With the loss of a mill, the multiplier effect, estimated to be between 2.5 and 4.2 for small area wood products economies, is also lost to the community (Connaughton and McKillop, 1979).

Not all workers who lose their jobs due to mill closures remain unemployed for a prolonged period; some readily find new employment. A State Employment Division study shows that younger workers quickly found subsequent employment. (Oregon Department of Human Resources, Employment Division, 1968). Eight months following the closure of the mills included in this study, only 14 percent of the workers under thirty-five remained unemployed; of those who found new employment, 75 percent found permanent jobs paying a higher wage than their mill job.

Others go longer without jobs. There is evidence that plant closures present a special problem for older workers. The picture becomes increasingly grim when the experience of older age groups is examined. Within the thirty-five to forty-five year age group, 90 percent found employment within eight months following the mill closure. However, a greater proportion of this age group found they had to accept a permanent job with a lower wage. The forty-five to fifty-four-year-old workers had a more difficult time. This group had an unemployment rate of almost 20 percent, and the majority of those who found new jobs had to accept lower wages. Mill closure was catastrophic for the oldest workers. For workers fifty-five to sixty-four years old, the unemployment rate was 42 percent, and this figure includes only those workers actively looking for jobs.

It should be noted that almost 70 percent of the employees of the closed mills included in this study were in the two older age groups. These older workers are less mobile, and employers outside of the wood products industry appear to be reluctant to make the investment to train older workers for new jobs.

A study by Stevens (1978) presents a more in-depth picture of the post-layoff experiences of older workers. Stevens found that workers with greater seniority and other evidence of employment stability have an advantage in obtaining subsequent mill employment. These workers were also found to pursue a more passive job search strategy, preferring to "wait out" the mill closure. Thus, the advantage gained by seniority operates only when alternative mill employment exists. As Stevens concludes, "should other mill opportunities not be available in their home communities, these core workers would be hard pressed to maintain their economic viability."

The difference noted by Stevens (1978) in the response of older and younger workers to the loss of mill employment has important implications for the demographic composition of Oregon's rural communities.

THE EFFECT OF STRUCTURAL ECONOMIC CHANGE ON THE DEMOGRAPHY OF RURAL OREGON

Population migration is among the most powerful forces shaping the cultural and economic landscape of an area. Sometimes as slow as a glacier, occasionally as sudden as an avalanche, the movement of people from place to place changes the character of the affected areas. The cultural and economic landscape is altered not only because of a net gain or loss in population but also, and perhaps more importantly, because of changes in the nature of the population.

While the root causes of large scale population shifts are varied, they are usually expressed through the push and pull economic forces acting on the individual. The strength of these forces varies with the attributes and circumstances of the individual. In this manner, economic forces sort and reshuffle the population to alter the most basic character of a community.

Over two-thirds (72 percent) of Oregon counties experienced two or more years of population loss between 1980 and 1985. Over a third (36 percent) of the counties lost population for three or more years during this period. Several additional trends can be seen in the county population data. First, none of the three counties within the Portland metropolitan area lost population during this period. Second, most counties within the Douglas-fir region (the coast range and the west side of the Cascades) lost population for three or more of the five years. Finally, there are the interesting exceptions to the general pattern of population loss in the rural counties and stability or gain in the major metropolitan counties. Four of the seven counties outside of the Portland metropolitan area that had stable populations are counties with a growing elderly population. While the number of persons over sixty-four years of age increased by about 12 percent for the state as a whole, the number of persons sixty-five and older in Deschutes County increased by 22 percent, in Lincoln County by 20 percent, in Crook county by 18 percent, and in Josephine County by 16 percent.

THE EFFECT OF STRUCTURAL ECONOMIC CHANGE ON DEPENDENT COMMUNITIES.

The geographic distribution of the wood products industry and the distribution of mill closures suggest that small communities would experience greater population loss than larger communities. In fact, however, communities with fewer than 3,000 persons tended to increase in population, while communities with populations between 3,000 and 5,000 tended to decrease very slightly. Thus, stability was found where decline was anticipated.

To explore this questions further, it is useful to examine in greater detail the experience of particular small communities. Six communities are included in this analysis. Each of these communities has substantial dependence on the wood products industry, and each has experienced economic instability over the past several years.

Figure 1 shows the population of each of the six communities for 1975, 1980, and 1985. Comparing the 1980 and 1985 populations, we find the same high degree of stability found in the statewide aggregate data on small communities. The question arises: If small communities are maintaining their population size in the face of economic instability, are the components of the population changing?

Figure 2 reports high school enrollment for each community for 1975, 1980, and 1985. High school enrollment is interesting in at least two respects. First, high school students soon become the young adult population—students who were seniors in 1975 are thirty years old today. In addition, the parents of high school

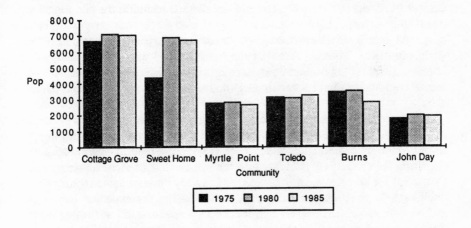

Figure 1. Community Population: 1975-1985. Source: Portland State University, Center for Population Research and Census. Population Estimates of Oregon: Counties and Cities, 1975-1986.

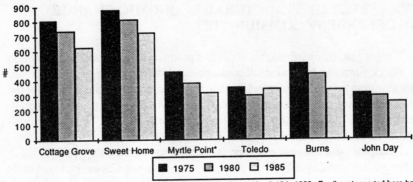

* Myrtle Point H. S. converted from including grades 9-12 to including grades 8-12 in 1982. Enrollment reported here has been adjusted to remove the effect of the additional grade.

Figure 2. High School Enrollment: 1975-1985. Source. Oregon State Department of Education. Approved Secondary Schools in Oregon: Estimated Enrollment, 1975-1985.

students are an important source for the mature, experienced leadership of the community. As Figure 2 reveals, with one exception, the communities have experienced a steady decline in high school enrollment. The apparent exception to this pattern, Toledo, is due to the high school's absorption of students from a nearby company-owned town that was dismantled when its mill was closed.

While the number of high school students was declining, the elderly population was increasing. Figure 3 shows for each community the percent change in the number of residents sixty-five years old and older from 1975 to 1985. Figure 4 reports the percent of each community's population that is over sixty-four years of age. As these figures show, the elderly population is large and growing. In 1985, slightly less than 13 percent of the population of Oregon was over sixty-four years of age. Each of the six communities exceeds the statewide proportion and four of the six communities have approximately double the statewide proportion of the elderly.

What process accounts for the increasing proportion of elderly in these communities? Selective out-migration is clearly a major contributor to this trend. In five of the six communities, the average age of those reporting an intention to remain in the community is higher than the average age of those reporting that they might or will leave. In every case, the average age of those reporting an intention to leave is younger than the age of those reporting an intention to remain in the community. Nearly 60 percent of the survey respondents under thirty years of age reported an intention to leave the community compared to 27 percent of those sixty-five and older.

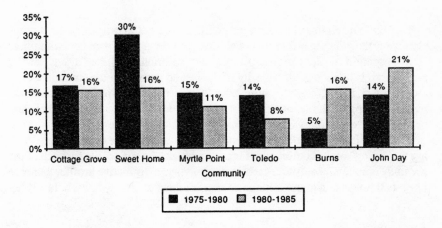

Figure 3. Percent Change in Population 65 Years and Older by Community. Source. 1) Number of OASDI Beneficiaries, U.S. Social Security Administration. 2) Portland State University Center for Population Research and Census. Population Estimates of Oregon: Counties and Cities.

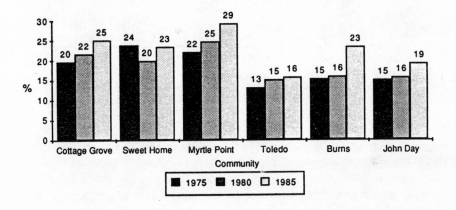

Figure 4. Percent of Total Population 65 and Older by Community 1975-1985. Source: 1) Number of OASDI Beneficiaries, U.S. Social Security Administration. 2) Portland State University Center for Population Research and Census. Population Estimates of Oregon: Counties and Cities.

Yet, the out-migration of younger families does not appear to account com-pletely for the growing proportion of elderly persons in small, rural communities.

In-migration of older retired persons also contributes to the "aging" of the population. While the great majority of the retired persons in the community are long-term residents, slightly more than 20 percent of the retired respondents reported living in the community for less than ten years, suggesting that they moved to the community upon their retirement.

The combination of selective in- and out-migration has the effect of accelerat-ing the "aging" of the community. Figure 5 presents the age profile for each of the six study communities. While each community has a distinctive profile, there are in general few young households and a large number of elderly households. What

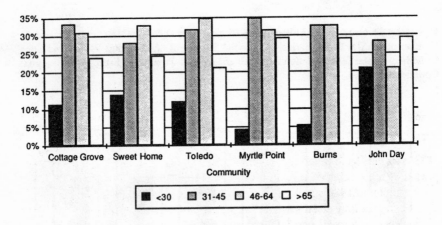

Figure 5. Age of Head of Household by Community. Source: Six Community Survey, University of Oregon Department of Planning, Public Policy, and Management, 1986.

is the consequence of this process for the continued vitality of a community and for the well being of its residents?

First, it is likely that the loss of younger residents will continue. As the community loses its ability to provide entry level jobs for new workers or "family wage" jobs for more established workers, these persons will leave the community in search for opportunities elsewhere. Twenty percent of the survey respondents reported that within the next five years they will look for work elsewhere. This trend is even more pronounced for the younger households: 37 percent of respon-dents under thirty, and 31 percent of those between thirty-one and forty-five years of age expect to look for work elsewhere.

High school students in these communities recognize the diminishing possibility of acceptable employment in the community upon graduation. This is reflected in the rate at which these students intend to join the military after leaving high school. Each year the Oregon State System of Higher Education surveys high school juniors about their post-high school plans. The trend since 1978 is for an increasing proportion of high school students in the six study communities to plan to enter military service following high school.

It is not clear that communities will continue to be able to hold older residents and attract additional elderly residents. On the one hand, retired persons receiving pensions or social security payments are insulated from the direct impact of community economic instability. On the other hand, economic instability may so detract from the quality of life available to elderly residents that the community loses its earlier attractiveness (Salazar, Schallau, and Lee, 1986).

SUPPORT FOR COMMUNITY INSTITUTIONS

So far, we have seen that the differential response of workers to the loss of mill employment has the affect of "aging" the community. Younger workers tend to leave the community in search of alternative employment, while older workers more often choose to remain in the community in the expectation that the mill will reopen and their employment will resume. What is the effect of the combination of economic decline and population change on the viability of the community?

Our studies have found that community economic instability is often accompanied by a lessening of support for community institutions and public services. For example, in 1982 small mill-dependent communities defeated 72 percent of all property tax levy elections. The lack of support for government services is not characteristic of small communities per se: the levy rejection rate for small communities which are not mill-dependent was only 57 percent.

The case of Oakridge, Oregon is illustrative. A case study of this community found that as confidence in the continued operation of the community's mill declined, voters became less willing to approve property tax levies necessary to maintain current levels of municipal services. For example, of the seven levies which had been put before the voters during 1981 and 1982, all were rejected. Further aggravating the city's financial condition was the expiration of a temporary levy previously adopted to support fire and police services, as well as an increase in the number of delinquent or uncollected property taxes. As a result, the property tax revenues to the city declined by 42 percent from 1978 to 1982.

The increasing proportion of elderly in the community suggests that support for public services will continue to erode. In our survey of the residents of six communities, respondents were asked about their support of eleven public services ranging from police and fire services to parks and libraries. For each service, retired respondents expressed less support than did the nonretired respondents. The differences were most pronounced for such community amenities as libraries and parks. When asked to describe the most important issue facing their community, retired persons were nearly twice as likely to mention taxes as the most important issue than were nonretired persons.

City governments cope with reduced resources in two ways: first, by reducing or curtailing city services; and second, by increasing their reliance on intergovernmental revenues to fund their operating expenses. One consequence of the increasing dependence on intergovernmental payments is the transfer of substantial decision-making authority from the local level to higher levels of government. As the community becomes increasingly vulnerable to revenue decisions made at other levels of government, much of the city budgeting process becomes mere ritual, and the public as well as city council members begin to play a less significant role in the actual budget process.

Along with diminishing financial support there is often a loss of support in the form of personal effort and commitment to continue some community institutions; service clubs go dormant, community celebrations are canceled, and high school activities are dropped for lack of a sufficient base of support.

SUMMARY

Oregon's wood products industry is undergoing a major transformation through technological innovation and plant modernization. This continuing process is driven by a combination of resource depletion and extraregional competition and is aided by tax policies that subsidize capital investment. One consequence of this trend will be a steady attrition of small, labor-intensive, community-based mills. Left alone, this transformation will leave in its wake a number of small, dying towns.

The immediate shock wave of the closures will cause additional economic failures and result in a number of personal tragedies. Employment driven outmigration will pull younger, more able, more ambitious, or more mobile residents from the community. The remainder, primarily older workers and their families, will be left in a decaying town with reduced economic resources. While an economist may describe this series of events as a simple case of labor market adjustments to greater technological efficiency, this technical description ought not be allowed to mask the human drama of a community in crisis.

While society as a whole benefits from the modernization of the wood products industry, the costs of modernization are inequitably borne by the residents of the affected communities. Further, this structural transformation of the industry takes place within the context of many supporting public policies. For these reasons, public policy intervention may be both proper and necessary to allocate more equitably the costs and benefits of technological innovations in the industry. Any intervention must be designed to serve the competing interests of facilitating plant modernization and guarding the interests of those communities disrupted by such modernization. There is a need to balance the interests of individuals, the community, and the regional economic system, and to view these interests in both the short and the long term.

NOTES

1. Since 1982, faculty and students in the Department of Planning, Public Policy, and Management have completed a number of studies of community economic instability. The results of these studies can be found in the following articles, papers, theses, and reports: Atkinson, R., "The Industrial Policy Debate: The Role of Ideology and Power" (unpublished thesis) Summer 1985; Barnes, M., "Plant Closures: Causes, Consequences and Policy Options (unpublished policy paper), December 1982; Brunelle, A., "Structural Change in the Oregon Wood Products Industry, 1978-1985" (unpublished issue paper) June 1986; Downes, B., "The Effects of Fiscal Stress and Cutback Management on Local Government Performance: The Case of Lane County." In Busson, T. and P. Coulter (eds.), *Policy Evaluation in Local Government*, Westport CT: Greenwood Press, 1986; Downes, B., "Fiscal Stress and Cutback Management in Small Oregon Cities: Some Preliminary Observations." *Oregon Governmental Notes*, Eugene, OR: Bureau of Governmental Research and Service, June 1985; Hibbard, M., "Community Beliefs and the Failure of Community Economic Development." *Social Service Review*, June 1986, 183-199; Hibbard, M. and L. Davis, "When the Going Gets Tough: Economic Reality and the Cultural Myths of Small-town America." *American Planning Association Journal*, Autumn 1986, 419-428; Hibbard, M. and H. Liggett, "Rethinking Community Economic and Social Development Policy." Presented at the Annual Conference of the Association of Collegiate Schools of Planning, October 1986; Liggett, H., "A Generative Model of Public Policy: A Textual Analysis Approach to the Politics of Local Economic Development." Presented at the Annual Conference of the Association of Collegiate Schools of Planning, November 1985; Liggett, H., "Reading the Economy." Presented at the Conference for New Perspectives on Planning in the West, March 1985; Low, J., "Mill Closures in Oregon: Issues of Equity" (unpublished thesis) December 1982; Mounts, D., "Central Business District Revitalization Strategies in Seven Small Oregon Cities: A Comparative Analysis" (unpublished policy paper) June 1984; Sorseth, C., "Unemployment Strategies in the Upper McKenzie Valley" (unpublished policy paper) August 1986; Weeks, E. and S. Drengacz, "Rocking in a

Small Boat: The Consequences of Rural Economic Decline." *International Journal of Mental Health*, Spring-Summer 1983, 12 (1-2), 62-75; Weeks, E. and S. Drengacz, "Reindustrialization and Mental Health. *Administration in Mental Health* 10 (4), 225-238; Weeks, E. and S. Drengacz, "The Non-economic Impact of Community Economic Shock." *Journal of Human Resources Administration*, Winter 1982, 4 (3), 303-318; Weeks, E., "The Effect of Community Economic Shock on Alcohol Sales and the Incidence of Alcohol-Related Problems: Final Report," January 1983. Submitted to the National Institute on Alcohol Abuse and Alcoholism; Weeks, E., "The Changing Demographics of Resource Based Communities." Presented at the Conference on New Perspectives on Planning in the West, Calgary, Alberta, March 12-14, 1987.

2. For all towns with populations under 3,000, data on the total number of manufacturing employees and the number of manufacturing employees employed in the wood products industry (SIC 24) were obtained from *The Directory of Oregon Manufacturers*. Oregon Department of Economic Development, 1981. The proportion reported is the number of wood products employees divided by the total number of manufacturing employees.

REFERENCES

Connaughton, K. and W. McKillop. 1979. "Estimation of 'Small Area' Multipliers for the Wood Processing Sector: An Econometric Approach." *Forest Science* 25 (1):7-20.

Crown Zellerbach. 1981. *Annual Report*. San Francisco, CA.

Ehinger, P.F. and Associates. 1986. *Periodic Statistical Reports on Oregon Mill Operations and Closures*. Eugene, OR: Paul F. Ehinger and Associates.

Howard, J. and B. Hiserote. 1978. *Oregon's Forest Products Industry, 1976*. Portland, OR: USDA Forest Service, Bulletin PNW-79.

———. 1984. *Oregon's Forest Products Industry: 1982*. Portland, OR: USDA Forest Service, Bulletin PNW-118.

International Paper. 1981. *Annual Report*. New York, NY.

Lane, P., J. Henley, R. Woodfin, and M. Plank. 1973a. *Lumber Recovery from Old-Growth Coast Douglas-fir*. Portland, OR: USDA Forest Service, Research Paper PNW-154.

———. 1973b. *Veneer Recovery from Old-Growth Coast Douglas-fir*. Portland, OR: USDA Forest Service, Research Paper PNW-162.

Oregon Department of Human Resources, Employment Division. 1968. *The Effects of Technological Change on Employment in the Lumber Industry*. Salem, OR: Department of Human Resources.

———. 1976 through 1986. *Oregon Resident Labor Force, Unemployment and Employment*. Salem, OR: Department of Human Resources.

Salazar, D., C. Schallau, and R. Lee. 1986. *The Growing Importance of Retirement Income in Timber Dependent Areas*. Portland, OR: USDA Forest Service, Bulletin PNW-359.

Stevens, J. *The Oregon Wood Products Labor Force: Job Rationing and Worker Adaptations in a Declining Industry*. Corvallis, OR: Oregon State University Agricultural Experiment Station, Special Report 529.

Tedder, P. 1979 "Oregon's Future Timber Harvest: The Size of Things to Come." *Journal of Forestry* 77:714-716.

U.S. Department of Commerce, Bureau of Census. 1970. *County Business Patterns—Oregon*. Washington, DC: Government Printing Office.

U.S. Bureau of Labor Statistics. 1984. *Employment and Earnings—States and Areas*. Washington, DC: Government Printing Office, Bulletin 1370, Pt. 12.

Weeks, E. 1983. *Plant Modernization and Community Economic Stability*. Eugene, OR: University of Oregon, Bureau of Governmental Research.

Weyerhaeuser. 1981. *Annual Report*. Tacoma, WA.

Young, J. and J. Newton. 1980. *Capitalism and Human Obsolescence*. Totowa, NJ: Allanheld, Osmun & Co.

11

Occupational Community and Identity Among Pacific Northwestern Loggers: Implications for Adapting to Economic Changes

Matthew S. Carroll
Department of Natural Resource Sciences
Washington State University

Robert G. Lee
College of Forest Resources
University of Washington

The stability of timber-dependent communities in the West and the welfare of forest products workers in those communities are issues that have long been debated in forest policy circles. During the 1960s and 1970s, the attention centered on the linkages between the regulation of timber supply (i.e., sustained yield versus market responsive approaches) and community stability (Waggener, 1969, 1978; Byron, 1977). In the current decade the focus has shifted to the effects of economic decline and structural change in the western forest products industry on such communities and workers. This paper reports results from a study of loggers in the Pacific Northwest which have implications for understanding their ability to adapt to declining job opportunities.

Preliminary field investigation suggested that identity and shared meanings are key factors in the logger's ability or inability to adjust successfully to dramatic shifts in the demand for labor.[1] In undertaking the study, we expected that the ability of workers to make changes in response to shifting labor markets has at least as much to do with shared meanings and social knowledge as it does with the economics of a particular industry or sector.

A common theme among the papers in this volume is that individual workers are subject to economic forces over which they have little or no control, but which have a profound influence on them. In the present case, the livelihoods of forest products workers are affected indirectly by such things as the prime interest rates, national rates of housing starts, the extent of local manufacturing as opposed to log exports, and the regulation of timber harvest in local and regional areas. Forest policy experts have sought to understand the workings of such political and economic developments, but little attention has been given to the indirect effects on workers and their communities. To understand how workers are likely to adapt to changes imposed by these "macro" forces, we must acquire an understanding of their "micro" social world. In particular, shared beliefs and shared meanings, values, and social knowledge are likely to influence individual behavior in the face of political and economic change.

A concept drawn from sociological literature which seemed at the outset of the research to have promise for conceptualizing the loggers' social world is that of occupational community. The basic notion of occupational community is that members of some occupations come to share a common (or community) life set apart from others in society (Salaman, 1974). This common life extends beyond the workplace and working hours and is, in many cases, independent of the particular neighborhood or geographic community in which the member resides.

A key defining characteristic of an occupational community is that its members' sense of identity is closely tied to the occupation:

> Members of such communities will not only see themselves in terms of their occupational role but will also value this self-image. The process is unlikely to occur among people who are in occupations that do not have occupational communities, and it is extremely unlikely among those workers who wish to escape totally from their work once they leave the work place (Salaman, 1974:22-23).

Members of occupational communities tend to spend a significant portion of their free time in the company of others in the occupation and members tend to look to each other as a primary reference group. Thus, the opinions and values of other "insiders" come to be seen as more important and valid than those of out-group members. The member of such a community looks to other members in developing and defining his or her own identity or sense of self (Blumer, 1969). The individual's identity literally becomes, at least in part, a reflection of the group, as he or she is primarily subject to the influences of other group members. This socialization process is common in many groups, but in the case of occupational communities, the distinctive values and world view which result tend to center specifically around the occupation and its culture.

This study was guided by the following working hypotheses: (1) loggers constitute an occupational community, and (2) the shared meanings and beliefs that evolve within the context of such a community strongly influence the ability of loggers to adapt successfully to externally imposed changes in opportunities for employment.

METHODS AND APPROACH

The field work took place in and around a group of logging settlements in northern California.[2] It was carried out in two phases. During the initial phase conducted in 1981, the first author engaged in six months of participant observation. He moved to a logging area and, keeping his identity as a researcher a closely guarded secret, sought employment in the woods. He was eventually successful in obtaining a job setting chokers on the rigging crew of an independent (gyppo) operator. During this period, he completed approximately 750 hours of active participant observation in addition to the time spent living in the town and observing its occupants and those of nearby settlements as well. The data gathered in this first phase consisted of a series of narratives and notes collected in a research diary in which entries were made on evenings and weekends. Having satisfied himself that a fairly realistic overall picture of the loggers' world in the particular location had been obtained, the investigator returned to the university to review his initial findings and to design the second phase of the field work.

The methodological strategy that guided the second phase of data gathering was analytic induction (Glaser and Strauss, 1980). The most important feature of analytic induction is that the researcher's developing conception, or "model," is confronted with all the available empirical evidence. If the model is contradicted by even one case, the model is reconceptualized to fit this new piece of evidence. This inductive process is continued until the model stabilizes. When conducting research using this procedure, the investigator does not define a sample in advance of the field work. Rather, the investigation proceeds inductively, gathering evidence from each of the categories[3] (in this case occupational categories) that are discovered in the social world under study. The initial conception of the categories themselves may change as the work progresses; the data gathering strategy is adjusted incrementally as the researcher gains additional knowledge of the social world being investigated.

The second phase took place in 1982 and 1983 and relied mainly on in-depth interviews together with some associated observation. The investigator returned to the field site, identified himself as "someone writing about loggers" and conducted a total of eighty-one in-depth interviews over the subsequent seven month period. Individuals to be interviewed were identified by means of chain referral, or "snowball" sampling. A minimum of six interviews was conducted with workers from each occupational category.[4] Interviews were concentrated in and around the half-dozen communities within a half-hour drive of the central field location. Responses to the interview questions exhibited no discernible variation that could be attributed to differences in locations within the boundary of the study area. The decision to terminate the data gathering was made when the interviews and observations ceased to yield novel information and when all substantively important occupational categories of logging had been adequately covered.

The interviews, typically one to two hours in length, took place in a variety of settings including the respondents' homes, the researcher's home, job sites, coffee shops, and the cabs of logging trucks. They were conducted in a semi-structured format. Interviewees were asked to describe their individual career history and particular attention was given to any mention of key individuals as teachers and role models. Subjects also were asked to describe their relationships with other loggers, the extent to which they spend free time in the company of others in the occupation, and the extent of their commitment to the occupation. Respondents were also asked to describe how they went about finding a job when necessary and the geographic extent of their job information networks. In addition, those interviewed were encouraged to talk at length about particular aspects of the occupation and its culture.

RESULTS

Bounding the Occupational Community

The loggers studied met the criteria describing an occupational community as defined in the sociological literature. Very clear social boundaries around the logger group were found. Individuals[5] involved in any part of the process of moving logs from the stump to the mill were considered loggers. This included workers who cut the trees (fallers and buckers), individuals who moved the logs from the stump to the landing where they are loaded onto trucks (rigging crew members), logging road builders, and log truck drivers. Workers who were not considered loggers included those whose primary duties were to cut and pile brush, clean up logging debris, or plant trees after the harvesting operations were completed. At first, these membership criteria seemed arbitrary, but further exposure to the loggers' value system revealed inherent logic; logging has historically been an extraction activity. Although the era of "cut and get out" logging is long over, some of the values that developed in that period seem to have survived in the group studied. One of the ideas that survived is that "real" logging involves getting wood to the mill. In addition to viewing themselves as highly individualistic and independent, a bond that links this group of workers is the commitment to the task of "getting the logs to town." Would-be loggers who are seen by their coworkers as lacking this commitment rarely last in the job. Informants for this study said that if a crew member displayed lack of commitment by failing to "pull his weight," he would either be "sent down the road" by a foreman or ostracized by his fellow workers.

For those studied, logging is clearly more than simply a means of earning wages; it represents a way of life complete with a set of highly developed traditions and shared values that have been cultivated and passed down through multiple generations. The boundary between loggers and nonloggers is very clear to members and they attribute considerable significance to group membership. A strong sense of shared mission and an almost militant esprit de corps was observed.

Despite the social boundary defining the loggers' community, the logging group was far from a seamless web. These results paralleled those of others who have studied occupational communities (see especially Miller and Johnson, 1981). There was clear role segregation and limited mobility between the four job categories. Although individuals occasionally move from one category to another (for example, a rigging crewman might try bucking in the hope of eventually becoming a faller), our informants and observations indicated a tendency for a worker to stay in a category once having become established there. Truck drivers, for example, stated time after time in the interviews that they wouldn't want to "get dirty" on a rigging crew and rigging crew members rarely expressed interest in driving a truck.

To serve as an illustration of role relationships, occupation-based categories, and career ladders within the loggers world, the configuration of a typical "cat" rigging crew[6] will be described. "Cat" refers to a bulldozer used to move (skid) logs to a cleared place known as a landing, from where they come to rest after trees are cut down by fallers and sectioned by buckers. The rigging crew consists of one or more cat skinners (or skidder operators when rubber tired skidding tractors are used) who operate the cats, one choker setter (sometimes two) per cat, one landing chaser (sometimes called a knot bumper), and one loader operator per crew. Additionally, there is usually a foreman (known as a side rod) who in the case of smaller, nonunion gyppo operations also usually runs a piece of equipment.

Choker setters occupy the bottom of the status hierarchy. The job is to fasten (set) a length of steel cable (a choker) around logs so they can be skidded to the landing by the cat. Up to seven or eight logs can be taken to the landing per trip or "turn," as it is called. Despite low status, the choker setter is a major determinant of the pace of a crew. Thus new choker setters are given a few days or a week to prove they can handle the pace and stay out of danger. Those who cannot are quickly fired.

As part of learning the job, the new choker setter is expected to very quickly learn the language of logging. He must know what it means "to get out of the bight," to "take a bonus log" or to put a "swede" or "bridle" on a log. If the terminology and behavior are not learned in short order, the individual acquires the dreaded reputation of having "no common sense." A new choker setter who learns the job, demonstrates willingness and ability to carry it out, and avoids acting like a "smart mouth" is accepted into the fold in a matter of weeks, virtually regardless of his lifestyle or views on religion or politics. If he is educated he is expected to "overcome his education" and demonstrate the common sense required for the job.

The landing chaser's job is to unhook chokers from logs as they are brought to the landing, trim any remaining knots or branches and "brand" each log with a branding hammer and spray paint. Chasers are usually former choker setters who have not graduated to equipment operator. In some cases chasers are young individuals waiting for an opportunity to run equipment, but many have reached the end of their career ladder. Cat skinners are typically former choker setters who took advantage of slack time or flat ground to learn the rudiments of operating cats and were then given the job permanently when an opening occurred. Loader operators have usually acquired their skills in the same manner.

The role of side rod can be compared to the popular stereotype of an army master sergeant. He generally has no more education or formal training than other crew members. He has typically come up through the ranks having experience in nearly every job on the crew. In addition, he has likely acquired a considerable repertoire of mechanical skills, which allow him to make minor and, in some cases, major equipment repairs. In short, he is an all around logger. The side rod usually has the power to fire crew members although he may or may not have hiring privileges. All of the side rod's duties are tied to one major responsibility: to see that a sufficient volume of logs is produced. It is his job to quickly deal with any obstacles to production and get the logs moving again.

Although specific job functions differ somewhat on yarder (cable logging) crews and for everybody but aviation people on helicopter rigging crews, status hierarchies and career ladders follow similar patterns to those of cat crews.

As the field investigation progressed, it became increasingly apparent that although all four categories of workers clearly were seen as falling within the boundary of the occupational community, a continuum existed within its internal organization. Fallers and buckers occupy the symbolic center and the high status position of the loggers' world. They are followed by rigging crewmen, with roadbuilders and truck drivers located closer to the periphery of the community. This center-to-periphery phenomenon was revealed both in terms of the relative esteem expressed by others within the community for occupants of various positions and also by the degree of attachment to the occupation demonstrated by members of the respective categories. Although members of all categories expressed relatively high degrees of attachment to logging as an occupation and way of life, fallers, buckers, and rigging crew members exhibited stronger and more consistent attachments. The implications of this for adaptability to other occupations are discussed below.

The Logger Identity

As the literature on occupational community led us to predict, the investigation uncovered highly developed occupational identities among most of the loggers studied. This was found to be particularly pronounced among fallers, buckers, and rigging crew members. The identities of those interviewed and observed tended to revolve around four interrelated themes: independence, pride in skill, pride in facing danger, and a sense of being in a unique category of workers. Loggers in all four categories were obviously fond of regaling listeners with stories of daring accomplishments with a chain saw, with a piece of heavy equipment, or behind the wheel of a truck. These accomplishments invariably were achieved by some combination of superior skill, physical strength, and unblinking "nerve." The expression of independence and rugged individualism surfaced repeatedly in the interviewing process. "You can't tell a logger what to do" was a statement recorded in interview after interview.

It became clear early in the participant observation that occupational identity is created and reinforced by in-group interaction. Logger-like behavior and attitudes are reinforced and nonlogger-like ones are discouraged or even ridiculed. One example of this is the loggers' view of the U. S. Forest Service, which manages much of the land in the study area. Nearly every logger interviewed made a negative statement about the agency. Perhaps the most direct insight into this was provided by an equipment operator on a rigging crew who tacitly admitted the existence of group influence by prefacing a monologue on the agency with the remark: "I'm a logger, so I'm supposed to hate the Forest Service...."

Occupational identity has two interrelated consequences for the logger. One is to foster what is often a very intense attachment to the occupation; the other is to provide the individual with an identity and its accompanying sense of empowerment and purpose. "Getting the logs to town" is seen as an important mission that is accomplished in spite of weather, steep ground, equipment failure, fires, and worst of all, interference from the Forest Service and assorted environmentalists.[7] Possessing the skills and courage to accomplish this difficult task leads the logger to set himself apart from ordinary people.

Shared Meanings

A set of interrelated values and shared meanings were found among the loggers studied. Taken together, these values and meanings constitute a group-based world view. Some of the more important themes are briefly summarized here.

One theme that emerged on virtually the first day of the observation and resurfaced repeatedly throughout the investigation is that loggers view themselves as extreme, rugged individualists (in both the physical and economic sense) whose survival and prosperity is based almost exclusively on individual initiative, skill, and hard work. Characteristic of this view is the tendency of loggers to favor compensation based on individual production. For example, fallers and buckers (including those who worked for a large unionized company) preferred to be paid on the basis of the volume of timber harvested rather than on the basis of day wages. Similarly, many truck drivers preferred to be paid on the basis of volume of logs hauled rather than by hourly wages. Arrangements whereby the worker is paid on the basis of individual production is referred to as "gyppoing" and the worker who refers to himself as a "gyppo" typically uses the term as a badge of honor.[8] One example of this is a truck driver who, in the course of an interview, stated proudly that he really was a gyppo even during a period in which he had been receiving an hourly wage. When asked to explain, he stated that he had worked as if his weekly pay was based on volume hauled even though that had not been the case. The gyppo arrangement allows the worker to claim that he really works for no one but himself and that whatever economic prosperity he and his family enjoy is attributable directly to his individual efforts. The loggers interviewed expressed pride in the fact that theirs is one of the few manual occupations left in which gyppo-type arrangements are possible. Related to the logger's individualism is a strong belief in the righteousness of entrepreneurship and a corresponding disdain for government regulation. Operators who turn a profit are seen as "good" or "smart" whereas government employees (and, one assumes, university researchers as well) are typically viewed as being impractical, lazy, or both. Many loggers aspire to someday having their own operations and most admire those who have such aspirations.[9]

A second theme that emerged from the observations and interviews is a "can do" or "do what it takes to get the job done" ethic. The loggers encountered in the study regard formal arrangements and abstract rules as unnecessary or impractical. Furthermore, they also were observed to be creative and innovative in solving the mechanical and logistical problems that often cropped up in moving the logs from the stump to the mill. Many loggers had become skilled mechanics by a process of trial and error. The ability to figure things out on one's own and to solve problems by improvising reflects common sense—a highly valued attribute in the loggers' world.

A third common theme among the loggers studied was an attachment to a rural way of life and an often strongly expressed dislike for cities. To the logger, the city represents a crowded, unhappy place where individualism and freedom are stifled. Many who were interviewed stated that they simply "couldn't" live in a city under any circumstances. One employee of a log trucking firm reported that he had turned down the offer of managing the maintenance of a fleet of trucks for a firm in Portland. He proudly stated that the offer included a doubling of his present salary and free helicopter rides to and from the city on Mondays and Fridays. He refused the offer because he valued his rural lifestyle and community attachments.

One of the ways that loggers (particularly those who work for gyppo operations) maintain a sense of independence is to change jobs on a frequent basis. Job changing is a time-honored custom among loggers in the study area and is apparently a tradition passed down from the very early days of western logging (Hayner, 1945; Holbrook, 1926; Williams, 1976; Stevens, 1979). In times of plentiful jobs, an individual may quit a particular operation for no stated reason and be hired back at a later time with no hard feelings. Gyppo operations often expand and contract from year to year, occasionally leaving no openings for individuals who performed entirely satisfactorily in the prior year. As a result, job switching is an acceptable and very common practice in the loggers' world.[10]

It became clear during participant observation that what at first appeared to be a lack of concern for job security, particularly among the gyppo loggers, was in fact an expression of confidence on the part of most that, under ordinary circumstances, another job could be obtained should the need arise. The individual would derive his sense of job security not from a necessarily long-standing relationship with a particular employer but rather from his marketability based upon his reputation in the occupational community. This reputation, reflected back to the individual from his peers, contributes to his occupational identity and sense of personal empowerment. In a sense, the logger's reputation is the primary product of his work and provides the basis of both identity and job security.

One of the questions the field investigator asked was how the information for job references made its way between employer and potential employee. Responses revealed that this process occurred almost entirely by word of mouth. Experienced loggers had developed reputations that were passed on through informal networks. Many of those interviewed indicated that jobs would come to them rather than vice versa. Informants stated that in the late winter, employees would begin calling around "to put a crew together" and those with the best working reputations were likely to have multiple job offers. In the case of larger company operations, union rules often would dictate who would be offered job slots first, but even in the case of larger companies, the remaining unclaimed slots usually would be filled through the use of informal networks.

DISCUSSION

During the first year of this study it was not clear that the early stages of long-term structural change in the forest products industry were underway. As a result, one initial focus of the research was on how the logger's occupational community might or might not equip him to respond to geographic shifts in the harvesting of available timber. Over the course of the study, the labor market for loggers in the study area became more and more depressed as the industry experienced the worst economic slump since the 1930s. In retrospect, it is clear that the study years marked the beginning of a transformation in which the industry permanently reduced employment substantially below levels common in the 1960s and 1970s. This unanticipated change in circumstances makes this study more valuable as the adaptability and welfare of forest products workers has quickly become a regional and national concern.

We feel safe in stating that the occupational community of loggers served a variety of very useful purposes in the lives of its members. Mutual support and helping behavior within the community were strongly evident. Members, for the most part, believed in their work and the group tended to reinforce the sense of independence and empowerment in its individual members. Experienced hands taught new members the tricks of the trade and helped one another adapt to technological developments in the industry. The community had even developed its own internal job referral network.

The community evolved over fifty or more years, during which there were periodic shifts in the forest products economy but few questions about the long-term prospects of employment (except, possibly, during the Great Depression). Loggers are, in our observation, extraordinarily adept at finding innovative and more efficient ways to "get the logs to town," but it is not at all apparent that they are equipped to adapt to circumstances under which the logs are either unavailable, no longer needed, or harvested with fewer workers. Rather, the very mechanisms that have embodied and maintained the loggers' community seem to impede problem-solving behavior that could possible lead to the creation of alternative livelihoods.

A highly developed and narrowly focused occupational identity can very quickly be transformed from an asset to a millstone around one's neck. Many of the loggers observed and interviewed were taught since childhood to believe that logging is the only acceptable way to make a living. In a typical case an individual may have followed his father's footsteps, devoting ten or twenty years to developing skills and a reputation as a good logger. In the course of that time he would have received numerous affirmations from those around him that served to strengthen his identity and commitment to the occupation. He would have developed a circle of friends largely from the occupational group and many of his leisure time activities would be, in one way or another, related to logging. If such an individual is suddenly faced with the fact that working in the woods is no longer a viable alternative, he not only loses a means of earning a wage, he loses an important part of his identity and a sense of personal empowerment as well. The more firmly attached an individual is to this occupational identity, the more traumatic and disorienting this kind of an experience is likely to be.

None of the job-getting strategies that the loggers' occupational community has evolved in the past adequately prepared its members to cope with the present set of conditions in the western forest products economy. The intergenerational transmission of values and shared meanings, the group influences, the tradition of hard physical work, the attachment to rural life, and the job information networks all seem to have evolved under conditions of reasonable levels of demand for labor. These strategies have not prepared loggers to look outside the occupation for work. Rather, the net effect seems to have been that of fostering and encouraging attachment to an occupation and a way of life that at least for some is no longer viable.

The most difficult problems of adjustment are faced by those relatively high status individuals closest to the "center" of the occupation—fallers, buckers, and rigging crew members. This is due largely to two factors: their characteristically higher degree of attachment to the occupation and the relatively lower trans-ferability of their skills to other jobs. Logging road builders and truck drivers generally share strong preferences to work in logging, but their occupational identities as loggers tended not to be as strong and their skills are more readily transferable to other occupations. It would be a less difficult transition (both in terms of identity and applicability of skills) for a log truck driver to take a long haul truck driving job or for a road builder to hire on to a general construction crew (assuming such jobs were available) than it would be for a timber faller or a rigging crew member to attempt to find alternative employment. Chain saw operation and choker setting are skills not in great demand outside of logging.

Policy Implications

At the time the field work for this study was conducted most loggers were unaware that their way of life was threatened by large scale economic changes. Whether a better understanding of this change by rank and file loggers has emerged since 1983 is not clear to us. Whether the logger's occupational community possesses the internal resources and information needed to help its members adjust to the current economic reality is an open question. The evidence gathered for this study suggests, however, that timely and effective adaptation without some form of outside intervention is unlikely.

Although forest products is not the only industry undergoing stressful decline in the present decade, its workers may be among the most severely affected. The combination of a highly developed occupational community and a lack of alternative economic opportunities in and around most logging areas presents displaced loggers with seemingly insurmountable obstacles to reemployment. An Appalachia-like cycle of poverty and hopelessness is emerging in many of the logging communities affected by structural changes in the forest products industry. Strong attachment to the occupation and a tradition of riding out the inevitable business cycles of the wood products economy have led to passive and perhaps ultimately maladaptive behavior on the part of loggers. Additional empirical research and monitoring is needed to study the effects on loggers of the changing economic circumstances in the wood products industry. There is an urgent need for information that can inform analysis and policy development.

How one interprets the relevance of the micro-level findings reported here for macro-level public policy depends on the assumptions one is willing to make about the future of the wood products economy and one's beliefs about the role that government can and should play in helping occupational groups under stress. If one assumes that the decline in employment is simply an unusually long and deep trough in the historic up-and-down cycle of the wood products economy, then intervention may be limited to short-term actions to preserve the occupational and industrial infrastructure until employment recovers. If, on the other hand, we are witnessing long-term employment decline, it may be cost-effective to intervene now with culturally relevant educational, self-help, and economic diversification programs rather than waiting for a cycle of poverty and hopelessness to become entrenched.

In conclusion, findings suggest that economic analysis alone is insufficient to understand the adaptability of occupational groups to economic changes. Rational behavior is shaped and influenced by one's life experiences, vision, and world view. These, in turn, are influenced by the social groups and micro-social setting in which the individual is embedded. It is therefore suggested that increased cooperation among economists, sociologists, and other social scientists would be beneficial in addressing the problems of occupations and communities under stress. Such analyses not only would be useful in understanding the difficulties faced by resource dependent communities, but the information generated could be used to help determine the circumstances and time frame in which intervention programs can be employed most effectively.

NOTES

1. The sociological theory used to guide the investigation was Blumerian symbolic interactionism. Briefly, this approach takes an inductive view of social organization and focuses on the individual's identity as a product of social interaction and on the importance of shared meaning in the creation and main-

tenance of cohesiveness and group boundaries. See Burrell and Morgan for an extended discussion of the basic assumptions of this theoretical perspective and Blumer (1969) for a discussion of its tenets and methodological approach.

2. The community from which the study was centered is located south of Portland, Oregon and north of Sacramento, California. The area chosen was deemed to be ideal for the study because the local economy was heavily dependent on timber extraction and the location provided access to a wide variety of types of logging operations. The central community had a population in 1980 of approximately 5,000 in a county of 38,700. There were no logging camps in the area and most loggers interviewed lived with their families and if necessary stayed in camp trailers near a particular job during the week. Loggers were interviewed in approximately ten smaller surrounding settlements as well.

3. The term "category" in this context relates to the way individuals in a social world group themselves. For example, as will be seen later in the text, fallers and buckers are seen by themselves and by other loggers as a particular group or subset of loggers. Individuals in the faller category are perceived by themselves and by others to have certain attributes not possessed by other loggers. In using analytic induction the researcher observes how the subjects categorize themselves rather than imposing preconceived categories on the group being studied.

4. It should be noted that the selection of individuals for interviews within categories was accomplished very readily through chain referrals but that the identification of additional categories was a more difficult task. It was accomplished in part by observation and in part by consulting with knowledgeable informants, some within and some outside the occupation.

5. All of the eighty-one individuals interviewed were men, although on several occasions interviews were conducted in the presence of spouses. Only one woman logger was identified among the several hundred who were encountered or whose names were located during the course of the study; however, problems in scheduling prevented an interview with her.

6. There are two other common types of rigging crews, those that use yarders (towers with cable rigging) and those that use helicopters.

7. It should be noted that the loggers interviewed were not all opposed to the value of environmental protection. One even claimed that loggers are more effective at protecting the environment than are those who call themselves environmentalists. What the loggers objected to most strenuously were the regulatory means by which environmental protection is sought. A number of those interviewed argued that flexibility and common sense are a better means to protect the environment than extensive formal regulation. The loggers interviewed typically viewed environmentalists (and to a lesser extent many Forest Service logging contract inspectors as well) as being ignorant of what it takes to get logs out of the woods. One colorful interviewee described a typical environmentalist as "(A)

one-way son-of-a-bitch who takes his annual walk in the woods and then goes home and votes against logging."

8. The term "gyppo" was originally derived from "gypsy"—meaning one who does not have forest land of his/her own from which to harvest logs and therefore moves around working for various landowners.

9. Approximately 85 percent of those interviewed for the study were gyppos, a percentage roughly reflecting the general populations of loggers in the study area.

10. It should be noted that a very small percentage of those interviewed or encountered in the course of this study had ever logged outside the Northwest or northern California. There was some evidence of individuals working temporarily in Alaska. For the vast majority, however, job information networks extended for approximately 100 miles.

REFERENCES

Blumer, H. 1969. *Symbolic Interactionism.* Englewood Cliffs, NJ: Prentice Hall.

Burrell, G. and G. Morgan. 1979. *Sociological Paradigms and Organizational Analysis.* Portsmouth, NH: Heinemann.

Byron, R. N. 1977. "Community Stability and Forest Policy in British Columbia." *Canadian Journal Forestry Research* 8:61-66.

Glaser, B. G. and A. L. Strauss. 1980. *The Discovery of Grounded Theory: Strategies for Qualitative Research.* New York: Aldine Publishing Company.

Hayner, N. S. 1945. "Taming the Lumberjack." *American Sociological Review* 2:217-225.

Holbrook, S. 1926. "The Logging Camp Loses Its Soul." *Sunset* (June):19-21, 62-65.

Miller, M. L. and J. C. Johnson. 1981. "Hard Work and Competition in the Bristol Bay Salmon Fishery." *Human Organization* 40 21:131-139.

Salaman, G. 1974. *Community and Occupation. An Exploration of Work/Leisure Relationships.* London: Cambridge University Press.

Stevens, J. B. 1979. "Six Views About a Wood Products Labor Force, Most of Which May Be Wrong. "*Journal of Forestry* 77:717-720.

Waggener, T. R. 1969. "Some Economic Implications of Sustained Yield as a Forest Regulation Model." Seattle, WA: University of Washington, College of Forest Resources Institute of Forest Products, Contribution No. 6.

——. 1978. "Sustained Yield Policies and Community Stability." Paper Presented for Agenda Item 2, The Interaction Between Stability in Forestry and Stability in Communities. October 16-28, Eighth World Forestry Congress. Jakarta, Indonesia.

Williams, R. L. 1976. *The Loggers*. New York: Time-Life Books.

III

Forest-Based Communities in a Service-Based Society

12

Social Bases for Resource Conflicts in Areas of Reverse Migration

Dale J. Blahna
Department of Geography and Environmental Studies
Northeastern Illinois University

A recent change in human migration patterns in the United States has sparked a great deal of research. During the 1970s, many rural areas grew significantly (Morrison and Wheeler, 1976; Price and Clay, 1980). While mid-decade census results for the 1980s suggest that this trend has slowed nationally, many rural areas are still growing, especially areas with natural amenity and recreational values (Luloff and Steahr, 1985; Fly, 1986). This paper is concerned with how rural communities have changed as a result of growth, and the implications of those changes for resource management. It focuses on small towns and unincorporated rural areas that grew as a result of reverse migration rather than on areas of suburban or industrial growth.

In areas of reverse migration, newcomers are often attracted by quality of life factors such as esthetic amenities and recreation opportunities (Graber, 1974; Price and Clay, 1980; Wellman and Marans, 1982; Voss, 1980; Fly, 1986). Many newcomers come from urban areas, and they tend to be older, retired couples or relatively young, affluent professionals and their families. Because of these distinctive characteristics, newcomers often act as "advocates of change" as they infuse into rural communities their own needs, competencies, and ideas of what constitutes the good life (Schwarzweller, 1979:16; Weeks, 1976).

The changes advocated by newcomers, however, are not always supported by long-term residents. For example, newcomers often lobby for expanding community services, but long-term residents have been found to oppose these policies due to the resulting increase in local taxes (Ploch, 1978; Dobringer 1969). Thus, while there has been no direct test of the hypothesis, it has often been postulated that reverse migration leads to increased instances of community conflict due to the contrasting preferences of migrants and long-term residents (Dillman and Tremblay, 1977; Price and Clay, 1980; Sofranko and Williams, 1980).

> Even modest increases for communities...now populated by homogeneous long-term residents, are likely to have dramatic impacts. New residents with city bred beliefs are likely to question the values of long-term residents and even their cherished ways of getting things done. Conflict may well be the result of sudden increases in heterogeneity (Dillman and Tremblay, 1977:129).

Price and Clay (1980: 563) use the term "culture clash" to characterize the tensions between long-term residents and newcomers. Culture clash has become the predominant theme for discussing social conflict in areas of rapid growth.

This paper examines the relationship between reverse migration and environmental conflict. The first section presents evidence suggesting that culture clash applies to questions of resource management and development. The primary tenet of the paper, however, is that normative clash between newcomers and long-term residents is only one of several possible forms that growth-related conflicts may take. The second section of the paper presents case study evidence from the literature and summarizes the results of several studies of reverse migration in Michigan, suggesting two additional forms of growth-related conflicts that cannot be explained by the culture clash model. Thus, it is argued that environmental conflicts may emerge as a result of social factors related to growth, even where the environmental attitudes of newcomers and long-term residents do not differ. In the third section of the paper the concept of cultural infusion is offered as an integrative framework that expands the culture clash perspective to include organizational and environmental factors important for understanding resource conflicts in areas of rapid growth.

CULTURE CLASH, MIGRATION, AND ENVIRONMENT

Early migration research was conducted in urban areas by Robert Park (1952) and other researchers at the University of Chicago. They found many social problems characteristic of certain urban areas experiencing rapid growth. These were called "zones of transition," which were characterized as areas of conflict between the new or "invading" and the old or "retreating" cultures (Menard and Covey, 1984: 112). With the influx of new residents came a disintegration of social organization in neighborhoods that reduced resident identification with the neighborhood and other residents, and increased anonymity.

In his classic treatise, *Community Conflict*, Coleman (1957) provided evidence that suggests population growth can lead to conflict in rural communities as well as in urban areas. He also argued that one of the specific sources of conflict was the diversification of values in the growing community.

> At some time or another, mass migration may deposit a whole new group of people into an existing community. Often these newcomers differ from the natives in their "styles of life"...The resulting "community" consists of two very dissimilar parts... Whenever a difference in values and in interests is created by the influx of new residents, it becomes a potential basis of conflict (Coleman, 1957:7).

While Coleman argued that several other factors were also critical determinants of community conflict, the notion of normative clash has become a dominant theme in the literature on reverse migration. While most studies of the normative cleavages between newcomers and long-term residents have focused on economic, social, or institutional issues, there is also some evidence that the culture clash concept applies to questions of environmental quality. For example, in rural Maine, Ploch (1978) found that newcomers were more likely than long-term residents to oppose development policies and to be concerned with preserving the environmental integrity and the rural atmosphere of the community.

There are also studies that support the applicability of the culture clash model to resource management. For example, Loomis (1982:18) found several instances of culture clash over range management issues in rapid growth areas of the West. He reported that conflicts arose "between the 'newcomer', who expects 'his' public lands to support wildlife, and the 'oldtimer' who sees 'his' public lands as a livestock forage source." This utilitarian versus preservation cleavage between long-term residents and newcomers was also found in road building controversies in southeastern Utah (Peterson, 1983) and the Upper Peninsula of Michigan (Teare, 1980) and in a conflict over mineral development in eastern Vermont (Ann Arbor News, 1985).

The explanation for these conflicts has been generalized as follows: Newcomers tend to oppose community growth and resource development in order to retain the natural, uncrowded conditions that attracted them in the first place (Graber, 1974; Frankena, 1980; Voss, 1980; Fliegel, Sofranko, and Glasgow, 1981; Wellman and Marans, 1982). This behavior is referred to as the "gangplank" or "last settler" syndrome. Many urban-to-rural migrants want the "best of both worlds," both the high quality pastoral environment that initially attracted them and the services they enjoyed in the cities (Dailey and Campbell, 1980). In effect, the urban oriented values of the reverse migrants clash with the more traditional, utilitarian values of long-term residents who favor economic growth and development (Buttel and Flinn, 1977; Ploch, 1978). Thus, whether implicit or explicit, most observers who discuss the issue of conflict do so from the culture clash perspective.

EMPIRICAL CHALLENGES TO CULTURE CLASH

The research record on the relationship between growth and conflict is not completely consistent (Sofranko and Williams, 1980). Several studies suggest that normative differences between newcomers and long-term residents often are not as distinct as generally believed. In two rapid growth counties in Michigan, Wellman and Marans (1982) found few demographic and attitudinal differences between newcomers and long-term residents. In addition, several authors reported that they had found little or no support for the gangplank hypothesis (Wellman and Marans, 1982; Fliegel, Sofranko, and Glasgow, 1981; Voss, 1980; Voss and Fuguitt, 1979). There is evidence from the Great Lakes region that newcomers have a more positive attitude toward growth than long-term residents (Price and Clay, 1980; Sofranko and Fliegel, 1983). Such findings led Wellman and Marans (1982) to question the validity of the assumption that reverse migration will result in increased social conflict.

Implicit in this question is the assumption that normative differences are the sole, or primary, determinants of growth-related conflict. It also implies that growth-related conflicts must be conflicts between newcomers and long-term residents. While this form of conflict has been documented in the literature, case studies suggest at least two other forms of growth-related environmental conflicts: (1) those between newcomers and public or private agencies, and (2) those instigated by newcomers but in which long-term residents join with newer residents to fight a common foe. These forms of conflict cannot be explained by the culture clash paradigm.

NEWCOMERS VERSUS AN AGENCY OR COMPANY

While conflict between subgroups of residents is common within communities, resource issues often occur in an entirely different form: citizens versus a public or private agency. Johnson (1983) documented six case studies of western national forests where rapid growth occurred in the forests' zone of influence. An increase in conflicts between the forests and local citizens resulted from an increase in the number of ownerships in or near the forests; most of the residents involved were relatively new to the area. These growth-related conflicts were not the result of complex sociocultural cleavages among residents, but arose around newer residents in subdivisions adjacent to forest resources. Another important factor was the political activism of the newcomers. For example, for the Eldorado National Forest:

> A major element in the forest's management situation is the political sophistication of many new residents. These individuals are integrating themselves into local political structures, and are vocal in presenting their views (Johnson 1983:41).

COALITIONS BETWEEN NEWCOMERS AND LONG-TERM RESIDENTS

The second form of growth related conflict not explained by culture clash is when newcomers and long-term residents agree on the issues and join to fight a common foe. Regardless of who that foe is —newcomers, long-term residents, or a company or agency—conflicts are growth related if newcomers are the catalysts initiating the conflict, or if they bring special skills and capabilities that influence the course of the conflict.

An example of newcomers acting as catalysts was documented by Graber (1974). She found that newcomers to a Denver exurban commuter town initiated a movement for historic preservation in the community. The newcomers were later "joined by a sizeable block of earlier residents, for historic preservation is a strategic issue around which newcomers and long-timers can unite" (Graber, 1974: 511). This case is one of the most cited examples of normative clash between newcomers and long-term residents, despite the fact that other social dynamics were taking place. And while Graber considers historic preservation a unique issue that deviates from the expected pattern, others have noted similar dynamics in different situations. For example, in Lakeview, Arkansas, newcomers fought against a proposed sewage treatment plant because they saw it as an inducement to future growth (Dailey and Campbell, 1980). Later those concerns were also voiced by natives who felt they were "watching their community change in ways they believe are for the worse" (Dailey and Campbell, 1980:261).

Coalitions between newcomers and long-term residents are also documented by Frankena (1983). Newcomers to Hersey, Michigan, who started a battle against the construction of a wood-fired electric power plant were concerned that the plant would increase pollution and that the wood requirements of the plant would decimate local forests. Most long-term residents who were active in the issue supported the plant opponents. The town council, which initially supported the project, changed to a neutral position in the the face of citizen protests. Frankena concluded that most newcomers and long-term residents were not in conflict in Hersey, as the "suburbanization" idea would suggest, but that they had joined together to achieve some common goals (Frankena, 1983: 85-86). He argued that the newcomers stimulated political awareness and, because of shared images of the countryside, long-term residents felt impelled to join the movement. Therefore, he suggested that newcomers should be viewed as contributing to qualitative changes in local politics by interjecting new values and capabilities (Frankena, 1983:82).

Finally, in his extensive research on reverse migration in rural Maine, Ploch (1980) documented a case where both culture clash and coalitions between newcomers and long-term residents occurred together. He found that while there were obvious situations of normative clash between newcomers and younger community members, older long-term residents often identified with newcomers. As a result of leadership experience, newcomers often advanced to community leadership positions quickly. Although participation of newcomers breathed new life into local activities, some residents were suspicious of newcomer motives, especially younger residents who stood to lose economic advantages and leadership positions. Under normal circumstances, young people in the small rural communities, would "replace their parents in positions of power and prestige" (Ploch, 1980:305). He concluded that:

> ...[T]he factionalism is complex. Some of the older members of the resident population are sympathetic to the interests and motivations of the son-daughter generation...In other cases, the older generation tends to identify with the newcomers...These older people...tend to see a kind of reincarnation of their own agrarian values in many of the in-migrants. In many cases they view their own children as 'migrants in place'...who seem more attuned to the values and norms of urban America than toward traditional local culture. In contrast, many of the in-migrants prefer a much simpler, more old-fashioned style of life (p. 306) ...Overall there appears to be a mutual desire upon the part of both migrants and nonmigrants to get on with the business of making their communities better places in which to live (p. 309).

In summary, these case examples suggest there are at least two forms of environmental conflict that cannot be explained by the culture clash paradigm. Growth related conflicts can often be expected to occur in areas of reverse migration even where there are little or no value differences between newcomers and long-term residents or little contact between the two groups. In order to test for the regional effect of reverse migration, two research studies were conducted in Michigan. The objectives were to (1) test for a relationship between population growth and environmental conflict, and (2) evaluate the differences in the attitudes and organizational behavior of newcomers and long-term residents. The next section summarizes the results from these studies.

MICHIGAN RESEARCH

Northern Lower Michigan (NLM) was selected for this research because it represents a classic case of reverse migration. Statewide, population in non-metropolitan areas grew 15.6 percent between 1970 and 1980 compared to 1.6 percent in metropolitan areas (Werner, 1982). The thirty-three counties of northern Lower Michigan (Map 1) grew an average of 22.7 percent (U.S. Dept. of Commerce, 1973; 1983). Growth was especially rapid (51 percent) in a region of nine contiguous counties in the central portion of NLM (shaded area of Map 1).

The region is predominantly forested and contains seven state parks, parts of six state forests, and one national forest. The economic base is tourism and resource development. Most of the migrants moved from urban areas in southern Michigan, attracted by the natural amenities and recreation opportunities (Fly, 1986); most of the growth occurred in the rural countryside. Despite this phenomenal growth, the population of many of the towns in the region remained stable or decreased during the ten year period.

Past findings on the relationship between social conflict and reverse migration have been based on two research methods: attitude surveys and conflict case studies. Because of certain weaknesses when the findings of these methodologies are generalized, we selected two research methods that had not been used: in-depth interviews with resource professionals and annual environmental conflict event counts gathered from secondary data sources.

Resource Manager Survey
In 1982, forty indepth, personal interviews were conducted with forest resource professionals from all public and private agencies with forest management respon-sibilities in the nine-county region shown in Map 1.[1] Results supported the notion of a positive relationship between population growth and environmental conflict. Twenty-eight (70 percent) of the respondents felt there had been an increase in resource conflicts, and of those, twenty-four (86 percent) felt that population growth was at least in part responsible. The open-ended responses suggested that the specific growth- related reasons were about evenly split between two explana-tions: (1) increased pressure on resources and (2) increased diversity of public opinion.

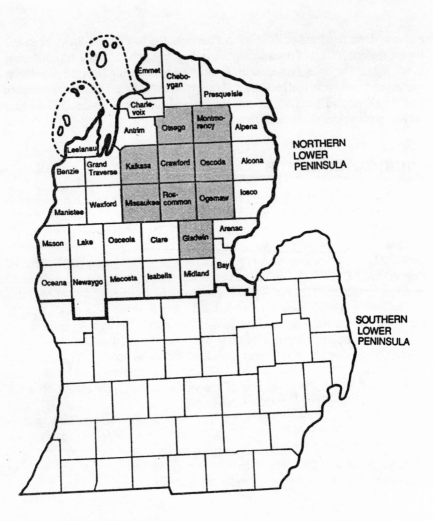

Map 1. Study Region in Northern Lower Michigan

Newcomers were most active in growth-related resource conflicts, especially conflicts over timber harvest practices such as clearcutting. As one Michigan Department of Natural Resources forester put it:

> Long-time residents...are not the ones that cause the turmoil. The ones that come in from the city, now that's different, especially if they come up and the realtor says: "We have a piece

of state land here, it shall remain forever in primeval conditions." Then we come in and cut timber. Well Holy Moses! Devastation! Rape of the land! The late 1800s loggers are coming back and just devastating!...[They say] "I realize why you have to do some cutting but don't do it in my backyard, do it someplace else."

Environmental Conflict Event Counts

While the interviews with the forests managers supported the notion that there was a relationship between growth and conflict, we felt their perceptions could have been influenced by other factors, such as the increase in environmental conflict in general. Thus, a second method of environmental conflict analysis was developed to test for the relationship between population growth and environmental conflict. We conducted a quantitative, longitudinal analysis of environmental conflict events, and compared the change in the number of events in rapid growth areas with the number of events in areas that grew more slowly.

The data for this study came from news articles in two state newspapers and the newsletters of two major environmental groups in the state.[2] Over 2,200 articles were collected that contained an environmental opinion about resources located within the thirty-three counties of northern Lower Michigan. From these articles, an operational definition of environmental conflict was developed. This definition utilizes the sociological concept of "contentious gatherings" (Tilly and Tilly, 1981; Schweitzer and Simmons, 1981). The final unit of analysis was termed a Local Citizen Group Environmental Action (LCGEA). This was defined as:

[A]n occasion in which five or more citizens of a local area or single county make a public claim that, if realized, would affect the interests of some other person(s) or groups(s), concerning a specific environmental action or policy, or proposed action or policy, for a natural resource located entirely or primarily within northern Lower Michigan, some time during 1967, 1970, 1975, or 1980, and was reported in one of the four primary data sources...

Using this definition and extensive coding of instructions (Blahna, 1984), 140 individual LCGEAs were identified. All the articles referring to each LCGEA were placed in a separate file. Pertinent aspects of each event, and all the stakeholders that could be identified for each event, were coded and entered in a computer data base. Due to the relatively small number of conflicts for longitudinal analysis, the data were collapsed into periods of early growth (1967 and 1970) and later growth (1975 and 1980). Sixty-nine took place in the early growth years and seventy-one took place in the later growth years.

Several different variables were used to test the hypothesis that there was a relationship between population growth and environmental conflict. The first measure was the location of the 109 events that occurred in the study region. The second measure was the location of the resources of concern in the LCGEAs that were county-wide or local in scope. The third measure was the location or "home" of citizen stakeholders. The results in Table 1 show that for all three measures there was a substantial increase in the number of observations in the rapid growth counties as compared to the slow and moderate growth counties, and that the change in the number of observations in the rapid growth counties was much higher than would be expected based on population change alone.[3]

Table 1. Location of Events, Resources, and Stakeholders by County Growth Period (numbers in parentheses are percents)

County Growth[1]	Percent Regional Population		Events Location[2]		Resources Location[3]		Stakeholders[4]	
	1970	1980	67-70	75-80	67-70	75-80	67-70	75-80
Rapid	20%	23%	17 (31)	27 (50)	11 (23)	26 (42)	6 (27)	49 (48)
Slow	80%	77%	38 (69)	27 (50)	36 (77)	36 (58)	70 (73)	53 (52)
Total			55 (100)	54 (100)	47 (100)	62 (100)	96 (100)	102 (100)

[1]Population growth from 1960 to 1980: rapid = 65% and over; slow = under 64% (U.S. Bureau of Census, 1973; 1983).

[2]Location of LCGEAs. (Of the total 140 events, 31 were held outside of the study region.)

[3]Location of resources involved in 109 county or local scope conflicts.

[4]Private citizen stakeholders whose members/participants and interests could be tied to one county in the study region. (Of the 669 stakeholders, 285 were citizen stakeholders and, of these, 198 were local or county scope groups.)

Resident Attitudes and Participation Characteristics

The final stage of research on the relationship between reverse migration and environmental conflict was a survey mailed to a random sample of resident property owners in the nine-county region of most rapid growth. The object was to test for differences between long-term residents and reverse migrants on (1) measures of socioeconomic status, (2) attitudes toward resource management and other environmental issues, and (3) participation in environmental issues.[4]

Survey results suggested there was little evidence for culture clash in the region. Although newcomers were more likely to be retired and to have spent most of their lives in urban areas, and long-term residents were more likely to own larger parcels of land, there were no significant differences between the two subgroups on four different measures of socioeconomic status (Blahna, 1985a).[5] Furthermore, newcomers were familiar with the region before settling there. Likewise, the existing residents were familiar with the migrants due to the annual migration of "flatlanders" during the tourist season.

As the culture clash hypothesis predicts, newcomers and long-term residents held significantly different attitudes on measures of satisfaction with social, economic, and service aspects of the community (Blahna, 1985a; 1985b). Measures of environmental attitudes, however, presented little evidence for culture clash. While newcomers favored policies emphasizing preservation, zoning, and the designation of public land more than long-term residents, and were more likely to oppose oil and gas development, there were no significant differences between newcomers and long-time residents for most of the environmental attitude measures on the survey. This included their perceptions of local environmental problems, such as water pollution and litter; their preferences for resource management and development practices, such as roading and timber harvesting; and their perceptions of the negative effects of population growth, such as crowding and environmental or social degradation. The two most surprising findings were: (1) that there were no differences between newcomers' and long-term residents' attitudes toward clearcutting, and (2) and that the newcomers were more likely than long-term residents to agree with statements suggesting there were positive benefits resulting from population growth (Blahna, 1985a; 1985b).

The results so far present a paradox. While the number of environmental conflicts in the study region increased substantially from the earlier to the later stage in the growth cycle, there were relatively few demographic and attitudinal differences between newcomers and the long-term residents. Some of this paradox can be explained by the differential participation rates of the two groups. While the migrants and long-term residents in the study belonged to approximately the same number of organized groups newer migrants were more likely to belong to conservation or preservation groups ($X^2 = 4.2$, p = .04) and property owner groups ($X^2 = 8.6$, p = .003). In the analysis of the environmental event counts discussed above, we found that most (72 percent) of the named citizen groups involved in the environmental conflicts were of these three types. The survey also showed that newcomers were likely to take more different types of environmental actions as compared to long-term residents, such as signing petitions, joining or donating money to a group, and attending public hearings ($X^2 = 11.8$, p = .003).

In summary, the results from the Michigan studies suggest that environmental conflicts increased in the rapid growth region, yet there were few socioeconomic and attitudinal differences between newcomers and long-term residents. While newcomers were more likely than long-term residents to support preservation and zoning policies, they exhibited about the same amount of support for resource development and population growth policies. The results suggest there will be no backlash against resource development in general, but that probably there will be large increase in the "not in my backyard" attitude. Thus, conflicts are likely to emerge between newer residents and agencies responsible for management of local resources. The clearcutting controversies provide evidence for this. The similarity in many environmental attitudes of the two subgroups also implies that there is ample opportunity for coalition between reverse migrants and long-term residents. And finally, since newcomers were more active in environmental groups and actions than long-term residents, there will be more people active in environmental issues in the region as a result of reverse migration.

CULTURAL INFUSION AND RESOURCE CONFLICT

Normative differences between newcomers and long-term residents are not the only factors that can trigger growth-related environmental conflict in areas of reverse migration. Newcomers in a rural community can contribute to environmental conflict due to their number, location, preferences, and environmental organization and leadership skills. Newcomers contribute to change by interacting with existing social, organizational, and environmental attributes of the receiving community. The potential for growth-related environmental conflicts can be increased by such "cultural infusion." [6] This section will discuss some general ways that cultural infusion can affect resource conflicts in areas of reverse migration.

The number of newcomers alone can stimulate resource conflicts simply because of the sheer increase in "squeaky wheels" in the community. Furthermore, population growth is related to increased levels of environmental degradation and competition for scarce resources (Loomis, 1982; Caldwell, 1983; Cutler, 1984). While all resource scarcity and degradation problems will not result in conflict, an increase in these problems indicates there will be an increase in the number of potential conflict initiating situations in the long run. [7]

The number of migrants can contribute to resource conflicts regardless of differences in the preferences of newcomers and long-term residents. To the extent that the recreational interests of newcomers are different from those of long-term residents, there may be demands to utilize resources for new recreational opportunities. However, if recreational interests of newcomers are similar to those of long-term residents, there may be increased crowding in areas where existing use is high. Also, whether or not timber harvesting or roading attitudes of newcomers clash with the attitudes of long-term residents, the newcomers' preferences have led to resource conflicts simply because they are associated with incompatible adjacent land uses. Thus, preferences of newcomers and long-term residents can be a misleading indicator of the potential for natural resource conflicts unless the particular characteristics of a situation are accounted for.

The organization and leadership experiences of newcomers can also contribute to resource conflicts. Newcomers were found to participate heavily in local community affairs, increasing the potential for resource conflicts. Conflicts can be exacerbated if newcomers have more organizational experience than long-term residents, or if they have experiences in different types of environmental actions. Newcomers may approach environmental issues in a manner fundamentally different from the community's traditional approaches. For example, in rural communities where residents traditionally contact decision makers in an informal, one-to-one manner, the migrants, who have fewer personal contacts in the community, may be more apt to organize formal opposition or to work with existing state and regional interest groups to bring about change.

When newcomers associate with long-term residents and cooperate in promoting reforms, they are more likely to have an impact on general community attitudes than when there are few or no links between migrants and long-term residents (Coleman, 1957), in which case, the dominant form of growth-related conflict is more apt to be culture clash.[8]

Finally, all of the cultural infusion factors discussed above are affected by the location of population growth. Since the natural amenities of rural areas are key attractions for many reverse migrants, migrants often relocate near lakes, rivers, and forests rather than in towns and villages (Frankena and Koebernick, 1984). Therefore, the settlement patterns involved in reverse migration are especially likely to affect resource management, because a much larger portion of the resource base has become "backyard" in both the physical and psychological sense.

CONCLUSIONS

This chapter provides empirical support for the notion that resource conflicts are likely to increase in rural communities affected by reverse migration. Growth-related conflicts are not due simply to normative differences between newcomers and long-term residents. Newcomers may also clash with private or public organizations, or they may initiate a conflict and obtain the support of long-term residents in actions that would not have occurred without the influence of newcomers in the community. These forms of conflict do not result only from differences in the cultures of newcomers and long-term residents, but from the way newcomers are integrated into the social and political life of a community. Cultural infusion suggests that, in addition to demographic and attitudinal differences of the migrants and long-term residents, the impact of reverse migration on rural communities is also dependent upon (1) the normal increase in conflict due to the sheer number of residents who are active in community decision making, (2) the interaction of newcomers' preferences and leadership skills with the community's existing organizational and attitudinal characteristics, (3) the environmental impacts resulting from growth, and (4) the location of housing, which may place more people in proximity to land-based resources.

Cultural infusion presents a special challenge for resource managers. It means there will be increased scrutiny of resource management practices by local residents, and that resource managers cannot always count on the support of long-term residents when conflicts emerge. In fact, long-term residents may lend support to newcomer demands. Thus, more flexible and innovative management strategies will be needed to adapt resource management goals to the demands of a more heterogeneous community. Residents in local communities will also have a wider variety of political and organizational strategies for influencing resource decision making. These trends suggest that, even in remote rural areas affected by reverse migration, public involvement and social impact assessment must play a key role in decision making if managers are going to understand, predict, and deal with resource conflicts.

For social scientists, the results suggest that we have suffered from professional myopia. Most research on the impact of reverse migration has focused on attitudinal and demographic characteristics of migrants. This has resulted in an oversimplified conception of the relationship between growth and conflict. As Firey (1978: 171) has pointed out, the sociological analysis of natural resources requires an integration of structural, attitudinal, and organizational factors. It also requires the integration of both social and physical factors (Firey, 1978; Humphrey and Buttel, 1982). In the case of reverse migration, as well as other forms of rural population growth, social adaptation to the physical environment is especially important for understanding the long-term implications for conflict. If one assumes the adaptation occurs after a period of social change, the normative distinctions between newcomers and long-term residents will diminish over time, to be replaced by potential conflict between future newcomers and "older" newcomers. The infusion of political sophistication will have a more enduring effect, but community and resource management institutions may be able to adapt to the new decision- making environment, again reducing the potential for conflict.

Integrating results from the physical and social sciences will require using new research paradigms. It will also require implementing multiple methods focused on a single research question, as suggested by Webb et al. (1981). In the Michigan research cited above, for example, relying solely on the resident survey would have led to the same conclusions reached by other social scientists in the past; there were few demographic and environmental attitude differences between newcomers and long-term residents, making it unlikely that many growth-related resource conflicts would occur. By looking only at counts of environmental conflicts, the assumption would have been that the increase in conflict events in rapid growth areas was simply the result of normative cleavages between newcomers and long-term residents. Thus, our conclusions, which have led to the expansion of the culture clash model, could not have been reached without triangulating results from several different data sources.

ACKNOWLEDGMENTS

This line of research has been supported by the U.S. Department of Agriculture (McIntire-Stennis Forestry Research) and the University of Michigan School of Natural Resources. The author thanks Pat West, Mark Fly, Fred Frankena, Carol Novak, and Paul Steinmetz for assistance and advice in the preparation of this paper.

NOTES

1. Sample subjects were selected using the following criteria: (1) at least two representatives (one administrator and one field manager) of every public agency office and every landowning forest industry in the region; (2) one administrator of each state park, (3) one field representative from each forestry extension and soil conservation unit; and (4) all forestry consultants in the region. From forty-five original sample subjects, forty useable surveys were obtained. Respondents represented the U.S. Forest Service, Michigan Department of Natural Resources, three different forest industries, two agricultural extension units, and four private consulting firms. Of the total sample, seventeen were foresters in public agencies, twelve were in parks or forest recreation, seven were industrial foresters, and four were private forestry consultants. All but three of the respondents had worked in the study region for five years or more.

2. The four primary data sources were the Bay City Times, Lansing State Journal, Michigan Out-of-Doors (monthly publication of the Michigan United Conservation Clubs), and the Michigan Audubon Newsletter. These publications were selected because they exhibited a relatively high level of environmental reporting, good coverage of northern Lower Michigan news, and consistent editorial policies throughout the study period.

3. The "rapid growth" counties were the eleven counties that grew at least 65 percent during the twenty-year period from 1960 to 1980. Sixty-five percent was selected to retain comparability with the counties used in the other two phases of the research, the resource manager study and the resident attitude survey. Using

65 percent, the eleven rapid growth counties consisted of the nine counties where the two surveys were conducted (shaded area of Map 1) plus Mecosta and Iosco counties.

4. A random sample of 705 resident property owners was selected from county property tax roles. A mail survey was conducted using a four wave sampling design (survey, reminder, second survey, second reminder). The results are based on 374 useable returns (53 percent response rate).

5. The year 1965 was used since it marked the beginning of the migration turnaround based on the census population levels and our measures of motivations for moving to the study region. Since many studies of reverse migration used 1970 or later as the cut point, most analyses were repeated using both 1970 and 1975 as cut points; the results were found to be similar regardless which cut point was used.

6. The term "cultural infusion" is used because it complements the concept of "cultural diffusion" which is used in demography and human ecology. Cultural diffusion is the process of internal migration in which representatives from certain regions migrate to other regions. This leads to a reduction of "intersectional and interregional differences" (Bogue, 1964:487). Reverse migration is an example of cultural diffusion because the rural areas that experienced growth became more like urban areas due to the increase in heterogeneity as a result of influx of middle class, urban residents (Dillman and Tremblay, 1977:129). Cultural infusion is a complementary concept: it refers to the process of social change that is experienced by the receiving community.

7. Price and Clay (1980: 593) refer to "institutional overload" as a source of "structural disturbance" in areas of reverse migration. This concept is applicable as a potential source of social conflict as well. In the case of environmental conflict, however, we must also consider ecological impacts (such as pollution from septic systems) as a form of institutional overload.

8. This suggests several specific ways newcomers can act as catalysts in resource conflicts. First, formal or informal interaction with newcomers may help to formulate a latent interest among long-term residents. Second, long-term residents may become involved in an issue in which they share an interest when new political activities are introduced (i.e., a protest). And third, the new activity or interest in the environment may actually change the attitudes of long-term residents due to the exposure to new ideas and methods.

People who stayed behind during the mass migration out of rural areas probably did so out of a strong attachment to the rural style of life. At the same time, out-migration may have planted a seed of doubt concerning the quality of rural life since so many people were opting for urban lifestyles. However, the recreation boom during the 1960s and 1970s brought many visitors and second home owners to rural areas. This phenomenon was followed by an influx of new residents, some of whom were actively fighting to preserve the rural way of life. For those rural residents who never left, these combined factors may have helped to reconstruct the latent positive image of life in the country.

REFERENCES

Ann Arbor News. 1985. "Vermont River: Oldtimers and Newcomers Battle Over Valley." April 15, p. C1.

Blahna, D. J. 1984. "A Method of Quantifying Environmental Conflict Utilizing Qualitative Data Sources and Relational Data Bases." Ann Arbor, MI: Unpublished technical report, the University of Michigan School of Natural Resources (Natural Resource Sociology Lab).

Blahna, D. J. 1985a. "Turnaround Migration and Environmental Conflict in Northern Lower Michigan." Ann Arbor, MI: Unpublished Ph.D. dissertation, University of Michigan.

Blahna, D. J. 1985b. "Rural Population Growth and Social Information Needs of Forest Management Agencies." In L. Wenner (ed.), *Social Science Information and Resource Management: Interagency Symposium Proceedings.* Washington, D. C.: USDA Forest Service, Office of Environmental Coordination.

Bogue, D. J. 1964. "Internal Migration." In P. M. Hauser and O.D. Duncan (eds.), *The Study of Population: An Inventory and Appraisal*, Fourth Edition. Chicago: University of Chicago Press.

Buttel, F. H. and W. L. Flinn. 1977. "Conceptions of Rural Life and Environmental Concern." *Rural Sociology* 42(4):544-555.

Caldwell, L. K. 1983. "'People Pressure' and Environmental Consequences." *Environment* 25(10): 68-70.

Coleman, J. S. 1957. *Community Conflict.* New York: The Free Press.

Cutler, R. M. 1984. "The Real Problem for Water Leaders—Future United States Population Growth." Paper presented at the annual meeting of the Colorado River Water Users Association, Las Vegas, NV.

Dailey, G. H. and R. R. Campbell. 1980. "The Ozark-Ouachita Uplands Growth and Consequences." In D. L. Brown and J. M. Wardwell (eds.), *New Directions in Turnaround Migration: The Population Turnaround in Rural America.* New York: Academic Press.

Dillman, D. A. and K. R. Tremblay, Jr. 1977. "The Quality of Life in Rural America: Annals of American Academy of Political and Social Sciences."

Dobringer, W. M. 1969. "The Natural History of a Reluctant Suburb." In R. O'Brien, *Readings in General Sociology,* Fourth edition. Boston, MA: Houghton-Mifflin.

Firey, W. 1978. "Some Contributions of Sociology to the Study of Natural Resources." In M. Barnabas, S. K. Hulbe, and P. S. Jacob (eds.), *Challenges of Societies in Transition.* Delhi: Macmillan Co.

Fliegel, F. C., A. W. Sofranko and N. Glasgow. 1981. "Population Growth in Rural Areas and Sentiments of the New Migrants Towards Further Growth." *Rural Sociology* 46(3):411-429.

Fly, J. M. 1986. "Tourism and Nature: The Basis for Growth in Northern Lower Michigan." Unpublished Ph.D. dissertation, University of Michigan.

Frankena, F. 1980. "Community Impacts in Rapid Growth Nonmetropolitan Areas: A Literature Survey." *Rural Sociology Series* No. 9. East Lansing, MI: Agricultural Experiment Station, Michigan State University.

———. 1983. "The Impact of Technical Expertise in a Nonmetropolitan Siting Dispute: A Case Study of the Hersey WFPP Controversy." Unpublished manuscript. East Lansing, MI: Michigan State University, Department of Rural Sociology.

Frankena, F. and T. Koebernick. 1984. "Effects of Environment and Location: The Pattern of Recent Housing Growth in a Nonmetropolitan County." Growth and Change 15(4):32-42.

Graber, E. E. 1974. "Newcomers and Oldtimers: Growth and Change in a Mountain Town." *Rural Sociology* 39(4):504-513.

Humphrey, C. R. and F. B. Buttel. 1982. *Environment, Energy, and Society.* Belmont, CA: Wadsworth Pub. Co.

Johnson, S. 1983. "Population Dynamics in National Forest System Zones of Influence." Washington, DC: USDA Forest Service Policy Analysis Staff.

Loomis, J. 1982. "Westward Migration: Putting Pressure on Public Lands." *Western Wildlands* 8(2):17-18.

Luloff, A. E. and T. E. Steahr. 1985. "The Structure and Impact of Population Redistribution: Summary and Conclusions." In T. E. Steahr and A.E. Luloff (eds.), *The Structure and Impact of Population Redistribution in New England.* University Park, PN: Northeast Regional Center for Rural Development, Pennsylvania State University.

Menard, S. and H. C. Covey. 1984. "The Impact of Rapid Population Growth and Energy Development on Court Caseloads." *Social Science Journal* 21(3): 111-122.

Morrison, P. A. and J. Wheeler. 1976. "Rural Renaissance in America: The Revival of Population Growth in Remote Areas." *Population Bulletin* 31(3): 3-23.

Park, R. E. 1952. *Human Communities.* New York: The Free Press.

Peterson, I. 1983. "Blacktop for a Desert Trail Spurs Southwest Tourism Debate." New York Times, October 25.

Ploch, L. 1978. "The Reversal in Migration Patterns—Some Rural Development Consequences." *Rural Sociology* 43(2):293-303.

———. 1980. "Effects of Turnaround Migration on Community Structure in Maine." In D. L. Brown and J. M Wardwell (eds.), *New Directions in Turnaround Migration: The Population Turnaround in Rural America.* New York: Academic Press.

Price, M. L. and D. C. Clay. 1980. "Structural Disturbances in Rural Communities: Some Repercussions of the Migration Turnaround in Michigan." *Rural Sociology* 45(4):591-607.

Schwarzweller, H. K. 1979. "Migration and the Changing Rural Scene." *Rural Sociology* 44(1):7-23.

Schweitzer, R. A. and S. C. Simmons. 1981. "Interactive, Direct-entry Approaches to Event Files." *Social Science History* 5(3):17-342.

Sofranko, A. J. and F. C. Fliegel. 1983. "Rural-to-Rural Migrants: The Neglected Component of Population Growth." *Growth and Change* 14(2):42-49.

Sofranko, A. J. and J. D. Williams. 1980. "Rebirth of Rural America: Rural Migration in the Midwest." Ames, IA: Iowa State University, North Central Regional Center for Rural Development.

Teare, J. 1980. "Pictured Rocks Key Controversy." *The Bay City Times*, August 3.

Tilly, A. and C. Tilly (eds.). 1981. *Class Conflict and Collective Action*. Beverly Hills, CA: Sage.

U.S. Department of Commerce (Bureau of the Census). 1973. Vol. 1. "1970 Census of Population, Pt. 24, Michigan." *Characteristics of the Population.* Washington, DC: Government Printing Office.

———. 1983. Vol. 1. "1980 Census of Population, Pt. 24, Michigan." *Characteristics of the Population.* Washington, DC: Government Printing Office.

Voss, P. R. 1980. "A Test of the 'Gangplank Syndrome' among Recent Migrants to the Upper Great Lakes Region." *Journal of the Community Development Society* 11(1):95-111.

Voss, P. R. and G. V. Fuguitt. 1979. *Turnaround Migration in the Upper Great Lakes Region.* Madison, WI: Applied Population Laboratory, University of Wisconsin, Department of Rural Sociology, Population Study Series No. 70-12.

Webb, E. J., D. T. Campbell, R. D. Schwartz, L. Sechrest, and J. Belew. 1981. *Nonreactive Measures in the Social Sciences* (2nd. ed). Boston, MA: Houghton Mifflin Co.

Weeks, S. B. 1976. "More About Controlling Demographic Change." *Small Town* 6(12):4-6.

Wellman, J. D. and R. W. Marans. 1982. "Social Conflict Associated with Turnaround Migration: Evidence from Northern Michigan." Unpublished research paper. Blacksburg, VA: Virginia Polytechnic Institute and State University, Department of Forestry.

Werner, L. 1982. "Rural Revival: Michigan is a Classic Case." *Detroit Free Press*, March 8, pp. 1a and 15a.

13

Power Plants and Resource Rights[1]

Louise Fortmann
Department of Forestry and Resources Management
University of California, Berkeley

Paul Starrs
Department of Geography
University of California, Berkeley

"If we, as citizens of Feather County do not stand up and take charge of our lives, the politicians will do it for us. Our Board of Supervisors are a bunch of foxes who are guarding the Feather County chicken coop" (Letter to the Editor, Plume River Bulletin, November 25, 1983).

Traditionally, the right to determine the nature of natural resource management and use has been one and the same as ownership of those resources. However, as with all forms of private property, the nature of private rights over natural resources is evolving (Geisler, 1984). For example, a number of states strictly regulate forestry practices. As the population of resource-dependent areas has changed, it has become clear that people who live adjacent to natural resources have deep and active concerns about their management. Inevitably, conflicts between users, concerned observers, and the holders of statutory property rights emerge.

Nowhere is this more true than in the western United States, where many rural residents rely on the use of land they do not own.[2] This is especially true in the case of forest residents. Loggers and millworkers who depend on timberland for a livelihood, people who collect fuel wood from the forests, visitor-oriented businesses that benefit from the aesthetic or recreational draw of the woods, all rely on forests owned either by the state or federal governments or large private owners. Since the land they use is rarely legally theirs, they seldom possess the right to make direct decisions about resource use and management.

In the last two decades local protest against the use and management of rural resources by nonresidents has become increasingly visible. We argue that much rural environmental protest is best understood as a new and effective strategy in local resource management that provides channels for reaching decision makers and influencing management decisions. We further argue that conflicts over resource management can only be understood if the existence of nonstatutory claims to property are recognized.

What follows is an analysis of the reaction of two forest-dependent mountain communities in California to identical wood-fired power plants proposed months apart for each town by the same company. One town accepted a plant; the other protested and blocked it. Data for this study were obtained from key informant interviews with Adamsville[3] and Woodlake residents, members of the U.S. Forest Service, and Megavoltz (the company) personnel; local newspapers; the U.S. Census; and documents obtained from the U.S. Forest Service and the County Planning Department. Two major questions arise:

First, why do communities mobilize? Protest against energy facilities is often referred to as "nimby" (not-in-my-backyard) protest. Nimby protest is directed against facilities that are deemed societally necessary by industry or government but judged to have unacceptably high local costs by prospective neighbors (Burt, 1979). The power plant protests in Woodlake and Adamsville are only partially interpretable as nimby protests because there was also a serious conflict between many residents and the company over access to woodfuel in the adjacent forest areas. Residents voiced a strong reaction against an "outsider"—in this case, a Southern California company—using local resources to produce a product for export only. To a lesser extent, residents sought to eliminate threats of air and water pollution feared to be associated with the plant. This protest, then, only marginally concerned the issue of environmental risk. The overriding issue was protection of rights to local resources— in particular, the right to gather fuelwood.

Between 1970 and 1980, the nonmetropolitan population of California grew by 42 percent, largely due to urban residents moving to rural areas. (Hope and Blakely, 1986:3). It is often held that this movement increased environmental conflict because of the urban characteristics and, in particular, urban environmental values of the new residents (Lee, 1984:126). But urban refugees, alone, do not a protest make. This is particularly obvious with these proposed power plants, since Adamsville and Woodlake are only two dozen air miles apart and have reasonably similar populations. Explanation of their differing reactions lies elsewhere.

Young (1964, 1970) has shown that solidarity movements, which include protests such as the one here, can be predicted by a community's structural characteristics. Reverse migration is relevant only to the extent that it affects community structure. The level of economic well-being, social organization, and the centrality of the two communities largely determined the extent of mobilization.

Second, why are some community mobilizations successful, while others are not? We will show that Adamsville's plant opponents were able to protect resources under the jurisdiction of a nationally responsive bureaucracy, the U.S. Forest Service, by moving the arena to a locally responsive forum: the county government. We will also show that preexisting social organization probably made a crucial difference in the ability to mobilize successfully.

CURRENTS IN CALIFORNIA ENERGY

> The catalyst in this case was the firewood issue. It hit people right where they were most afraid. It was the Forest Service giving their firewood away to a company from Los Angeles (Adamsville resident).

California ranks second, nationally, in total energy consumption, and increases in its population have kept utilities searching for energy sources and new energy technologies. After the energy crisis of the 1970s, attention in California turned to wood. A combination of standard state and federal investment tax deductions, alternative energy tax credits, and laws specifically passed to require public utilities to buy power produced by nonutility-owned sources made the construction of small wood-fired power plants in California financially attractive. And favorable tax credits made it at once possible and profitable to build power plants largely for reasons of "taxfarming." The only catch was that plants had to be built before January 1, 1986, to seize most of these benefits.

Under these circumstances, a Southern California company, Megavoltz, Inc., developed plans for building a string of wood-fueled power plants including one in Woodlake, Volcano County, and one in Adamsville, in Feather County, California. Megavoltz argued that its plants offered significant economic, environmental, and energy independence benefits including creation of fifty to seventy-five new local jobs with each project, an increased local tax base from property and salaries, local construction jobs for a typical $20 million, eleven megawatt project, and improved forest management. Although Megavoltz carefully explained to local residents that it only proposed plants where there was sufficient suitable wood, "we always encounter the firewood issue," said one senior company official.

In early 1982 California was in the throes of a timber industry depression, so when Megavoltz began a search for plant sites, the company had every reason to expect some enthusiasm from local communities. Megavoltz looked for areas with an "availability of wood fuels, depressed labor market with logging skills, and a reasonable attitude toward growth compatible with the county's master plan," a location near a national forest or "cooperative private landowners," "existing logging infrastructure, and a healthy community spirit." (Megavoltz V.P. to Volcano and Feather Counties Planning Directors, 1982 and 1983).

The irony is that the same abundance of fuelwood and relative poverty of the people that attracted Megavoltz in the first place also led, in one sawshop owner's words, "probably 90 percent of the people in Adamsville," to depend to some extent on woodstoves and fireplaces for heating. Among the unifying architectural themes in Woodlake and Adamsville has long been firewood in multiple-cord stacks. An organizer of Adamsville's plant opposition would later comment:

> Firewood was the critical issue. There was a slick big-city image
> that Megavoltz projected that hurt them. But the firewood was
> the big thing. There was also a general distrust of the Forest
> Service and their policies (Adamsville plant opponent).

It was primarily around the perceived threat to this fuelwood supply that the controversy revolved.

A TALE OF TWO CITIES

> Volcano County is run from Janetown by businessmen. The
> same story might be true in Adamsville except that people there
> are more able to influence local politics (Woodlake resident).

Similarities between Adamsville and Woodlake are notable. Mountain communities dating from the mid-nineteenth century, they are both surrounded by national forests. Their economies are natural resource-based—timber in the case of Woodlake and timber, mining, and ranching in the more diversified Adamsville. Both towns are the site of a lumber mill. About the same proportion of the population in each town are high school graduates, recipients of social security or public assistance, and working women or men out of the labor force (Table 1).

Despite these similarities, Table 1 shows that Adamsville and Woodlake differ in profound ways. The median income in Woodlake is two-thirds that of Adamsville and the proportion of households below the poverty line is triple Adamsville's. A higher percentage of Adamsville's male population is unemployed. Woodlake has a larger proportion of in-migrants, but nearly three times as many Adamsville residents have moved to town from out-of-state. On the

Table 1. Demographic Characteristics of Adamsville and Woodlake

Characteristics	Woodlake	Adamsville
1980 population	2,117	4,451
Income 1979		
Median Income	12,628	18,255
Percent households—social security income	27.4	24.9
Percent households—public assistance	11.1	11.0
Percent persons below poverty line	18.8	6.2
Employment and Education		
Men over 16 worked	73.7	61.7
Did not work	4.3	14.4
Not in the labor force	21.9	23.9
Women over 16 worked	50.7	50.7
Persons over 25—percent high school graduates	75.2	75.4
Persons over 25—percent college education	33.2	40.7
In-migration		
Percent persons living out-of-county in 1975	47.1	39.7
Percent persons living out-of-state in 1975	3.5	14.9

Source: (Census of Population and Housing, 1980: Summary Tape File 3A (California) machine readable data file/prepared by the Bureau of the Census. Washington, D.C.: The Bureau [producer and distributor], 1982; Bureau of the Census. 1983. 1980 Census of Population. Volume 1, Chapter C General Social and Economic Characteristics, Part 6 California. Tables 166-168).

whole, Adamsville is a larger, more differentiated, wealthier, better educated, and more organized community.

Adamsville is the Feather County seat, is the site of a community college, has over 400 members in the Chamber of Commerce, and maintains linkages to Nevada and California cities. Access to Adamsville is relatively easy and the newspapers of major cities are found in its newsstands. All six local papers of both Feather and Volcano Counties are published there. Access to Woodlake, in contrast, can be a problem, and during the deep snows of winter it is not uncommon for the town to be cut off. Woodlake recently went for sixteen months without a resident doctor, has only fifty surviving businesses, and in 1985 lost its only bank (personal communication, editor, Woodlake Press).

Adamsville is a lively town—"it's really busy here, much more so than in the city because everyone's active," in one resident's words. Adamsville has the Elks, the Rotary, the Lions, the Rebekahs, the Grange, a VFW chapter, the 4-H, the Chamber of Commerce, environmental groups, wildlife groups, and numerous churches, in just a sample of its 150 organizations. Woodlake, with half the population, has far fewer than half the number of organizations—only intermittently active service clubs and a smattering of churches. On a summer afternoon in 1985, all the posters in town publicized events in nearby towns, and none in Woodlake itself.

Both communities had prior experience with protest. Woodlake has a history of sporadic but dramatic swings into action. It was the site in 1937 of a serious strike that closed the mill in the then-company town. Violence followed that put Woodlake in the national spotlight. Woodlake residents in 1978 organized a power blackout, boycotting the utility company. The action was highly successful in mobilizing participation but failed to lower rates. A similar campaign in the summer of 1985 ("Unplug C.P. National Day") was an almost complete failure.

Woodlake's blackout protest, based on clear pocketbook losses, was in marked contrast to the town's reactions to the power plant proposal. Any power plant protest demanded balancing the possible firewood loss and pollution dangers against a corporate promise of local jobs for a depressed area. Any protest would have had to transcend the local pocketbook issues around which the earlier boycott was organized. Further, while an electricity boycott could be planned and carried out at leisure, a power plant protest required the ability to move quickly: researching, marshalling, and publicizing facts before various government—particularly planning commission—deadlines ran out. Woodlake had no such ability. The Adamsville-based Friends of Feather Wilderness had experience in exactly this kind of organizing.

FRACAS IN THE FOREST

It wasn't that we perceived this as OUR LAND—that's not true, it's government land. We assume multiple use of our resources, but our major need is to have an economic future with our wood resources. We've seen it overlogged and over-roaded, but this proposal was just too much. Sure it's not our wood, but we're here, and the Forest Service needs to remember what the general people think... (Adamsville resident).

The Adamsville protest was a multi-issue campaign that brought together diverse local interests. As one opponent summarized the town's feelings, "Not everyone objected to the same thing. Each person might have a different pet peeve, but the net effect was almost universal opposition." The most important and most emotional issue was the perceived threat to local fuelwood supplies. "Wood is the primary heat for most people here," commented a Forest Service employee, and wood—obtained mostly from the surrounding national forest—was already a lively issue before Megavoltz ever came to town.

In 1982, the U.S. Forest Service imposed a fee on woodcutting on national forest land, inspiring a brief "Woodcutter's Rebellion." In an already depressed local economy, more than one unemployed logger wrote the local paper to complain that free firewood was the only thing that brought his family through the past winters. Wood became a rallying point. As one Adamsville former logger put it:

> Once there was information put out, everyone got going against it. Here's the Forest Service pushing woodcutters onto marginal land—they've kept getting stricter and stricter. Fifteen years ago, you could go anywhere and get your wood. Now, they charge you money, make you get a permit, send you off, and you can only cut wood on selected areas that they show you on their maps. You get there and there's nothing worth cutting... The Forest Service bigwigs were pushing the plant. They wanted to get rid of all that small stuff no woodcutter would ever take, but they're blocking firewood cutting.

Local residents also resented what they considered to be interlopers from Reno, Nevada, driving pickup trucks into Feather County to collect fuelwood. Out-of-the-area woodcutters were as numerous as locals in the national forest, taking altogether 18,000 cords in 1982—twice as much as in 1981. At Rotary Club meetings in Adamsville, members had even queried visiting Forest Service officials about allowing outside woodcutters to use "our" wood. The proposed wood-fired plant was easily made out to be the granddaddy interloper of them all, requiring 120,000 wet tons of wood per year.

Residents feared that the de facto control they had hitherto exercised over "their" supply of firewood, as some perceived it, would be severely diminished with the building of a wood-fueled power plant. That fear inspired many to join the developing protest. Other issues included the fear of unacceptable levels of air pollution, concern over groundwater depletion and heated waste water, and, with large numbers of chip-laden trucks moving to the plant, alarm was voiced about traffic increases in school areas. Plant opponents argued that the plant might be converted to coal, leading to more pollution, and the effect of wood removal on forest nutrient cycling was debated. Public relations was a continuing problem. The approach taken by the plant's proponents, including Megavoltz itself, seriously alienated many Adamsville residents. There was, finally, an active campaign by some plant opponents to portray the alternative energy plant as a greedy exploiter of federal tax-credit largesse.

In Woodlake, too, plant opponents raised the issues of depletion of firewood and threat of air pollution but did so far less adeptly. The only consistent theme in Woodlake was skepticism about the speed with which the planning commission declared an environmental impact report unnecessary and granted a use permit:

> Some people did feel that this was happening really fast and that maybe there should be some questions asked before embracing the whole plant (Woodlake resident).

Despite the reservations of some residents, little opposition to the plant emerged in Woodlake until the facility was finished and into its testing phases.

In both communities the protest organizing attempts began with a small group of concerned people. Yet in Woodlake the effort never went beyond a few letters to the local newspaper and the county planning office, and a handful of questions in company-sponsored public meetings. Adamsville anti-plant efforts began with a few members of Friends of Feather Wilderness who had prior experience in environmental protests. This core group of some forty Adamsville residents rapidly enlisted support from numerous and widely varied people numbering in the hundreds. The Anti-Plant Committee was the focus for plant opposition. Core members of the committee realized that the protest could easily be portrayed by plant protesters as an "environmentalist" battle and countered that possibility by refusing to allow the campaign to be narrowed to one or two issues. They brought in new members, gathered signatures on petitions, raised several thousand dollars in contributions, published and distributed brochures, and ultimately were credited by everyone from county supervisors to Megavoltz company officials with stopping the plant project. Many of the Adamsville plant opponents were novices at public protest. One of the pivotal new activists on the Anti-Plant Committee commented:

> There were a number of people, like me, who got really involved against [Megavoltz] who hadn't been involved in anything like this before... I'd like to think this'll have a lasting effect. People will remember that their energy changed the supervisors' minds.

Long after the protest was over only a few townspeople would publicly admit to having supported the plant. One Forest Service employee noted:

> There were not very many vocal supporters. They really stayed back, if there were any. Maybe they were afraid of being verbally attacked if they came out in favor.

THE ANATOMY OF OBJECTION

> If we'd let it happen with this power plant, why we'd be just like another Owens Valley... they'd be coming from Southern California taking out water and trees, and leaving us nothing in return (Adamsville resident).

> Up here we're used to L.A. taking our water—Look at Loon Lake and Lake Bebe. There wasn't much more Megavoltz could do. They're just taking one more thing—the only local worry was about firewood (Woodlake resident).

The explanation for the contrasting reactions to plants in Adamsville and Woodlake can be found in three factors: variation in the economic well-being, the level of social organization, and the relative centrality of the two communities. In this study, the poverty rate is used as a measure of community well-being; the numbers of businesses and social organizations as a measure of social organization, and access to county level government as a measure of centrality.[4]

While unemployment, especially seasonal unemployment, was substantial in both communities, and indeed higher for men in Adamsville, Woodlake was by far the poorer community. For Woodlake, the Megavoltz promise of twenty-five to seventy-five local jobs was far more attractive than for Adamsville. Not only would these jobs affect a greater percentage of the households than in Adamsville, but the income was needed more. When the decision to approve or not approve the plant was being made, the prospect of jobs was harder for Woodlake to resist: "It was like putting food in front of starving rats," claimed one resident. But after the plant was built, Woodlake residents discovered to their dismay that Megavoltz defined "local" not as in Woodlake, but as within the greater Feather-Volcano County area, a forty mile radius around Woodlake. In the end only five permanent jobs went to Woodlake residents.

The extent of existing social organization differed markedly between the two communities. The Sierra Valley Biomass Committee was able to tap into a community organizational structure that aided its organizing effort. For example, a member of a local church could call on an existing network of fellow churchgoers even though the church was quite uninvolved in the protest. Although few Adamsville organizations formally joined in the protest campaign, their very existence increased the reach of the few experienced members from a variety of viewpoints—contact was easy, as the fuelwood issue affected the majority of the community—and the campaign spread quickly along the multitude of preexisting networks. As one organizer noted:

The opposition was successful [in Adamsville] because there was a structure already in place that could react fast—the Friends of Feather Wilderness and other [individuals] who were always ready. But Woodlake had no effective group involved in environmental issues, so the plant was pushed through with no knowledgeable opposition.

In Adamsville, the experience and knowledge of a few people was magnified by access to nonenvironmental organizational networks. The smaller size of Woodlake, with its potential for easy information dissemination and neighborhood intimacy, was no substitute for organizational capacity.[5]

Finally, the differences in the centrality of Woodlake and Adamsville proved crucial. Adamsville was the county seat. Protesters could and did drop in at the county courthouse to talk with members of the county government, go to County Board of Supervisors' meetings, and in general make their presence and views felt.[6] Plant opponents broadened the plant opposition to communities ten and fifteen miles away, and an issue originally of local concern became, through fears of a fuelwood depletion, a countywide question. Opponents and proponents, alike, could track the process of permit approval on which defeat of the proposal ultimately hinged and had easy access to information about the case.

In contrast, Woodlake is twenty-three winding miles over a mountain pass from the county seat, and during the plant discussion there was no Woodlake resident on the County Board of Supervisors. Official notices were printed in the county seat newspaper but not always in the Woodlake paper; planning commission meetings were held in the county seat in the dead of winter, when travel was the most difficult for Woodlake residents. Woodlake had felt for years that it received less than its fair share of county resources; as one county employee in Woodlake remarked, "Janetown likes to act as if Woodlake is in Feather County," that is as if it were not a responsibility of the Volcano County Board of Supervisors.

Adamsville citizens had direct access to the seat of decisions while Woodlake drifted in a sort of political and bureaucratic limbo. The activities of the Anti-Plant Committee were covered (at times with considerable editorial vitriol) on a weekly basis in the Adamsville newspaper, while the activities of Woodlake's "handful" of plant opponents got minimal local coverage and none at all in the county seat newspaper. The logistics of trying to affect the planning decision were much more easily managed in Adamsville than in Woodlake. And there were parallel issues: while Adamsville residents debated the desirability of Megavoltz' proposed power plant, Feather County residents simultaneously were discussing a proposed national forest wilderness and were embroiled in revisions of the county general plan. All received extensive coverage in local media. Adamsville was also more central in terms of individual links to the national environmental movement. Plant opponents in Adamsville hired an outside environmental consultant to help them block the plant. Although no appeal to a state or national organization was ever made, many members of the Adamsville Biomass Committee were members of national environmental groups and were familiar with their organizing techniques.

SEEDS OF SUCCESS

> Most of all, these people here don't care to be treated as a bunch of hicks who are incapable of understanding or reacting to what's happening to them (Feather County planning official).

The Adamsville protesters won against a well-funded corporation in a short period of time without having to go to court. How did it happen?

The previous experience of some plant opponents in the Friends of Feather Wilderness helped. Generally, Megavoltz would make quiet overtures to members of the business community, the Forest Service, and local government to determine whether there was a favorable climate for investment. If responses were positive, they then proceeded with public information meetings and the formal application process. They expected the approval process to move expeditiously once the company's interest was public knowledge, and since tax credits important to the plant's profitability had an exipiration date, Megavoltz needed haste. This meant that any protest also had to be organized quickly and effectively. Some of the 600 Feather County residents on the Friends of Feather Wilderness mailing list already had considerable experience obtaining and disseminating technical information, identifying issues, and participating in public meetings.

Reverse migrants and long-term residents are equally important here. Conventional wisdom among industry and resource bureaucracies is that the values of reverse migrants put them at odds with rural residents and economies, causing an abrasive relationship between in-migrants and "natives". This argument is not totally persuasive; Woodlake, with a higher proportion of reverse migrants than Adamsville, produced no significant power plant protest. Further, protesters included both reverse migrants and long time residents in Adamsville, and after the plant was built, both groups objected in Woodlake, although to a much lesser extent. However, reverse migrants may have been necessary to the protest, not because of their imported values but because of their skills and their connections to outside networks: they were more skilled at gleaning factual information, ideas, and techniques.

Long-term residents were essential to the protest because of their connections to local networks and because they lent weight and credibility to arguments against the plant. They brought in additional long-term residents because their involvement legitimized the conflict, proving it was more than a newcomers' issue. They served as "center persons" (Sacks, 1984) who coordinated and mobilized other loggers, millworkers, business people, and retirees who had their own networks. They joined reverse migrants, who knew the details of organizing, who possessed skills in technical research and fund raising, and who had connections to other networks of protest and environmental concern. The Adamsville reverse migrants brought to a rural area sophisticated urban organizing skills and used them against a sophisticated urban company.

The key to success was focusing considerable and persistent pressure on susceptible government and bureaucratic entities. Every publication by the Anti-Plant Committee included the names and phone numbers of county supervisors and encouragement to contact them. The county supervisors and planning commission were easily lobbied. The U.S. Forest Service is, however, a national organization with a national mandate that does not tailor its decisions to the needs of the local community and thus, by design, is less sensitive to local than to national pressures (Kaufman, 1960; Twight, 1983, 1984). Still, the Forest's Timber Management Officer was careful to remind company representatives that the Forest Service was bound by national policies that gave primary importance to leaving sufficient materials in the forest to replenish soil nutrients, put second emphasis on personal fuelwood gathering, and allocated third priority to commercial biomass harvesting. And although the officer calculated that there was sufficient wood to abide by these policies and meet Megavoltz needs, Adamsville residents worried that the Forest Service had overestimated the amount of wood actually available for power plant consumption and had underestimated the local difficulty of finding decent firewood. Commented a neutral bystander in Adamsville:

> The Forest Service honchos did figuring on wood availability and they came out with a standard line, you'll just have to readjust your thinking on what you'll burn. People here are very picky and that didn't fit well. People don't want to burn white fir.

Feeling that the Forest Service would not protect the interests of local woodcutters by prohibiting Megavoltz from harvesting fuelwood on national forest land, people elected to do it for themselves by preventing the construction of the plant through manipulation of the permit process. For those who were worried about air and water pollution, the county process was, of course, the only possible arena. The County Board of Supervisors was vulnerable to pressure by local interests, and ultimately, the board, through the planning commission, had to rule on a stack height variance essential to the plant. Supervisors at meetings in their districts found themselves subject to intense lobbying, including thinly veiled threats of recall elections. The jurisdiction of the County Board of Supervisors served as a resource for those who were attempting to affect the management of fuelwood on the national forest.

Finally, the very fact that Megavoltz consisted of Southern Californian outsiders worked in favor of the protesters. Local residents characterized Megavoltz representatives as smooth-talking city slickers trying to pull a fast one on a bunch of hicks. This perception led Adamsville residents to assert, in the words of one, "We may be hicks but we're smart hicks."

CONCLUSIONS

The Adamsville protest was remarkable for its rapid development, the diversity of its members (loggers to environmentalists, young reverse migrants to long-time resident grandmothers), the proportion of the town opposing the plant (nearly everyone except the newspaper editor and a few influential residents), and its success. It demonstrated that, while the skills and networks of reverse migrants might be different from those of local residents, so long as care was exercised not to take extreme positions, they could meet on the common ground of their concerns. It also demonstrated that a community could achieve some control over local resources through protest when no other channel existed. Finally, it demonstrated the crucial importance of community structure in community mobilization.

The Adamsville experience has important implications for the study of natural resource management. First, statutory rights do not include the full gamut of claims to natural resources that people exercise and seek to protect. The realization that distant bureaucracies and local government elites can be forced into action by public pressure has resulted in activity that makes these nonstatutory claims both more obvious and more powerful and leads to new understandings of property rights.

A second and corollary implication is that communities mobilize partly to protect these nonstatutory claims to property. This means that instead of searching for an ideological basis to explain community protest attention might be better directed toward identifying disputed claims to property.

Finally, Walter Firey (1978) has observed that the state of communities dependent on a resource and the state of the resource itself are interdependent. In many times and places, recognition of this fact has resulted in community management of resources. The phrase "community management of resources" may for some conjure up visions of third world villagers managing irrigation schemes or communal pastures. Rarely do images of rural America, complete with VCRs,

Chevies, and equipment dealerships, leap to mind. Nonetheless, residents of rural America have historically managed natural resources not only as individuals but also as communities. For example, in 1639, in Hampton, New Hampshire, three men were appointed wood's wards to control forest use and to assign a cutting quota to each head of household (Pennsylvania Department of Forests and Waters, 1932). Few rural American communities have the kinds of social organization conducive to direct day-to-day management of natural resources (See Panel on Common Property Resource Management, 1986). Nonetheless, communities press their claims to and concerns over resources, and protest will affect use and management decisions. What transpired in Adamsville can be understood as a new sort of community management of resources. This new community management works through bureaucracies and legislative bodies rather than through direct control of the resource. It is a kind of community action that can be expected to grow in the future.

NOTES

1. This research was funded by the Forest and Rangelands Resource Assessment Project of the California State Department of Forestry. The views are those of the authors and not of the funding agency. The comments of W. Burch, L. Huntsinger, R. Lee, D. MacCannell, and E. Roe are gratefully acknowledged.

2. The issues discussed here also pertain to ranchers, miners, commercial fishermen, and proprieters in tourist-based industries among others. The Sagebrush Rebellion was, at a different level of social organization, another manifestation of the phenomenon discussed here (see Fairfax, 1984).

3. To protect the identity of the towns and company, pseudonyms have been used.

4. Young (1970:300-301) defines centrality as the "degree to which the system 'recognizes' the subsystem" and uses measures such as political representation.

5. Thompson (1983:247) comments, "there may be some threadbare social fabrics so lacking in manipulative and information-handling ability as to be unable to mobilize any sort of nimby at all... As any civil engineer experienced in motorway construction will tell you, the best soil conditions are always to be found in working-class areas."

6. Ease of access is not in itself sufficient. One protester noted, "Sometimes decisions get made without anyone hearing about it. The Feather County Board of Supervisors does it and there's nothing to be done. But we told them we wanted it done differently this time."

REFERENCES

Burt, R. S. 1979. "Community Conflict in the Nuclear Power Issue: A Review Exploring the Network Structure of Conflict Escalation." Berkeley, CA: Project in Structural Analysis. Survey Research Center Working Paper 6.

Fairfax, S. K. 1984. "Beyond the Sagebrush Rebellion: BLM as a Neighbor and Manager in the Western States." In J. G. Francis and R. Ganzel (eds.), *Western Public Lands: The Management of Natural Resources in a Time of Declining Federalism.* Totowa, N J: Rowman and Allenheld.

Firey, W. 1978. Some Contributions of Sociology to the Study of Natural Resources. In M. Barnabas, S. K. Hulbe and P. S. Jacob (eds.), *Challenges of Societies in Transition.* Delhi: Macmillan Company.

Geisler, C. 1984. "A History of Land Reform in the United States: Old Wine, New Battles." In C. C. Geisler and F. J. Popper (eds.), *Land Reform, American Style.* Totowa, N J: Rowman and Allanheld.

Hope, J. and E. Blakely. 1986. *A Rural Development Agenda for California.* Prepared for the California Senate Office of Research.

Kaufman, H. 1960. *The Forest Ranger: A Study in Administrative Behavior.* Baltimore, MD: The Johns Hopkins.

Lee, R. 1984. "Implications of Contemporary Community Organization and Social Values for Forest Management on the Residential/Wildland Interface." In G. A. Bradley (ed.), *Land Use and Forest Resources in a Changing Environment.* Seattle, WA: University of Washington Press.

Panel on Common Property Resource Management. Board on Science and Technology for International Development. Office of International Affairs. National Research Council. 1986. *Proceedings of the Conference on Common Property Resource Management.* April 21-26, 1985. Washington, DC: National Academy Press.

Pennsylvania Department of Forests and Waters. 1932. "Interesting Forest Facts." Service Letter 3 (149, June 16)

Sacks, K. 1984. "Kinship and Class Consciousness: Family Values and Work Experience Among Hospital Workers in an American Southern Town." In H. Medick and D. W. Sabean (eds.), *Interest and Emotion.* Cambridge: Cambridge University Press.

Thompson, B. W. 1983. "Postscript: A Cultural Basis For Comparison." In H. C. Kunreuther, et al. (eds.), *Risk Analysis and Decision Process: The Siting of Liquified Energy Gas Facilities in Four Countries.* Berlin: Springer-Verlag.

Twight, B. W. 1983. *Organizational Values and Political Power: The Forest Service versus the Olympic National Park.* University Park, PA: Pennsylvania State University Press.

——. 1984. "The Missions: The Case of Family Fidelity" Paper Presented at the CHEC Forest Symposium, December 13-17, 1984. San Francisco, CA.

U.S. Department of Commerce (Bureau of the Census). 1982. Census of Population and Housing 1980: Summary Tape File 3A (California) (machine readable data file prepared by the Bureau). Washington, DC: Government Printing Office.

——. 1983. 1980 Census of Population. Vol 1C, General Social and Economic Characteristics, Pt. 6, California. Tables 166-168. Washington, DC: Government Printing Office

Young, F. 1964. "Location and Reputation in a Mexican Intervillage Network." *Human Organization* 23:36-41.

——1970. "Reactive Subsystems." *American Sociological Review* 35:297-307.

14

Depopulation and Disorganization in Charcoal-Producing Mountain Villages of Kyoto Prefecture in Japan

Hisayoshi Mitsuda
Department of Sociology
Bukkyo University, Japan

This paper describes the causes of rapid out-migration in several Japanese mountain communities in Kyoto Prefecture and analyzes the impacts of this process on social structure and community development efforts within these communities. By means of a comparative field study undertaken before and after the oil crisis of 1973, which occurred during Japan's period of rapid economic growth, the paper examines the capacity of these communities to cope with the problems of depopulation.

In the late 1950s, Japan went through a "heating fuel revolution," a rapid conversion from the use of charcoal and firewood to the use of petrochemical fuels in everyday life. This changeover had a disastrous impact on many mountain villages that were dependent upon charcoal and firewood production for their basic economic livelihood. Consequently, most of the mountain area communities have been drastically depopulated and disrupted due to the fading of this traditional form of employment. This demographic shift was associated with a worsening of the standard of living and the general welfare levels in these areas, a regional economic depression widely known as the "Kaso" problem (the problem of rapid population loss and related social disruption in the hinterlands) in Japan. This stands in marked contrast to the "Kamitsu" problem (the urban problem caused by hypergrowth in metropolitan areas) (Ito, 1974).

The government of Japan identified the Kaso problem for the first time in 1966 and began to address this depopulation problem in earnest. In 1970, the Japanese Diet agreed to establish the Kaso Act for the development of areas suffering from rapid population loss. According to this Act, national, prefectural, and local governments had to initiate comprehensive development plans to improve the industrial and social infrastructure within these regions (Japan, Ministry of Home Affairs, 1972).

In addition to these governmental efforts, there were many local community corrective efforts, including attempts to develop new industries, e.g., mushroom farming, mountain vegetable production, and tourism; a "renaissance" movement to protect traditional rural cultures; and youth, 4-H, and other programs for the preservation of community identity and pride. These actions, along with the slowdown in the rate of nationwide economic growth that began in the late 1970s, have helped bring about a marked decrease in the rate of depopulation (Japan, National Land Agency, 1982).

Nevertheless, the following problems remain unsolved in the depopulated areas: First, the out-migration of young adults has caused an increase in the dependency ratio in the population, which is exacerbated by the rise in the percentage of elderly people living in these communities. This loss of young adults means that remaining members of the labor force have more potential dependents to support in their communities. Second, the disappearance of traditional leaders and potential new leaders has destroyed the traditional heirarchical decision-making apparatus in many of these communities. Remaining community members have, so far, been unable to institute a new form of community organization and decision making, which means that these communities are often unable to reorganize themselves to cope with change. Third, services and infrastructures in these communities, i.e., public transportation, water and sewer systems, hospitals, schools, community centers, and industrial facilities, have deteriorated. These unsolved, disruptive problems have become serious obstacles not only to the improvement in the quality of life in such communities, but also to the overall economic development and environmental quality of these areas. The same problem appears to have existed in the Appalachian area of the southeastern United States in the 1950s and 1960s (Price and Sikes, 1975).

Many previous studies dealing with this depopulation problem in Japan have focused primarily on the economic and demographic impacts in mountainous areas. However, there has been little research that scientifically analyzes changes in the social structure of these communities, i.e., community leadership, community solidarity and autonomy, and the residents' values, attitudes, expectations, and lifestyles, since these sociological concepts are not easy to measure (Adachi, 1973). There have also been few studies aimed at alleviating the rural poverty of those who have been left behind in marginal areas while urbanites have benefited from Japan's rapid economic progress. More attention needs to be focused on the social consequences of heavy out-migration in mountain areas in order to encourage community development efforts aimed at helping these communities maintain local control of community issues and their sense of community cohesion and identity (Mitsuda, 1978, 1979a, 1979b).

The primary focus of this paper is on Japanese community experiences in coping with the impacts of rapid depopulation in mountain areas. Using a comparative study of community reorganization movements before and after the oil crises of 1973 and 1979, I analyze the changes in community structure, values, attitudes, and expectations of members of these communities as well as their vitality and ability to adjust to important changes in their economic environment.

My analysis is based on an intensive field study undertaken in two charcoal producing villages, Haiya and Ashu, located in the Hokuso forest area of Kyoto Prefecture. Detailed survey data, collected by the author in four different periods (1972, 1978, 1981, and 1983), are presented as a basis for analysis and policy recommendations. These villages were selected for the following reasons: First, they are characterized by common and marked features often found in depopulated and depressed areas; a large number of farm forestry households in the villages, the deteriorated economic condition of forestry and agriculture, the isolation and remoteness from urban areas, and a self-contained socioeconomic life. Second, these communities had a different type of community power structure, which changed during the process of depopulation.

Field interviews were carried out with the heads of all households in these villages as well as informants in the surveyed area. Questionnaires from all community members over twenty years old, including temporary forest workers, were used to investigate: what inducements have led residents to migrate from these areas; how the community power structure has changed in the process of depopulation; how different community structures, especially the community leadership structures, affect and determine the methods of adjustment in rural development efforts evolving in these communities; the change in community values, attitudes, and expectations that have taken place as a result of the social structural changes of the communities; and the capacity of the community to cope with the problems presented by the process of heavy out-migration.

HISTORICAL PERSPECTIVE: DEPOPULATION AND ECONOMIC GROWTH IN JAPAN

This section describes the historical process of depopulation and its relationship to the cycle of rapid economic growth from 1956 to 1972 and the economic slowdown after the oil crisis of 1973.

Heavy Out-migration During Rapid Economic Growth

From 1960 to 1973, the average growth rate of the gross national product was more than 10 percent per annum. This rapid economic expansion, especially in the nonagricultural sectors, radically changed the labor force structure. As the labor force shifted from the primary (extractive) sector to the secondary (industrial) and tertiary (service) sectors, rural people, especially youngsters who had just graduated from school, left the countryside for urban areas in large numbers in search of better job opportunities and higher standards of living.

As a result, the ratio of municipalities in which the decrease in population reached more than 10 percent in relation to all other municipalities, increased from 6.5 percent (227 out of 3,280) in the 1955-1960 period to 26.6 percent (897 out of 3,376) in the 1960-1965 period and then to 28.8 percent (938 out of 3,330) between 1965 and 1970. These areas constituted 44 percent of the national land area in 1965-1970. Rural depopulation was acute in remote, mountainous, and heavy snowfall areas, especially in the regions peripheral to the Tokyo-Nagoya-Osaka megalopolis, i.e., Hokkaido, Kyushyu, Shikoku, Chugoku, and Tohoku (Map 1).

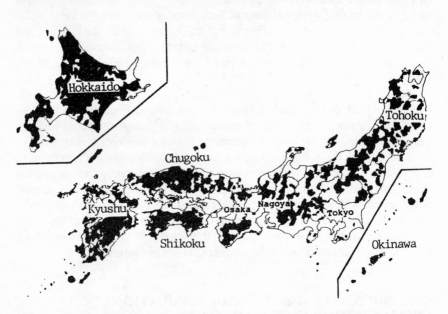

Map 1. Distribution of Kaso Areas in Japan. Source: White Paper of Kaso (1972). Note: The black areas indicate Kaso areas.

The rural depopulation process that occurred before the oil crisis of 1973 went through three stages (Figure 1); roughly from 1956-1960, 1960-1970, and 1970-1975. Before 1960, drastic population decreases were limited to the most isolated mountainous villages. At first, mass media attention to this problem was scarce, and the general populace was unaware of the situation. At that time, many economists and forestry researchers interpreted this migration phenomenon as a

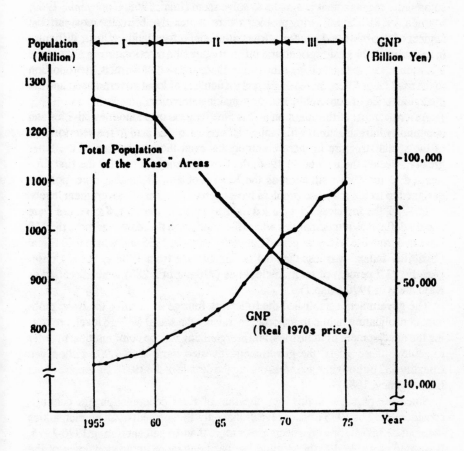

Figure 1. Depopulation and Gross National Product: 1955-1975. Source: Yearbook of Japan Statistics.

reasonable labor force shift from a marginally depressed zone to a more viable one. Little attention was paid to the social consequences of out-migration. Continued economic expansion during the 1960s accelerated rural-urban migration throughout Japan. Most of the municipalities located in mountainous areas suffered from serious problems associated with depopulation. A number of scholars, journalists, and government officials began investigating demographic, economic, social, and fiscal changes and proposed some regional policy and community management programs to solve them (Imai, 1968; Yoneyama, 1969; Masuda, 1978). The following problems were indicated as being the most serious: neglect of desirable and needed afforestation and reforestation efforts; difficulty in maintaining the basic agricultural infrastructure; the deteriorating quality of the labor force, i.e., the increasing ratio of the aged, and also of women, in proportion to the total labor force; increasing fiscal difficulties of local governments; and the disorganization of community decision-making structures.

As a rule, most of the attention at this time focused on economic activities and community infrastructure, while much less concern was paid to the deterioration of the social structure in these communities even though the fate of the latter greatly affected the former. In 1966, the Government of Japan for the first time referred to the above situation as the Kaso problem. Since that time, policies designed to tackle the Kaso problem have been initiated at all government levels.

In 1970, the Japanese Diet passed the Kaso Act. In this Act, Kaso areas were legally defined as municipalities where the population decrease was more than 10 percent during the five-year period between 1960 and 1965 and where the "Fiscal Capability Index" was less than 0.4 on the average from 1966 to 1968. Consequently, 23.7 percent of all municipalities (776 out of 3,280) were classified as Kaso areas in 1970 (Map 1).

The government established the following four goals to solve the Kaso problem: consolidating public transportation, raising the social welfare level, promoting the development of industries, and reorganizing village communities. In order to achieve these goals, the government invested more than 7,902 billion yen (roughly $32 billion) in Kaso areas during the decade of the 1970s (Japan, National Land Agency, 1982).

Since the passage of this Act, the rate of rural depopulation has declined considerably. The 1975 Census reveals that only 13.6 percent of all municipalities (443 out of 3,257) showed a decrease of more than 10 percent during 1970-1975. It is quite probable that this decline has been due more to the slowdown of the Japanese economy after the oil crisis of 1973 than to anything else.

After the oil crises of 1973 and 1979, incentives for rural people to leave their villages decreased as Japan's economic growth began to slow. Some peripheral communities were successful in decreasing or even stopping out-migration and a number of smaller municipalities began a trend of population increase. For example, 15.9 percent of Kaso areas (178 out of 1,119 Kaso municipalities) grew in population between 1975 and 1980. This growth reflects a combination of one or more of five factors: geographical expansion of neighboring cities, development of bedroom communities, arrival of new rural industries, creation of new local economic initiatives, and an increase in exploitation of energy resource development, e.g., dam construction. Accompanying this rural growth has been the movement of people, especially youngsters and retired persons, from large cities to the countryside in search of new lifestyles.

FACTORS AFFECTING DEPOPULATION IN MOUNTAIN AREAS

This section will discuss the theoretical model of the depopulation process and identify the factors that significantly affect depopulation in mountain areas.

Push-Pull Factors of Depopulation

The inducements to move away from mountain areas can be divided into external factors (pull factors) and internal factors (push factors), as is shown in Figure 2 (Mitsuda, 1976). The major pull factors are: the drastic change in the nationwide labor force structure during the period of rapid economic development, and the urban-rural differences in availability of employment, income, and standard of living and welfare levels. These pull factors have been strengthened by the expansion of urbanization and industrialization during the 1960-1970 period.

The push factors may be divided into economic, social, fiscal, psychological, and demographic factors. Major economic push factors are: the depressed position of forestry due mainly to the fuel revolution, the impact of increased imports of timber, and the low productivity of agriculture and the relatively poor agricultural infrastructure in mountain areas.

Before 1960, charcoal making and firewood cutting had provided moderate income for many mountain villagers. However, after the fuel revolution, production of charcoal decreased rapidly due to the shift away from charcoal use by Japanese households. In 1960, 1.5 million tons of charcoal were produced in Japan. Production declined to 0.6 million tons in 1965; 180,000 tons in 1970; 70,000 tons in 1975, and 35,000 tons in 1980. In other words, charcoal production in 1980 was less than 3 percent of what it was in 1960.

The same phenomena took place in firewood production. Countrywide production of firewood in 1975 was 5 percent of the 1955 production figure. This drastic change resulted in the loss of many job opportunities in forest communities. This development hit small landowners especially hard because they received a large proportion of their income from charcoal and firewood production.

Figure 2. Process of Depopulation in Mountain Area Communities

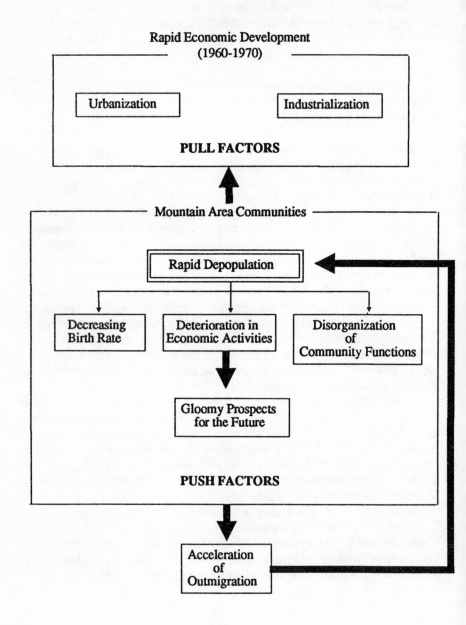

The Push-Pull Theory

Rapid Economic Development
(1960-1970)

Urbanization

Industrialization

PULL FACTORS

Mountain Area Communities

Rapid Depopulation

Decreasing
Birth Rate

Deterioration in
Economic Activities

Disorganization
of
Community Functions

Gloomy Prospects
for the Future

PUSH FACTORS

Acceleration
of
Outmigration

Starting in the 1960s, government policy deemphasized the importance of domestic timber production and this led to a rise in the amount of timber imported into Japan. In 1970, the amount was 6.6 times what it was in 1960. The rapidly increasing supply of imported timber has caused severe damage to domestic forestry. Ninety-one percent of forest landowners having less than 5 ha (12.5) gave up working their forest land because they could not afford to extend their businesses. Thus, the number of forest workers decreased from about 67,000 to 37,000 in 1970.

Farms in mountain areas were usually very small. For example, in 1970 each farm household in mountain areas had an average of only 0.8 ha (2 acres each), mostly in terraced fields. The nationwide average was 1.07 ha (2.68 acres). In addition, the agricultural infrastructure was so poor that the net farm income in the mountain areas in 1970 was only 66.8 percent of the national average. In order to supplement their incomes, 86 percent of farm households engaged in part-time employment. But remoteness from urban employment opportunities has limited the gain from off-farm employment for the villagers. Most of them had to work as temporary workers, often for low wages.

The social push factors include: the lack of social or welfare facilities, such as roads, water and sewer systems, school, and hospitals; and the difficulty of maintaining these community functions. Differences in the availability of social and welfare facilities were extreme between Kaso areas and non-Kaso areas in 1975 (Japan, Ministry of Home Affairs, 1975). For example, the percentage of paved roads in Kaso areas was only 11 percent; by contrast, that of non-Kaso areas was about 24 percent. The rate of extension of water systems in Kaso areas was 67 percent while that of non-Kaso areas was 90 percent. The number of hospital beds per 1,000 population was 87.1 beds in Kaso areas compared to 129.3 beds in non-Kaso areas. Since local governments located in the malfunctioning Kaso areas have always been in financial difficulty they could not completely provide the residents with the needed, desired public services.

It is obvious that the residents, especially youngsters, felt that future prospects in their own communities were dim, and thus they preferred to leave for the cities as soon as possible. This may be called the psychological push factor. The demographic factor is that the increasing proportion of the aged in the population structure results in a decrease in the birth rate and of the population itself. The process of depopulation can be theoretically described as circular and cumulative causation. Push-pull factors operate as a downward spiral to continue and strengthen the process of depopulation.

To sum up, the external influences, i.e., urbanization and industrialization, have drastically changed the community structure in mountain communities. These structural changes resulted in the loss of economic vitality, community cohesion, and control over decisions, and in the weakening of community pride and identity.

Finally, people lost the community ideology on which they could base redevelopment or reorganization plans. The result is a community that exists physically, but does not exist sociologically.

IMPACTS OF OUT-MIGRATION ON COMMUNITY STRUCTURE

The following two case studies provide some insight into the impacts of depopulation on community social structures and what some communities have done to cope with depopulation.

Deterioration of a Traditional Community Structure: The Haiya Case

The village of Haiya was initially established around the sixteenth century as a forest village to provide charcoal and timber for the city of Kyoto, especially the Imperial Palace of the pre-Tokugawa era. Haiya was built along the banks of a small stream and is surrounded by steep mountains. Forest lands have always dominated the village while farmlands in the hilly fields have traditionally been few and small in size. The standard of living has generally been extremely poor, and because of its geographical isolation, Haiya village has been economically and socially self-sufficient.

The deterioration of the traditional social structure of Haiya began with the fall of a prominent pioneer family, the Wada, around 1920. During the Meiji and Taisho eras (1868-1924), the family owned over half of the forest lands and farmlands in the village. They were also the core family of the large extended family system, and, as such, exercised influence over the actuator of the branch families. The Wada family had had near absolute power in economic, social, and administrative activities during the Meiji and Taisho eras.

At this time, the community structure of the villages was based on traditional communal ties, i.e., the landowner and tenant relationship, or "Honke and Bunke" relationship (the relationship between main stem family and side stem family). In the early Showa era around 1930, the former head of the Wada household died after mismanaging all of the family properties and left huge debts. The position of the Wada family deteriorated rapidly.

In the following years, substantial numbers of local landowners sold their forest property to outside businesses or landowners and left Haiya for the cities. This depopulation deprived Haiya of many potential leaders who could have organized community development. No other family took over the role of community leader.

Out-migration from Haiya continued after the war, primarily because of the fuel revolution. Forty-four percent of the total population in 1960 left for cities during the decade of 1960-1970. The deterioration of charcoal production deprived villagers of their major source of income, and forest landowners were confronted with the task of transforming their community economy from charcoal production to timber production. However, local people had difficulties in making this change because of the pattern of small scale land ownership in the area (the average landowner had less than 10 ha).

It should be noted that in the Haiya case the larger forest landowners were the first to leave because they were pessimistic about the future of the forestry industry. Then forest workers, because of the low wages and large number of accidents associated with their professions, looked for opportunities to work in nearby towns or migrated to large cities.

After the migration of landowners, most of the forest lands in the village were purchased by outside businesses and speculators, who hired temporary workers. The migrant temporary workers began to flow into village sites and developed into a rootless labor force. Although they established links with the local labor force in production activities, in social life they were alienated and segregated as outsiders. Outside control became stronger and the oldtimers lost their autonomy over decisions on developing the natural resources near Haiya.

To summarize the case study of Haiya, the traditional community structure deteriorated because of heavy out-migration and loss of community leaders, inability to create a new economic foundation industry, i.e., a new forest management industry, and inflow of outside temporary workers. The loss of community decision-making ability to cope with the out-migration problems weakened the sense of solidarity among the villagers, and most members eventually gave up trying to push for local community development. Consequently, out-migration accelerated. Today, about 40 percent of the remaining household heads, mostly aged people, are out of work and have only gloomy prospects for the future (Figure 3).

Revitalization of Community: The Ashu Case

Ashu village has one of the largest old-growth forests in Japan. After 1923, Kyoto University bought 4,162 ha (10,405 acres) for research. Ashu had been a major producer of charcoal, and most families either produced charcoal as a family operation or were employed by the University. However, after the fuel revolution caused charcoal production to deteriorate, the occupational structure of the village changed from a uniform structure (charcoal making) to a threefold structure (employees at the research grounds of Kyoto University, forest workers who were employed in the forest work union, and employees of the "mountain vegetable" processing industry).

The families employed by Kyoto University research were guaranteed their status and income as civil servants and were not influenced by the fuel revolution. Because of their stable income and status, these families rank quite high on the socioeconomic scale of the community.

On the other hand, the families not involved with the University have suffered

Figure 3. Depopulation and Deterioration of Mountain Villages During Rapid Economic Growth: The Case of the Village of Haiya

During Rapid Economic Growth

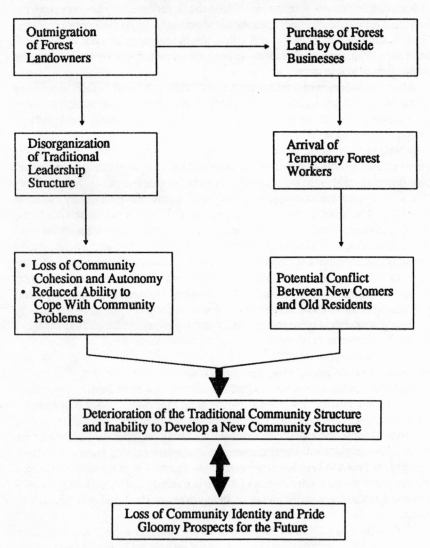

severe damage because of the fuel revolution. Since they lacked measures to reforest their lands after the heavy use of lumber resources in the years following the war, most of this forest land is now bare and the economic value is nil. There was no transformation of the forest industry into a forest management program.

Meanwhile, Kyoto University introduced a new employment policy that restricted employment opportunities in the research field. Consequently, most forest workers were forced to seek employment as low wage laborers. Most of them became migrant workers because it was impossible to sustain themselves on other kinds of employment.

After the 1960s, many villagers emigrated from the community, usually as entire families. Consequently, between 1960 and 1970 the population of Ashu declined from 138 to 98 people, and the number of households in the village decreased from 45 to 33.

Members of the Ashu community seriously discussed the methods of stopping out-migration. Development of the production of so-called "mountain vegetables" (Sansai) and a corresponding processing industry was attempted by the community and a local production cooperative was founded. In the beginning, because production was not stable, the industry operated in the red, and many members dropped out. However, over a period of seven years, three leaders, who were cousins, continued to to improve production methods and management. During Japan's period of rapid economic growth, urbanites began to prefer these "natural" foods. Since then, the Sansai industry has stabilized with sales of approximately 80 million yen (about $320,000) in 1978. Youth returning from urban areas, and other community members joined the group.

During the process of promoting the Sansai industry, members of Ashu village learned the importance of community solidarity and consensus among members, and the permeation of progressive ideas of community leaders. As a result, the Sansai cooperative began to take the lead in decision making for many community problems. As the Sansai industry achieved sales of 100 million yen per year (about $400,000), the leaders of the Sansai cooperative began to gain the community's respect for their abilities and accomplishments.

In conclusion, the case of Ashu village presents an example of successful community development by promoting a substitute industry suited to the geography of the area and based on community participation. In addition, the principle of "cooperation and equality" was established under the leadership of those who had excellent abilities and respect from community members (Figure 4).

Figure 4. Creation of New Industry and Community Reorganization: The Case of the Village of Ashu

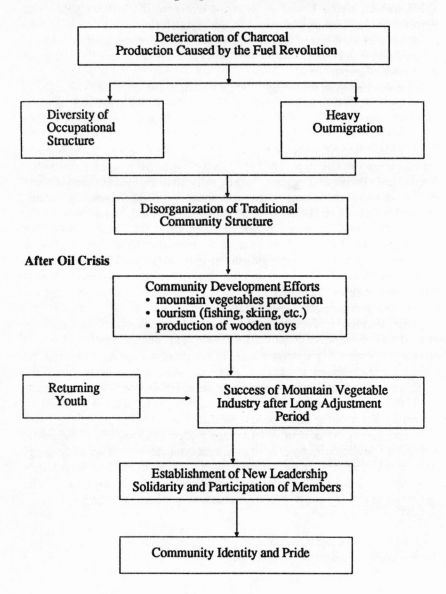

During Rapid Economic Growth

Deterioration of Charcoal Production Caused by the Fuel Revolution

Diversity of Occupational Structure

Heavy Outmigration

Disorganization of Traditional Community Structure

After Oil Crisis

Community Development Efforts
• mountain vegetables production
• tourism (fishing, skiing, etc.)
• production of wooden toys

Returning Youth

Success of Mountain Vegetable Industry after Long Adjustment Period

Establishment of New Leadership Solidarity and Participation of Members

Community Identity and Pride

CONCLUSIONS AND POLICY IMPLICATIONS

The findings of this study lead us to the following brief conclusions:

(1)The "pull factors" of Japan's economic growth and fuel revolution in the 1960s rapidly accelerated the migration of rural population, especially from remote and mountainous areas into urban areas.

(2) The "push factors" which most significantly affected out-migration were: low population density, a high percentage of unproductive forest lands and fields, and a high percentage of household income in primary industry sectors.

(3) The process of depopulation can be described as a downward spiral of circular and cumulative causation of push-pull factors, including economic, social, fiscal, and psychological ones.

(4) It seemed unavoidable that communities experiencing rapid out-migration would lose their community solidarity and autonomy.

(5) The deterioration of the traditional social structure often caused disorganization in community decision-making abilities, as well as a reduced ability to institute new forms of community organization and decision making. This is a serious obstacle for community development efforts.

In my opinion, these conclusions indicate that the following policy recommendations for community development of depopulated areas should be considered:

(1) The creation of new industries that make best use of the geographic setting of the region; e.g., tourism, mountain vegetable industry, wood toy factory, educational centers, and so on.

(2) The development of human capital and community organizations through the participation and consensus of all community members.

(3) A concerted effort to cope with depopulation problems and to help local people and community institutions improve the quality of life through development of local plans.

Much additional research will be required to clarify and solve depopulation problems in mountain areas. Among other things, research is needed: (1) to identify depopulation problems left unresolved; (2) to examine what kinds of community development efforts have succeeded in coping with the impacts of heavy out-migration; and (3) to study ways to establish and reform new community structures in mountain villages, especially decision-making structures.

ACKNOWLEDGEMENTS

Adapted from a paper by the same title in H.K. Steen (ed.). 1984. *History of Sustained-Yield Forestry: A Symposium.* Santa Cruz, CA: Forest History Society.

REFERENCES

Adachi, I. 1973. "Mura to Ningen no Houkai (The Collapse of Community and Individual)." Tokyo: Sanichi Shobo.

Imai, S. (ed.) 1968. "Nippon no Kaso Chitai (Depopulated and Depressed Zones in Japan)." Tokyo: Iwanami Shoten.

Ito, Y. 1974. "Kamitsu Kaso Eno Chosen (The Challenge to Kaso and Kamitsu)." Tokyo: Gaykyo Shobo.

Japan, Ministry of Home Affairs. 1972. "White Paper of Kaso." Bureau of Printing.

Japan, Ministry of Home Affairs. 1975. "Reports of the Situation of Public Facilities." Bureau of Printing.

Japan, National Land Agency. 1982. "White Paper of Kaso." Bureau of Printing.

Masuda, S. (ed.) 1978. "Sonraku no Hendo to Byori: Kaso no mura no Jittai (Rural Changes and Problems: The Situation of Depopulated Villages)." Tokyo: Kakiuchi Shuppan.

Mitsuda, H. 1976. "A Regional Planning for Depressed Areas." *Journal of Rural Problems* 12:1, 18-25.

———. 1978. "Public Policy Needs of Households in a Depopulated Village." *Journal of Rural Problems* 14:2, 15-21.

———. 1979a. "Mura no Jichi (Autonomy in Rural Communities)," in Masuda, S. (ed.), *Sonraku no Hendo to Byori: Kaso no mura no Jittai*, Tokyo: Kakiuchi Shuppan.

———. 1979b. "Murazukuri to Riida ni kansura Kenkyu (Community Reorganization and Community Leaders)," in Yamaoka, E. (ed.), *Chiikishakaigaku no Shomnondai*, Kyoto: Koyoshobo.

Price, D. O. and M. M. Sikes. 1975. "Rural-Urban Migration Research in the United States: Annotated Bibliography and Synthesis." Washington, D.C.: DHEW Publication No. (NIH) 75-565.

Yoneyama, T. 1969. "Kaso Shakai (Depopulated and Depressed Communities)." Tokyo: NHK Shuppan.

15

Community Stability as Social Structure: The Role of Subsistence Uses of Natural Resources in Southeast Alaska

Robert M. Muth
USDA Forest Service
Juneau, Alaska

In many areas of the United States, natural resource development and community growth and decline have historically gone hand-in-hand. Partly due to the boom-and-bust cycles of development experienced by many rural communities, natural resource management agencies have often adopted policies designed to foster orderly community development and stability. In the area of forest management, for example, providing for the stability of forest-dependent communities has been an objective of Congress and public-sector resource agencies for many years, manifesting itself in such policies as sustained-yield harvest and provision of a nondeclining even-flow of timber from national forest lands (Waggener, 1977; Schallau, 1983).

To date, however, community stability objectives have become part of policy more through an act of faith than through empirical fact. Although a body of systematic analysis has begun to emerge (e.g., Byron, 1978; Jackson and Flowers, 1983; Haynes, 1983; Lee, 1985), definitive evidence regarding the relationship between natural resource management and community stability is yet to emerge from applied studies in economics, demography, or the policy sciences.

Perhaps a more fruitful approach for analyzing the relationship between natural resource development and community stability may be that provided by structural sociology. Applied to the area of natural resources, structural sociology helps determine how features of the biophysical environment are mediated through culture to acquire meaning or functional importance and become institutionalized into social structure. Drawing on this perspective, this paper argues that community stability is best understood in terms of the stability of community institutional structure (Muth and Lee, 1986), rather than in terms of such traditional indicators as employment stability, the stability of resource supply, economic stability, or population stability.

The concept of social structure is widely used in the social sciences, often with little consensus regarding its precise specification. (Readers wishing to explore this concept further are encouraged to consult the vast sociological and anthropological literature on the subject.) Common to all definitions of social structure, however, is the idea of persistent patterns of human behavior. The term institutional structure is used here to refer to persistent patterns of relationships among elements of society that follow organized and enduring patterns of behavior—social practices regularly and continuously repeated that embody values or specialized meanings necessary for the functioning of society (Berger and Luckmann, 1966). Elements of social structure that pattern human behavior include values, norms, roles, rewards and sanctions, and artifacts. One reason to focus on institutional structure in analyzing community stability is that social institutions, by patterning social behavior, lend stability to peoples' lives. In the words of Berger (1977, p. xv), "Every social institution, no matter how nonrepressive or consensual, is an imposition of order..." From the standpoint of the stability of resource-based communities, one important institutional pattern that readily lends itself to structural analysis is the use of natural resources for subsistence purposes.

SUBSISTENCE RESOURCE USE AS A SOCIAL INSTITUTION

Subsistence use of resources is a complex resource allocation issue in Alaska, where it has been codified into both state and federal law. The Alaska National Interest Lands Conservation Act (U.S. Congress, 1980, p. 2423) contains the following definition:

> ...the term "subsistence uses" means the customary and tradi-
> tional uses by rural Alaska residents of wild, renewable resour-
> ces for direct personal or family consumption as food, shelter,
> fuel, clothing, tools, or transportation; for the making and sell-
> ing of handicraft articles out of nonedible byproducts of fish and
> wildlife resources taken for personal or family consumption; for

barter, or sharing for personal or family consumption; and for customary trade.

It is important to note that the statute conveys subsistence rights to all Alaskans residing in rural communities and settlements, Native and non-Native alike. (Following conventional usage, the term Alaska Native is employed to refer to any of the aboriginal people of Alaska—Aleuts, Eskimos, and Indians. Non-Native refers to individuals belonging to groups not indigenous to Alaska). The law also gives priority to subsistence users over commercial and sports users in the taking of fish and wildlife, when sustained-yield populations of resources are in jeopardy.

Although the legal definition of subsistence uses provides an overarching policy mandate for resource management, it is of little utility in analyzing the stability of human behavior patterns from a structural perspective. More helpful are the traditional social science approaches, in which the term subsistence refers to a loosely-defined pattern of social and economic activities. These activities include hunting, fishing, gathering, herding, cultivating, trading, tool-making, crafting, fuel production, trapping, and food processing and storage. In Alaska, although these activities generally take place within the context of an economy containing a subsistence sector-private sector-public sector mix, they generally provide for near-term consumption and are governed by traditional distribution and exchange patterns rather than profit maximization and large-scale commercial market transactions (Langdon and Worl, 1981; Wolfe, 1984; Glass and Muth, 1986; Muth, Ruppert, and Glass, 1987).

As an institutional pattern of structured behavior within the socioeconomic environment of Alaska, subsistence consists of an interrelated sequence of highly-prescribed activities, which includes preharvest and harvest elements, processing and transportation, distribution and exchange, preparation, consumption, and barter. To understand how this particular institutional pattern developed in southeast Alaska, and to understand the reasons for its persistence in the contemporary era, it is necessary to examine the evolution of subsistence from a historical perspective.

HISTORICAL OVERVIEW OF SUBSISTENCE IN SOUTHEAST ALASKA

The northwest coast of North America, and southeast Alaska in particular, is truly a land of abundance (Suttles, 1968). The physical configuration is characterized by a mainland and an associated archipelago environment with a relatively moderate climate. It possesses a wide variety of fish, shellfish, wildlife, waterfowl, marine mammals, and plant species. At the time of Euroamerican contact, the indigenous Indian population of the northwest coast had developed mechanisms for using this variety of flora and fauna for food, fuel, shelter, clothing, tools, medicine, and trade.

But even amidst this abundance, physical survival could be tenuous in the face of a variety of life-threatening situations (Suttles, 1968). Potentially catastrophic events—e.g., severe climatic conditions (such as major storms or prolonged cold or drought), disruptions in salmon migration patterns, avalanches or landslides, paralytic shellfish poisoning, canoe accidents, bear encounters, raiding parties— gave rise to uncertainty and insecurity even within this land of abundance. Given the particular constellation of biophysical features of the natural environment, however, adaptive institutional mechanisms emerged to provide security and ensure survival despite periods of resource scarcity, accidents, or other unanticipated events.

The most highly-organized institution that developed for coping with uncertainty was the subsistence economy—the means by which scarce resources were produced, allocated throughout a social system, and consumed. Thus, a distinctive cultural pattern of subsistence harvest, distribution and exchange, and consumption developed and, over time, became incorporated into social structure.

Within this broad institutional complex, perhaps the most important adaptive strategy for coping with uncertainty within the biophysical conditions of the northwest coast were the patterns of resource sharing, distribution, and exchange (Krause, 1956; Drucker, 1965; Oberg, 1973). Most significantly, these institutionalized patterns of distribution and exchange were based on norms of mutual obligation and reciprocity. Those lucky or skilled enough to have a surplus supply always distributed it among other members of their kin group or village (Oberg, 1973). That this sharing took place even during periods of resource abundance served to reinforce norms of obligation and reciprocity, thereby imparting to people a sense of security that they would be provided for during future periods of resource scarcity.

Within the context of uncertainty induced by the natural environment of southeast Alaska, this structural feature of the subsistence institution—distribution and exchange based on mutual obligation and reciprocity—served as a form of social insurance for members of society in a time of need. If a landslide buried an individual salmon stream, a clan would be secure in the knowledge that it would at least survive on resources provided by others until it could discover or claim another productive stream. Although resource distribution and exchange served a variety of social functions, including the reinforcement of status hierarchies and the maintenance of respect and authority, the social insurance function of subsistence was perhaps its most important feature. It lent stability to people's lives during periods of uncertainty.

From the subsequent accounts of many early explorers, traders, and ethnographers, it appears that these adaptive mechanisms were working quite well at the time of contact. In 1741, however, an event occurred that dramatically altered the course of cultural development in Alaska. Vitus Bering discovered Alaska and claimed it for the Russian Empire.

FROM SUBSISTENCE TO A MIXED ECONOMY: THE PERIOD OF POST-CONTACT TO THE PRESENT

The period of post-contact produced tremendous cultural stress among the aboriginal populations in all institutional domains (Drucker, 1965; Oberg, 1973). But from the standpoint of the historical evolution of subsistence, the most important changes took place in the economy. The uncertainty of survival previously associated with biophysical features of the natural environment became supplanted by the uncertainties associated with the boom-and-bust cycles of a commercial market economy.

The cyclical nature of economic development in southeast Alaska since Russian discovery and subsequent purchase by the United States has been due to the region's dependence on exploitation of its natural resources. Discovery by early Russian explorers of vast numbers of sea otters, fur seals, and other valuable furbearers gave rise to extensive harvest during the first hundred years of Euroamerican contact. Although reliable data pertaining to southeast Alaska in particular are sketchy, statistics for Russian America in general are illustrative. During the period 1797-1821, approximately 1,305,268 fur seals and sea otters were exported by the Russian-American company, which had been operating under a monopoly charter granted by Czar Paul I. In contrast, due to overharvest and changing market conditions, export of fur seal and sea otter pelts declined dramatically during the period 1842-1862 to a total of 398,793 (Kresge, Morehouse, and Rogers, 1977). The downward cycle in the furbearer economy continued after the purchase of Alaska by the United States. Commercial harvest on the high seas by Russian, British, Japanese, and American sealers nearly drove certain species to extinction. By 1909, of the extensive herds that once existed prior to Russian contact, approximately 200,000 fur seals remained in Alaskan waters (Kresge, Morehouse, and Rogers, 1977).

By the late nineteenth century, commercial fishing and fish processing had become the mainstay of the southeast Alaskan economy. The first salmon cannery in southeast Alaska was established in Klawock in 1878. According to Rogers (1985), salmon production increased from 70,000 cases in 1878 to over 1,000,000 cases in 1908. Salmon harvest increased to an annual average of approximately 20 million fish during the decade 1905-1914 and peaked at an annual harvest of

41 million fish from 1915 through 1924. The salmon fisheries' decline began in the 1940s; by the 1950s, salmon production totaled only 13,253,000 fish in 1955 and 12,773,000 in 1957. Production bottomed out to an annual average harvest of over 8 million fish during the period 1973-1976, but has since recovered substantially.

The decline in the salmon harvest had serious repercussions on the regional economy. At the peak of the salmon boom, one observer noted that a cannery inhabited the mouth of nearly every productive salmon stream in southeast Alaska (Drucker, 1965). According to Rogers (1960), there were eighty-two canneries operating in southeast Alaska in 1920; in 1958, less than forty years later, only twenty-four were still in operation.

Coinciding with the salmon boom was the gold rush, a period in which the major economic contributions to the regional economy were derived primarily from the three gold lode mining operations located in Juneau, Douglas, and on Chichagof Island. During 1906 to 1943, annual production of gold equaled 162,347 ounces. In contrast, annual production averaged only 2,464 ounces during the period 1944-1956 (Rogers, 1960).

In the 1950s, an era of intensive timber management began on the Tongass National Forest, which had been under a custodial level of management since its creation in 1907. As Rogers (1985:12) has noted, "The economic plight of the region at mid-century brought increased pressure on the Forest Service to create an expanded timber industry within the region." Community stability was one of the stated motives for this decision:

> ...Regional Forester Arthur Greeley summarized the U.S. Forest Service's philosophy as managing forest areas "so that (1) long-term technical forestry needs which require developing a pre-determined pattern of stocking, ages, and growth are meshed with (2) long-term economic needs of both the landowner and the timber user in a way that (3) recognizes dependence of local communities or other human institutions on the forests of that area." (Rogers, 1985:1)

With the construction of two pulp mills in southeast Alaska, in 1954 and 1959, and with the subsequent development of sawmilling operations, timber harvest increased sharply. During the period from 1949 to 1953, the annual timber harvest from the Tongass National Forest averaged 56 million board feet per year; by the early 1970s it had increased tenfold, when a peak of between 500 and 600 million board feet was being cut. Since then, production from national forest lands has decreased substantially, to 250 million board feet in 1984 (Rogers, 1985). The decrease in harvest volume from the Tongass National Forest has been made up for somewhat by timber harvested from Native Corporation lands (202 million board feet in 1984) in southeast Alaska. However, since timber harvested from private land is not subject to the requirement that it receive primary processing in Alaska prior to export, direct and induced timber industry employment in the region has decreased from a high of 4,365 jobs in 1980 to 2,790 in 1985 (Mehrkens, 1985).

Cyclical economic fluctuations based on natural resource extraction in southeast Alaska continue through the present time. Petroleum revenues accruing to the state government during the 1970s and 1980s fueled a government-sponsored construction boom, as well as a proliferation of government-related services and employment. But the recent decline in petroleum revenues due to the expanding world oil supply has resulted in dislocations of an unknown future duration.

Historically, tourism-related sectors of the regional economy have been a rather insignificant factor in southeast Alaska. Although American and Canadian cruiseship companies have plied the inside passage almost continuously since the turn of the century, tourism has recently increased to unprecedented levels, spawning an expanding (although seasonal) industry currently undergoing a "boom" phase of its own. This increased tourism, highly dependent on such external factors as international monetary exchange rates and the health of the United States economy, has resulted in the proliferation of seasonal, tourism-related services whose contribution to the regional economy of southeast Alaska is poorly understood.

As the foregoing overview suggests, the historical pattern of the market economy in southeast Alaska is characterized by instability. As Rogers (1985:15) has persuasively argued:

> Before statehood, Alaskans fought verbal battles against the absentee owners, absentee government, and nonresident workers. Alaska and its southeastern region were the classic colonial economy—limited and specialized exploitation of a few natural resources to provide raw materials for outside markets and industry. Despite the reformation of the past three decades, we are still an economic colony, with the addition of Japan as another of the absentee masters and markets. If anything, the people are less self-sufficient than they were earlier in the century when subsistence hunting and fishing and a modest agriculture provided at least some of their basic material needs.
>
> Seasonal instability has been significantly reduced, but the people have recently learned that the new economy has another

type of instability. With timber and much of fish production dependent upon world markets and competition, and government tied to world oil prices, employment has leveled off and declined and the people are left with a sense of insecurity because of economic forces which go beyond those of the Nation alone.

Within this context of seasonal and cyclical patterns of employment and economic development, personal use of renewable natural resources takes on special importance. Subsistence activities play an important role in supplementing cash incomes during the periods when the opportunity to participate in a depressed or unstable wage economy is either marginal or nonexistent.

THE CONTINUING IMPORTANCE OF SUBSISTENCE IN SOUTHEASTERN ALASKA

The process of modernization has made its impact felt in all areas of institutional life in southeast Alaska. But despite over 200 years of contact between Native and Euroamerican culture, and despite continued institutionalization of the cash economy, traditional patterns of resource use adapt and persist.

Data from recent research confirm the continuing participation of southeast Alaskans in hunting, fishing, and gathering activities. In 1979, state and federal agencies cooperated in conducting a study referred to as the Alaska Public Survey. This survey, administered to a random sample of over 1,200 people in nearly all the communities in southeast Alaska, posed questions about food-producing activities. Research results indicate that local, wild food resources were used extensively by southeast Alaskan residents. As reported by Alves (1980), approximately 80 percent of the adult population in southeast Alaska participated in hunting, fishing, or gathering activities (such as berry-picking and seaweed-gathering). By means of these activities, people directly procured for themselves a sizeable portion of their own food budgets: "Our data indicate that about 80 percent of the households surveyed provided some of their own food; on the average, households in the region directly supplied 30 to 40 percent of the meat, fish, and fowl consumed" (Alves, 1980:V-3.)

In addition to resource harvest, resource sharing contributed to household food budgets as well. According to Alves (1980:V-3), through a combination of harvest and sharing,"...benefits of local food resources touch 90 percent of all households" in the region.

More recently, research in the form of four community case-studies cooperatively funded by the Alaska Department of Fish and Game and the U.S. Forest

Table 1. Estimated Annual Usable Weight (Lbs.) Per Household of Selected Resources Harvested in Four Southeast Alaskan Communities (148 Sample Households), 1984-1985.

Species	Mean Weight (Lbs.) Per Household
All Edible Resources	920.9
All Salmon (5 Species Total)	308.7
Sitka Black-tailed Deer	122.4

Table 2. Estimated Mean Weight (Lbs.) of Salmon Harvested in Four Alaskan Comunities, by Native and Non-Native Households, 1984-1985.

Community	Native	Non-Native
Angoon	333.7	279.8
Klawock	237.5	262.3
Tenakee	125.3	144.3
Yakutat	467.6	351.1
All Four Communities	336.2	286.7

Service in 1984 and 1985 provide detailed, resource-specific information on subsistence uses. A random sample of 148 households was surveyed in four remote southeast Alaska communities—Tenakee, Angoon, Yakutat, and Klawock—regarding household harvest and sharing activities. The total population of the four communities during the study period was 1,784. Although these data are not meant to be representative of the region as a whole, they are presented as illustrative examples of the magnitude and extent of resource use in selected rural southeast Alaskan communities.

The study confirmed the continuing reliance of rural households on a wide variety of renewable natural resources. Use data provided by respondents indicate that, in terms of total weight harvested, deer and salmon—the two principal subsistence species in southeast Alaska—continue to make substantial contributions to household food budgets in the study communities (Table 1). The average number of pounds of salmon harvested in the four communities was 336 pounds for Native households and 287 pounds for non-Native households (Table 2).

In addition, rates of household participation in harvesting and sharing activities suggest the continuing importance of renewable natural resources to the lifestyles of southeast Alaskans. Data on participation in harvest activities indicate that three-fourths (74.5 percent) of the Native households in the study communities harvested salmon for personal use, while two-thirds (69.3 percent) of non-Native households harvested at least one of the five salmon species present in southeast

Table 3. Percentage of Households Annually Harvesting, Giving, or Receiving Salmon (All Species) in Four Rural Southeast Alaskan Communities, by Native and Non-Native Household, 1984-1985.

Community	Households Harvesting		Households Giving		Households Receiving	
	Native	Non-Native	Native	Non-Native	Native	Non-Native
Angoon (N=25 Natives) (N=13 Non-Natives)	68.0	76.9	20.0	32.8	30.8	23.1
Klawock (N=17 Natives) (N=19 Non-Natives)	76.5	68.4	47.1	42.1	52.9	47.4
Tenakee (N=03 Natives) (N=21 Non-Natives)	100.0	57.1	33.3	38.1	100.0	66.7
Yakutat (N=16 Natives) (N=34 Non-Natives)	81.3	70.6	50.0	50.0	43.8	67.6
All Four Communities	74.5	69.3	35.3	42.8	42.4	54.3

Alaska (Table 3). Sharing patterns also appear to have retained their vitality. Slightly over one-third (35.3 percent) of the Native households and 42.8 percent of the non-Native households gave salmon to other households (Table 3). In terms of receiving, 42.4 percent of Native households and 54.3 percent of non-Native households received salmon from harvesters outside their own households (Table 3).

In terms of total weight harvested, Sitka black-tailed deer is the principal land mammal taken by hunters in southeast Alaska. Native households had a mean harvest of about two deer, while non-Native households averaged slightly over one deer per household (Table 4). The Alaska Department of Fish and Game has established a conversion formula which ascribes 80 pounds of useable meat, on the average, to each Sitka black-tailed deer. Using this conversion ratio, Native households harvested a mean of 162.4 pounds of deer meat, while non-Native households averaged 87.2 pounds of deer (Table 4).

Although the residents of the four study communities harvested far fewer pounds of useable deer meat than pounds of salmon, they shared it with friends, family, coworkers, and others at rates approaching those for salmon. On the average, nearly one-third of all households (31.2 percent of Native and 30.8

Table 4. Estimated Mean Weight (Lbs.) of Sitka Black-tailed Deer Harvested in Four Alaskan Communities, by Native and Non-Native Household, 1984-1985.

Community	Native		Non-Native	
	No. of Deer	Lbs. of Deer	No. of Deer	Lbs. of Deer
Angoon	3.4	272	2.6	208
Klawock	1.9	152	1.2	96
Tenakee	1.3	104	1.6	128
Yakutat*	0.12	9.6	0.08	6.4
All Four Communities	2.03	162.4	1.09	87.2

*The low number of Yakutat households harvesting deer may be largely attributed to the fact that the community is situated nearly 100 miles beyond the northern extremity of the range customarily inhabited by Sitka black-tailed deer.

percent of non-Native households) gave deer meat to other households (Table 5); while, at the same time, 35.1 percent of Native and 33.9 percent of non-Native households received deer meat from other households (Table 5). Clearly, the mean

Table 5. Percentage of Households Annually Harvesting, Giving, or Receiving Sitka Black-tailed Deer in Four Rural Southeast Alaskan Communities, by Native and Non-Native Household, 1984-1985.

Community	Households Harvesting		Households Giving		Households Receiving	
	Native	Non-Native	Native	Non-Native	Native	Non-Native
Angoon (N=25 Native) (N=13 Non-Native)	64.0	46.2	48.0	53.8	44.0	46.2
Klawock (N=17 Native) (N=19 Non-Native)	58.8	52.6	29.4	42.1	35.3	42.1
Tenakee (N=03 Native) (N=21 Non-Native)	33.3	52.4	0.0	47.6	100.0	52.4
Yakutat (N=16 Native) (N=34 Non-Native)	6.3	5.9	6.3	8.8	12.5	17.7
All Four Communities	47.2	32.8	31.2	30.8	35.1	33.9

total rates of deer harvest, giving, and receiving would be considerably higher if the low participation rates of Yakutat households were deleted from the calculations.

Although the aboriginal system of production, distribution, and exchange has undergone considerable change, and although no data were gathered on the number of pounds of salmon and deer given or received, these data on the nature and extent of use suggest that in spite of over 200 years of acculturation, normative patterns of distribution and exchange continue to operate in rural southeast Alaskan communities.

Considerable controversy remains regarding the extent to which Natives differ from non-Natives in such things as the variety and amount of species harvested, the breadth of sharing among friends and relatives, and the amount of traditional foods appearing in food budgets. However, as the data reported here suggest, levels of harvest and sharing of salmon are fairly comparable between Native and non-Native households. And, although the difference in the amount of deer harvested is considerable (and close to being statistically significant at the .05 level), no statistically significant differences were detected between Native and non-Native households in the rates of harvest, giving, or receiving of salmon or deer[1].

It is often difficult to sort out recreational and commercial uses of resources from subsistence uses. Natives and non-Natives alike participate in hunting, fishing, and gathering activities for a variety of reasons. Clearly, much of the resource harvesting that takes place in rural communities is motivated by recreational considerations. Although data from recent research suggest similar patterns of harvest and sharing among different groups, the actual meanings (i.e, norms, attachments, moral codes) associated with resource use may be very dissimilar for different segments of the population. The social insurance function of resource use important to subsistence users may mean very little to the trophy hunter who can avail himself of other social insurance options (e.g., unemployment benefits, transfer to a job out of state, or reliance on outside investments). Similarly, the social meanings attached to resource sharing will vary with different subpopulations. Consider the meanings ascribed to resource sharing by a young Tlingit Indian man, who, out of respect and obligation, gives deer meat to his maternal uncle. The meanings associated with resource sharing will be much different for him than for an urban sportsfisherman who, prior to replenishing his salmon supply, cleans out his freezer in the spring and gives leftover fish to casual acquaintances.

Ultimately, these differences will only be identified as behavioral scientists delve into the social meanings ascribed to natural resources by different user groups. Further research will also be necessary to determine the extent to which resource sharing retains its instrumental (as opposed to expressive) value, to identify the extent to which norms of mutual obligation and reciprocity are still operant in Native society, and to discover the extent to which these norms have diffused to non-Native society.

Data cited above, as well as information from other studies (e.g., Mills, 1982; Gmelch and Gmelch, 1985) conducted in southeast Alaska, confirm the continuing existence of resource harvest and sharing patterns in the current lifestyles of southeast Alaskan residents. Further, it is evident that subsistence utilization has retained its value for a number of psychological, social, cultural, and economic reasons (Newton and Moss, 1984; Mills, et al., 1984). Among other things, the boom-and-bust cycles of the contemporary market economy may have served to underscore and reinforce the importance of resource harvest, distribution, and exchange as a stability-inducing form of social insurance during the twentieth century among residents of southeast Alaska—both Native and non-Native alike.

From the standpoint of structural analysis, these data suggest the existence of normative patterns of participation possessing characteristics of a social institution. Subsistence utilization is not the random behavior of isolated members of society. Instead, it constitutes a pattern of resource use common to individuals who may be otherwise only loosely connected by the traditional institutional affiliations of social class, kinship, or occupation.

CONCLUSIONS

The traditional lifestyle of southeast Alaska may be gradually disappearing. But that institutional sphere known as subsistence, rather than being extinguished, appears to be undergoing a transformation. Subsistence activities may not be as pervasive as they were in the past, but they have shown considerable persistence, adaptability, and stability. To maintain the opportunity to engage in subsistence as mandated by state and federal law, three things are necessary:

Resource availability. Suitable and adequate habitat is necessary to provide for the sustained yield of renewable natural resources. Although this has been the subject of considerable scientific study and intensive management by a variety of resource agencies in southeast Alaska, the long-term, cumulative effects of habitat modification on many fish and wildlife species remain poorly understood. In addition, predation, disease, and climate affect the population levels of fish and wildlife, often in a cyclical fashion. Management attention to the biophysical conditions that provide for healthy resource populations will help ensure their continued availability.

Specialized knowledge. Specialized knowledge concerning subsistence must be sufficiently incorporated into social structure so that individual members of society can draw on that knowledge to more fully participate in subsistence activities if desired. Informal participant observation, anecdotal evidence, and available research suggest that the institutional aspects of subsistence—the specialized knowledge extant in social structure—retain sufficient vitality during the contemporary period, allowing significant numbers of southeast Alaskans to engage in a wide variety of traditional food gathering activities.

Harvest regulations. A regulatory environment is necessary that provides sufficient opportunity for continued participation in subsistence as a total institutional pattern—harvest, processing, distribution and exchange, preparation, and consumption or barter. It does little good, for example, to retain millions of acres of pristine habitat if harvest regulations limit the taking of subsistence sockeye salmon to twenty-five fish. Such regulations have the effect of undermining the distribution and exchange aspects of subsistence just as surely as damming up all the salmon streams would destroy the harvest aspects of subsistence. This issue— the effects of regulations on subsistence patterns—has been sorely neglected as a topic of study in southeast Alaska.

If these three conditions—resource availability, specialized social knowledge, and a supportive regulatory environment—can be maintained, southeast Alaskans who desire to participate in subsistence activities as a component of a chosen lifestyle would be able to do so. Subsistence harvest, distribution and exchange, and consumption lend stability and social cohesion to rural communities facing the highly cyclical economic fluctuations characteristic of regions such as southeast Alaska. Resource management that is sensitive to subsistence as an institutional element of social life is needed to help ensure that subsistence uses of renewable natural resources continue to serve these and other vital social functions.

ACKNOWLEDGMENTS

This chapter benefited greatly from the technical review and statistical analysis provided by personnel with the Alaska Department of Fish and Game, Division of Subsistence. The contributions of Robert Wolfe, Robert Walker, and Cheryl Scott were especially helpful and are gratefully acknowledged.

NOTES

1. Analysis conducted by Robert Walker, Alaska Department of Fish and Game, indicates that considerable differences in resource use exist when household size is taken into account. On a per capita basis, for example, Native households harvested approximately 79 pounds of salmon per household member,

while non-Native households averaged about 100 pounds. On the other hand, Native households harvested approximately 40 pounds of deer per family member, while 29.5 pounds of deer were harvested on a per capita basis in non-Native households (Walker, 1987). Further analysis is necessary to shed light on ethnic differences in resource use in southeast Alaska, and reasons for those differences.

REFERENCES

Alves, W. 1980. *Residents and Resources: Findings of the Alaska Public Survey on the Importance of Natural Resources to the Quality of Life in Southeast Alaska.* Anchorage, AK: University of Alaska, Institute for Social and Economic Research.

Berger, P.L. 1977. *Facing up to Modernity.* New York: Basic Books, Inc.

Berger, P.L. and T. Luckmann. 1966. *The Social Construction of Reality.* Garden City, NY: Doubleday and Co.

Byron, R. N. 1978. "Community Stability and Forest Policy in British Columbia". *Canadian Journal of Forest Resources* 8: 61-66.

Drucker, P. 1965. *Cultures of the North Pacific Coast.* Scranton, PA: Chandler Publishing Co.

Glass, R.G. and R.M. Muth. 1986. "Natural Resource Allocation Decision-making in Alaska: Systematic Evaluation of Socioeconomic Impacts on Subsistence Lifestyles." Paper presented at the First National Symposium on Social Science and Resource Management, May 1986, Corvallis, OR.

Gmelch, G. and S.B. Gmelch. 1985. *Resource Use in a Small Alaskan City—Sitka.* Juneau, AK: Alaska Department of Fish and Game. Division of Subsistence, Technical Paper No. 90.

Haynes, R. W. (technical ed.). 1983. *Competition for National Forest Timber: Effects on Timber-dependent Communities.* Portland, OR: USDA Forest Service, General Technical Report PNW-148.

Jackson, D.H. and P.J. Flowers. 1983. "The National Forests and Stabilization. *Western Wildlands* 8(4): 20-27.

Krause, A. 1956. *The Tlingit Indians.* Seattle, WA: University of Washington Press.

Kresge, D.T., T.A Morehouse, and G.W. Rogers (eds.). 1977. *Issues in Alaska Development.* Seattle, WA: University of Washington Press.

Langdon, S. and R. Worl. 1981. *Distribution and Exchange of Subsistence Resources in Alaska.* Juneau, AK: Alaska Department of Fish and Game. Division of Subsistence, Technical Paper No. 55.

Lee, R.G. 1985. "Comparative Analysis of Stability in Forest-Dependent Communities of Japan and the Pacific Northwest United States." Paper presented at the annual meeting of the Rural Sociological Society, August 1985, Blacksburg, VA.

Mehrkens, J.R. 1985. *Timber Supply and Demand.* Juneau, AK: USDA Forest Service, Alaska Region. ANILCA Section 706(a) Report No. 4.

Mills, D. 1982. *The Procurement and Use of Abalone in Southeast Alaska.* Juneau, AK: Alaska Department of Fish and Game. Division of Subsistence, Technical Report No. 40.

Mills, D., V. Sumida, G. George, and M. Kookesh. 1984. *Salmon Use by Residents of the Chilkat and Chilkoot River Drainages, 1983.* Juneau, AK: Alaska Department of Fish and Game. Division of Subsistence, Technical Report No. 95.

Muth, R.M., D.E. Ruppert, and R.J. Glass. 1987. "Subsistence Use of Fisheries Resources in Alaska: Implications for Great Lakes Fisheries Management." *Transactions of the American Fisheries Society* 116:510-518.

Muth, R.M. and R.G. Lee. 1986. "Social Impact Assessment in Natural Resource Decisionmaking: Toward a Structural Paradigm." *Impact Assessment Bulletin* 4(3/4):168-183.

Newton, R. and M. Moss. 1984. *The Subsistence Lifeway of the Tlingit People: Excerpts from Oral Interviews.* Juneau, AK: USDA Forest Service.

Oberg, K. 1973. *The Social Economy of the Tlingit Indians.* Seattle, WA: University of Washington Press.

Rogers, G. W. 1960. *Alaska in Transition.* Baltimore, MD: The Johns Hopkins Press.

———. 1985. "The Southeast Alaska Regional Economy and Communities: Evolution and Structure". Juneau, AK: Report to USDA Forest Service, Region 10, unpublished mimeo.

Schallau, C. 1983. "Departures from What?" *Western Wildlands* 8(4):8-13.

Suttles, W. 1968. "Coping with Abundance: Subsistence on the Northwest Coast." In R.B. Lee and I. DeVore (eds.), *Man the Hunter*. New York: Aldine Publishing Co.

U.S. Congress. 1980. Alaska National Interest Lands Conservation Act. P.L. 96-487, 94 Stat. 2423. Washington, DC: Government Printing Office.

Waggener, T.R. 1977. "Community Stability as a Forest Management Objective. *Journal of Forestry* 75(11):710-714.

Walker, R. 1987. Personal Communication.

Wolfe, R.J. 1984. "Subsistence-based Socioeconomic Systems in Alaska: An Introduction." Juneau, AK: Alaska Department of Fish and Game. Division of Subsistence, unpublished mimeo.

16

Building Trust: The Formation of a Social Contract

Margaret A. Shannon
Faculty of Forestry and Faculty of Environmental Science
College of Environmental Science and Forestry
State University of New York, Syracuse

Understanding the evolving role of citizen participation in national forest land management planning processes entails understanding both the idea and the problem it was intended to solve[1]. What is new about citizen participation is not that Forest Service officials talk to local people, but to whom they talk, to whom they must listen, and what they must do with what they learn from these conversations.

Statutory changes in the 1970s opened land management decisions to review and critique by external parties—the public—in response to a crisis of both authority and legitimacy (Coggins and Wilkinson, 1981; Dana and Fairfax, 1980; LeMaster, 1984; Shannon, 1983). Expanded citizen participation requirements, among other tools, were intended to change both how agencies did business and their actual decisions and policies (Reich, 1966:1260). This paper will place citizen participation in a broad organizational context and seek to explain how it led to forest plans, as social decision processes, becoming "social contracts" between the government and the public.

THE PURPOSES OF CITIZEN PARTICIPATION

One might fairly term participatory democracy a theory in search of practice (Wengert, 1976). The traditional political values of the United States underlie our shared commitment to the conception of the ideal citizen as a participant in the public realm of politics.

> Democratic faith is faith in the capacities of ordinary men and women as responsible co-creators with one another, and with nature, of the common world (Engel, 1980:41).

In dealing with the problems of public discontent with government, Congress has since 1970 consistently responded by giving rights of participation to the discontented interests. This practice is consistent with a pluralist model of government where all interests are assumed legitimate and public policy reflects consensus based on accommodating interests (Lowi, 1969; Stewart, 1975). Democracy is rooted in the belief that participation by all interested and affected citizens leads not only to the best process for making collective decisions, but also to merging individual personal interests into the public interest (Bellah, 1985).

> Such participation, it is claimed, will not only improve the quality of agency decisions and make them more responsive to the needs of the various participating interests, but is valuable in itself because it gives citizens a sense of involvement in the process of government, and increases confidence in the fairness of government decisions (Stewart, 1975:1761).

Why then were new statutory requirements (e.g., National Environmental Policy Act and National Forest Management Act) for citizen participation in planning and decision-making processes greeted so unenthusiastically by federal land management agencies? The traditional model of public administration centers upon an objectivist concept of rational decision-making—action is rational only when it serves to directly contribute to meeting organizational goals. When "rational" decisions exclusively refer to the choice of the most direct and efficient means for achieving predetermined goals, then participation by citizens only interferes with the technical assessment of means to ends. This is the classical model of rational-bureaucratic decision making (Burrell and Morgan, 1979; Gerth and Mills, 1974; Ladd, 1975).

Pressures for citizen participation grew from the view that administrative decisions were not simply technocratic, but entailed choices amongst values. People recognized that agency decisions affected their everyday lives and their deeply felt moral concerns, yet were made by officials "far away" and unattached to the affected social relationships (Krause, 1968). Thus, citizen demands to participate arose from the desire to make public decisions responsible.

When the process includes decision-making, the demand for
participation is a demand to *be* a decision-maker rather than
simply to have the opportunity of exerting influence *on* the
decision-maker" (Ladd, 1975:108). (emphasis added).

Note that influence is not participation, for it does not entail responsibility for
the outcome. The once firm line separating the public from the decision-making
responsibility of the agency became fuzzy with requirements for citizen participation in agency decision-making processes. To participate is to be a part of the joint
action required to make a social decision. Since citizens often define participation
as joint action where the outcome is significant, then participants must give an
account of the reasons for their decision (Ladd, 1975:108). Especially when the
decision affects social relationships beyond those of the direct participants, the
reasoning for the decision is the basis for the legitimacy, or acceptance of the
decision among the affected individuals.

This paper will examine how the U.S. Forest Service (USFS) responds to
expanded citizen participation and the challenge posed by such participation to
traditional norms of bureaucratic accountability. It also examines the emergence
of a natural resource community from the practice of citizen participation. Finally,
it attempts to deepen our understanding of how public land management agencies
are now forums for making social decisions.[2]

BUILDING TRUST THROUGH DIALOGUE

Statutory requirements for citizen participation shifted the point of public
access from the Washington, D.C. office to the numerous local offices of the
USFS. Whereas forest staff traditionally responded "the Congress" when asked
who they considered their ultimate boss, now field officials discovered they had
to heed carefully the values and viewpoints of the public.

Citizen participation is purposive social action aimed at achieving goals
through collective decision processes. Thus, how citizens choose to participate in
administrative processes depends upon their view of how the organization works
and what has to change before their goals can be realized. There is a close
correlation between how citizens view the USFS and how they try to achieve their
objectives.

How Citizens Get Involved

Every national forest has its own particular social environment and a long
history of local relationships. However, local citizens generally view themselves
as either in a personal relationship with individuals working on the forest or in an
impersonal relationship with a large agency and its agents. How they view the

agency affects how they participate in the planning process and what they expect to achieve through their participation.

There are two major categories of public involvement processes in the Forest Service, formal and informal. The formal processes include identifying planning issues, the regular mailing of newsletters to interested people, notification and review of tentative decisions, and the array of public meetings held by a forest. The informal processes range from simple conversations to, in one instance, a group of local business people inviting the forest supervisor to be a permanent guest at their regular meetings. Four general types of relationships and styles of interaction with the public can be described.

PURPOSIVE STYLES OF CITIZEN PARTICIPATION

STRUCTURE OF THE INTERACTION	TYPE OF RELATIONSHIP	
	Personal	Impersonal
INFORMAL	Citizens work directly with individuals in the agency to change their values and thus their actions as well as formal policy	Citizens use the media, rumor, or bluff to influence the climate of public opinion to which the agency is responding
FORMAL	Citizens work with their political representatives, circulate petitions, sponsor mass mailings, write comments on EIS/Forest Plan documents in order to broaden the political scope of the issues.	Citizens work through administrative appeals processes, judicial review, and legislative forums to change the legal and political requirements for and constraints on agency management decisions.

Personal Relationships
The basis of the personal relationship is that every staff member of the agency is viewed as an individual. While citizens may perceive them as "good" (meaning that they personally share many of their own beliefs), or "bad" (meaning that they don't listen or have different beliefs), they see the agency as composed of individuals and thus, as fallible as individuals. In addition, the bad actions of good agency people are attributed to the bad policies of the organizations which tell the good person what to do. Empathizing with the common experience of employee dependence, citizens can forgive the good person for such actions.

Because the officials of the organization are seen to embody the policy and values of the Forest Service, local people believe they can change policy by changing how the officials think. Not only do local citizens try to change decisions by changing the values of the decision-makers, they also try to affect the prioritization of resource values used to make technical allocation and management decisions.

Local citizens have a long tradition of "going on in to the Ranger's office to talk about what's happening." But in these conversations, the Forest Service has viewed itself as informing and educating the public about its management activities. Authentic citizen participation requires the agency to recieve, not just send messages. Thus, informal networks can provide useful information only if the agency staff perceive themselves as listening to what citizens are trying to get them to understand and then using this understanding in management decisions and practices. Yet, all too frequently, resource managers look to "science" and not to "understanding other values and perspectives," when choosing a course of action.

Thus, when informal approaches fail to elicit the desired response or change, other approaches must be used. Local political networks provide a direct tie between local concerns and politicians. When citizens are unhappy with a USFS decision, they can simply contact their political representatives and ask them to take action. Bureaucrats prefer to avoid this kind of exposure, but citizens know that when an issue gets "hot," it gets agency attention.

Impersonal Relationships

In contrast, the impersonal relationship involves characterizing the agency as "other," despite some of the "nice" people who work for it. In interviews, citizens often showed they were quite aware that there were nice people working on the forest, people who were even trying very hard to "do the right kind of management." But they also clearly stated that to keep "my anger with the outrageous policies of the agency, I have to think of it as just an impersonal organization." Thus, Forest Service staff came to be viewed only in their roles as agents.

Means of informal influence range from keeping political representatives informed of proposed agency actions to changing local public opinion. The local or regional media can be a very effective way to raise the awareness of the local public and activate their concerns. Civic organizations also provide a ready forum—especially groups that meet frequently and are always eager to find programs, such as the Lions or Rotary Clubs—to publicize and question proposed forest planning actions.

The formal category of this relationship is the most visible because the issue is raised to the highest level of public prominence. Typically, however, it is the last mode of influence sought by local citizen groups. When all other attempts at changing the actions and policies of the agency have failed, when their concerns have been dismissed as irrelevant, when no one will listen; then the forum of discussion is changed. When changes in policy cannot be achieved through internal agency adjustments, citizens seek to challenge existing authority and policy and to change the substance of the legal mandate entrusted to the agency. Larger, well-organized and funded interest groups (e.g., Sierra Club Legal Defense Fund, Natural Resource Defense Council, Wilderness Society, National Wildlife Federation) play a critical role in pursuing judicial and legislative means to change the purposes and responsibilities of the agency (Coggins and Wilkinson, 1981; Shannon, 1983).

THE SOCIAL CONTEXT OF CITIZEN PARTICIPATION

USFS programs for involving citizens in planning and decision processes need to be cognizant both of how people prefer to participate (affected by the factors discussed above) and of how the very act of participation creates values and interests. Several agency planners reflecting on their experience realized that what information was presented and how it was presented greatly influenced how interests coalesced into organized groups. However, since most models of planning view values and interests (or preferences) as prior conditions affecting the planning process, agency planners were surprised that people changed their views and developed new interests during the process itself. This section discusses several features of the social context of land management planning that strongly affect the nature and effectiveness of citizen participation in the process.

First, and often overlooked, people in local communities generally have some way of addressing common problems. While some local areas may have leaders who organize and direct the local response to all kinds of social issues, issue-specific leaders/organizers are more common. For example, one forest supervisor, in describing a community in which he had worked for some years, observed that individuals who emerged as leaders in organizing the community to respond to particular problems moved to the background after the crisis passed. He believed that the local people were afraid of influence and power becoming concentrated in a long-term leader. Community leaders came and went, and the agency could not expect to interact with the same individuals for very long.

Second, the "community of interests" associated with each resource use do not have the same geographical distribution. For some resource values and uses the affected public is easily bounded geographically, fairly localized, and organized. For others, like outdoor recreation uses, members of the relevant community of interests may be geographically dispersed and only loosely aware of one another. Clearly, there is variation in the mode of communication most effective for reaching these different users.

Third, not even the best participation technique can force the agency to listen.

It must choose to "hear" the messages sent by the public. The degree to which the public is heard and responded to on any particular forest is critically dependent upon the style of management employed by the forest supervisor. Not only does the staff take its cue from the supervisor on how to respond to the public, but most importantly, the way the supervisor treats and listens to the staff is highly correlated to the way the staff treats and listens to the public (Shannon, 1985). This means that when the supervisor encourages dialogue among the staff concerning policy and management choices, and when the staff participates fully in designing policy options responding to changing social values, they learn a responsive style of management. To be challenged and questioned when expressing one's judgments becomes viewed as a positive means for seeking viable ways of accommodating diverse needs. The professionals learn how to listen to the new meanings of the forest emerging from new ways people use its resources. They then can respond to what is new within the framework of the agency's jurisdiction and responsibilities.

Fourth, the degree to which the agency explicitly recognizes the creativity of the participation process is critical. It is creative in two different ways. First, amorphous and individually defined experiences will, during the course of the planning process, become both clarified in content and collectively defined. The result is the creation of interests. This process can often create surprises for the agency. Seeking to simplify and manage their political environment, resource managers began to include the environmental interest groups in the broad structure of informal external relationships they maintained for both gathering information and testing ideas. Often, the corollary of including the organized groups was the unanticipated development, and exclusion, of other interests. When the social significance of the forest planning process came to be recognized by local people, all sorts of local groups suddenly organized to contribute to the shaping of the future national forest. Forest plans are also creative in that they express community visions of how the forest will be used and be a part of people's lives.

The planning process must create these visions and articulate them clearly enough to inform both the balancing of resource uses and diverse measures of good land management. To the extent that the forest staff explicitly recognize their creative role, they listen not just to the resource-specific information contained in public comments, but also to the broader message of what values take highest priority. To make citizen participation work well, as several forest supervisors stated, the USFS may need to take the initiative in providing opportunities for local people to identify their collective vision of the future.

PUBLIC DIALOGUE AND THE IDEA
OF A SOCIAL CONTRACT

The concept of community aptly captures the creative, organizing capacity of federal action when broad citizen participation is an integral part of the policy process. The idea of community expands our definitions of the affected public and of participation. Rather than a discrete number of organized interest groups, we see a loose, fluid structure of social actors involved in and affected by forest planning decisions.

The basic purpose of citizen participation is to create a new way to decide what is appropriate land management. No longer are bureaucratic decision and planning processes simply a way for experts to choose the technically best ways of solving predefined problems or meeting already accepted objectives. Now, land management planning processes must establish a dialogue between political and social knowledge (located within social and political organizations) and technical knowledge (located within professionals from a diverse array of scientific disciplines).

> Technical knowledge would be viewed as only one rather uncertain input into a situation that also requires common sense, ethical insight, and a great deal of conversation with those affected before a policy can be formulated or a decision made. The important point is that technical knowledge does not necessitate anything. Decisions and commitments must emerge from the practical context of communicative action (Bellah, 1983:55-56).

Question: What Is Public Dialogue About?

The purpose of public dialogue is to create from practice—everyday experience of people—governing generalizations (policies) for making choices about how to use, allocate and regulate public forest resources. As a democracy, we institutionalized public dialogue as our form of government. Now, administrative decision-making processes are also explicitly designated as forums for public dialogue. It is the practice of citizen participation that creates the vision of the future necessary to make today's resource management decisions.

> The purpose of practice is not to produce or control anything but to discover through mutual discussion and reflection between free citizens the most appropriate ways, under present conditions, of living the ethically good life. To that end technological knowledge may be helpful provided that it is used in

the context of practical—that is, ethical and political—knowledge that has precedence over it (Bellah, 1983:55).

But over time agencies become forces of convention as they follow policies and rules formed in the past. And formal organizations often seek goals of autonomy and survival rather than reevaluate the efficacy of their programs in light of changing circumstances. Thus, the practice of participation changes the role of the public administrator from a neutral implementor of policy to that of a co-creator—with the citizenry—of policy (Reich, 1985).

Question: How Are Forest Plans "Social Contracts?"
Since citizen participation entails responsibility, the participants as well as the agency are obliged to abide by the policies set out in the forest plan. In this way, forest plans become social contracts between the participants and bind both agency and public to the agreement. Given the strong desire of the community of interests to have certainty and accountability in the policies governing agency actions, forest plans need to articulate clearly both the governing policies for future management and how they will be implemented (Barber, 1983).

Just what is a social contract? First, to be "social" the contract is to be binding on all members of society, not just those individuals who participated in drafting it. Second, to be a "contract" there must be mutual agreement to terms which adequately accommodate the differences in values, objectives, and goals of the resource management community based on a principled and reasoned analysis.

As a public agency, the Forest Service is obligated to carry out mandated purposes. Indeed, to be an agent is to abdicate personal goals to organizational purposes. To the extent that organizational purposes are expressions of public purposes, the organization also functions as an agent of public interest. However, where values are conflicting or ambiguous, the difficult problem of the agency is to define governing principles and then bring them to bear on specific decisions. This remains the challenge of forest planning.

CONCLUSIONS

Citizen participation is not just an addendum to a technical decision process. As envisioned in both theory and practice, citizen participation is constitutive of public decision-making. Thus, we can see public agencies as forums for public dialogue. Public dialogue presumes that accommodations to specific interests will be measured against enduring collective values (Nonet, 1977).

Public policy thus becomes a product of the processes of interpretation, action, and reinterpretation in the light of new information or new understandings of the meaning of the action to the community of natural resource interests. The USFS is challenged to find organizational structures that can respond to ongoing processes of change without losing their sense of direction or purpose, while also retaining the ability to incorporate new ways of doing business (Korten, 1981).

But such challenges are being met within the decentralized structure of the agency. Individual members of the agency—particularly forest supervisors—with a vision of how to practice responsive management are paving the way for organizational adaptation. Vigilant citizen organizations determined to change the way the agency interprets its objectives are forcing the agency to hear their voices. The process of citizen participation no longer gets shuffled to the sidelines. Now, savvy forest staff seek out public views and incorporate them into the development of both policy and activity-specific management practices.

The familiar caveat of citizens, "I won't know if I like the Forest Plan until I see it on the ground," expresses clearly the criteria for trust. The USFS must truly hear the voices of the people and see the forest through their eyes and then incorporate a shared vision of the future forest into specific management policies and practices.

NOTES

1. In this paper, I use the term "citizen participation" to refer to the political role and position of the public vis-a-vis the USFS and to distinguish it from more general uses of the term public.

2. This analysis draws upon a decade of research on the implementation of the forest planning requirements of the National Forest Management Act and Regulations (36 CFR Part 219). In 1984, I interviewed citizens who had been participants in federal land management planning processes for several years. Most of my research efforts were supported by the USFS. Several times I was employed by the agency and assigned to a special project designed to increase its understanding of the effects of forest planning on both the agency and on the social environment.

REFERENCES

Barber, B. 1983. *The Logic and Limits of Trust.* New Brunswick, NJ: Rutgers University Press.

R.N. Bellah. 1983. "Social Science as Practical Reason." In D. Callahan and B. Jennings (eds.), *Ethics, the Social Sciences, and Policy Analysis.* New York: Plenum Press.

———. 1985. *Habits of the Heart: Individualism and Commitment in American Life*. Berkeley, CA: University of California Press.

Burrell, G. and G. Morgan. 1979. *Sociological Paradigms and Organizational Analysis*. London: Heinemann.

Coggins, G.C. and C.F. Wilkinson. 1981. *Federal Public Land and Resources Law*. New York: Foundation Press.

Engel, R. 1980 "The Democratic Faith in America." Six Minns Lectures.

Dana, S.T. and S.K. Fairfax. 1980. *Forest and Range Policy: Its Development in the United States*, Second Edition. New York: McGraw-Hill.

Gerth, H.H. and C.W. Mills. 1974. *From Max Weber: Essays in Sociology*. New York: Oxford Press.

Korten, D.C. 1981. "The Management of Social Transformation." *Public Administration Review* 41:609-618.

Krause, E.A. 1968. "Functions of a Bureaucratic Ideology: 'Citizen Participation'." *Social Problems* 16:129-143.

Ladd, J. 1975. The Ethics of Participation." In J.R. Pennoch and J.W. Chapman (eds.), *Participation and Politics, Nomos XVI*. New York: Leiber-Atherton.

LeMaster, D.C. 1984. *Decade of Change: The Remaking of Forest Service Statutory Authority During the 1970's*. Westport, CT: Greenwood Press.

Lowi, T. 1969. *The End of Liberalism*. New York: W.W. Norton.

Nonet, P. 1977. "Taking Purpose Seriously." In G. Dorsey (ed.), *Equality and Freedom: International and Comparative Jurisprudence*. Dobbs Ferry, NY: Oceana Publications.

Reich, C. 1966. "The Law of the Planned Society." *Yale Law Journal* 75:1227.

Reich, R.B. 1985. "Public Administration and Public Deliberation: An Interpretive Essay." *Yale Law Journal* 94:1617-1641.

Shannon, M.A. 1985. "Assessing Communication Effectiveness in Developing Forest Plans and EIS Documents". Washington, DC: USDA Forest Service, Report to the Director, Land Management Planning.

Shannon, R.E. 1983. *Wildlands Management Law*. Missoula, MT: University of Montana School of Forestry.

Stewart, R. 1975. "The Reformation of Administrative Law." *Harvard Law Review* 88:1669.

U.S. Congress. 1969. National Environmental Policy Act of 1969 (NEPA). 83 Stat. 852 amended; 42 U.S.C. 4321.

———. 1976. National Forest Management Act of 1976 (NFMA). P.L. 94-588; 90 Stat. 2949.

Wengert, N. 1976. "Citizen Participation: Practice in Search of a Theory." *Natural Resources Journal* 16:23.

17

Counties, States, and Regulation of Forest Practices on Private Lands

Debra J. Salazar
College of Forest Resources
University of Washington

The relationship between human communities and adjacent forest lands has been studied from a variety of perspectives. Sociologists have examined how alternative timber management strategies and practices affect local social structure.[1] Economists have studied the relationship between harvest scheduling and local economic stability.[2] However, very little research has addressed the relationship between local politics and forest land use and management. This paper examines how political decision making at the local level constrains the management of private forest land. More specifically, the paper asks why local governments in particular types of counties and towns have sought to regulate the practice of forestry on privately owned lands. In addressing this question, I focus on how the economic role of the forest in the community circumscribes the kinds of forest policies a local government will adopt.

Forest practice regulations consist of statutes and administrative rules that address a variety of practices employed in the culture and harvest of forest stands. Regulations may deal with reforestation, silvicultural systems, harvest method, design and maintenance of transportation networks, slash management, and the use of chemicals. Forest practice regulations are not equivalent to rules that control land use. Laws that regulate the location and intensity of residential, commercial, industrial, and agricultural development are only peripherally addressed here. Land use laws often serve different constituencies and purposes than forest practice laws. However, land use laws sometimes contain provisions that can be used to regulate forest practices.

Since the 1940s, regulation of forest practices has been widely regarded as a policy prerogative of the states (Clepper, 1971; Greeley, 1951). However, during the 1970s and 1980s local governments have become increasingly active as regulators of forest practices on private lands.[3] The purpose of this paper is to explore reasons for this increased level of activity and to propose an explanation for variation in the nature of regulations that county governments have enacted.

Toward those ends, this paper first describes recent developments in local and state regulation in several regions of the country annd then presents a conceptual framework that relates community characteristics, patterns of political participation, and the content of local forest practice regulations. Data on local governments in Oregon and California are then examined in order to evaluate the explanation developed in the previous section. The paper concludes with a discussion of how changing resource values have motivated political changes in forest-based communities.

THE LAST FIFTEEN YEARS OF
FOREST PRACTICE LEGISLATION

During the 1930s and 1940s fifteen states enacted legislation that required or encouraged owners of forest land to provide for reforestation after timber harvests. State governments' forest practice policies changed very little until the 1970s. The renewed interest in forest practice regulation at that time was closely tied to the burgeoning environmental movement. During the late sixties and early seventies environmentalists fought for air and water pollution control and land use planning legislation. By the late 1960s it was becoming apparent to some in the wood products sector that environmental protection policies eventually would affect private forest lands.

During the late 1960s and early 1970s members of the wood products sector in several western states initiated consideration of new forest practice legislation (Salazar, 1985). They sought legislation that would authorize a state board of forestry or a forestry agency to promulgate and enforce forest practice rules. The forest practice statutes adopted during the 1970s went beyond those of the 1930s and 1940s. Whereas, the earlier laws were concerned almost exclusively with reforestation, the 1970s statutes incorporated provisions regarding water quality, fisheries, wildlife habitat, air quality, recreation, and scenic quality in addition to reforestation.

While western states were adopting legislation specifically for the purpose of regulating forest practices, such regulation in the eastern states occurred primarily as an indirect result of other types of legislation. Forest practices in Maine were regulated through a land use planning law. A wetlands protection law regulated some forest practices in Massachusetts. In other eastern states water pollution control and stream protection legislation resulted in regulation of some forest practices. While the regulatory strategies employed differed in the different regions of the country, the states were the primary source of regulation through the mid-1970s.

Local governments in California created the major exception to that generalization. The California Board of Forestry contended with proposals for county logging ordinances throughout the 1950s (Arvola, 1976). In 1957 the Board prevailed upon the legislature to amend the forest practice act so that it would preempt local governments. There was no further local action until 1969. During that year, San Mateo County denied Bayside Timber Company logging and roadbuilding permits for a planned timber harvest.[4] Bayside appealed the denial arguing that the California Forest Practice Act preempted county authority. The state courts upheld the county permit system and ruled that the state law was unconstitutional because it delegated rulemaking authority to individuals with a pecuniary interest in logging (Lundmark, 1975). The turmoil surrounding forest practices set the stage for new state legislation in 1973. The Z'berg-Nejedly Forest Practice Act explicitly permitted counties to adopt rules "stricter than" those promulgated by the state (State of California, 1973:1615).

Six California counties exercised their authority to adopt separate rules (DeMaria, 1983). Loggers and owners of forest lands perceived some of the county rules as unduly restrictive and costly. They proposed an amendment to the forest practice act that would eliminate county authority to adopt separate rules. In 1982 the state legislature enacted this amendment, including a provision that allowed each county to petition the Board of Forestry to promulgate special rules for that county. Through this petitioning process as well as through the courts, county governments in California continue to battle with the state Board of Forestry over forest practice regulation.

Outside of California, local governments were generally inactive with respect to forest practices until the late 1970s. Since that time, local governments throughout New Jersey, New York, and Connecticut have adopted logging ordinances. Some local governments in Pennsylvania and Georgia also have enacted such ordinances. Local governments in Florida and Hawaii regulate forest practices through zoning ordinances. Most of these ordinances have been motivated by concerns about water quality, wildlife habitat, noise, log hauling on public roads, and scenic values.

The wood products sectors in different states have adopted different strategies to deal with local regulation. In Connecticut, members of the forestry community have proposed state forest practice legislation in order to provide more uniform and acceptable operating conditions (Cubbage and Siegel, 1985). Members of the wood products sector in Massachusetts successfully pursued a state forest practice law in 1982. One purpose of their effort was to stop the proliferation of local logging rules. Members of the forestry community in Georgia, New York, New Jersey, and Pennsylvania have chosen to work with local governments rather than to seek state legislation.

The behavior of local governments and of interested citizens and groups has been influenced by the states' roles in forest practice regulation. In the eastern states, regulation of forest practices is generally a wide-open policy field. Very few eastern states have state legislation that restricts local authority in this arena. However, even in the West where state forest practice laws have preempted the field, local governments are no longer silent. As noted earlier, some California counties continue to press for local forest practice rules. In Oregon, a state law requiring counties to protect natural resources through zoning created openings for local regulation of forest practices.

Thus, throughout the timber-growing regions of this country local governments have sought increased control over the practice of forestry on private land. Local governments in the Northeast have been most active; but local regulation appears to be of increasing importance even in the South and in the West. How can we account for the growth of local forest practice regulations as well as for the inter- and intra-regional variation in the nature of such regulations?

THE POLITICS OF LOCAL FOREST PRACTICE REGULATION IN A FEDERAL SYSTEM

In order to predict or explain the behavior of local governments, one must account for the structural context in which they make policy. County commissioners and city council members face opportunities and constraints presented by the courts, by federal and state policies, and by the policies of other local governments. Internal demands are not the sole determinants of local public policies. Thus, an analyst concerned with explaining the occurrence of local forest practice regulation should examine external as well as internal factors.

Cubbage and Siegel (1985) argued that the courts will influence the future role of local governments with respect to the regulation of forest practices. They contended that the results of legal challenges of western states' preemption of regulatory authority will also influence the state/local distribution of authority in the East. They argued that if the courts in the western states uphold the states' preemption of forest practice regulation, then members of the wood products sectors in the eastern states may seek state legislation in order to stop local regulation. But if the courts increase the scope of local authority, there will be no reason for the forestry communities in other regions to seek state forest practice legislation.

Recognizing that courts and state legislatures may limit the scope of local authority, what other factors influence how local jurisdictions will use that authority? To address this question, I have used Peterson's (1981) analysis of urban politics. Peterson argued that the kinds of policies cities can undertake are limited by competition from other cities. He observed that cities are composed of individuals and groups with a variety of often conflicting interests. However, Peterson argued that one objective unites residents of a city and constitutes the city's interest. This objective is the protection and improvement of the city's "economic position" (p. 20).

A city's economic position is a function of its attractiveness as a locale for economic activity. Cities use their land base and infrastructure to attract capital and a high quality labor force. Cities are considerably more constrained in these efforts than are nations. Whereas nations exert at least partial control over labor and capital migration, cities must rely on the creation of positive incentives. Thus, cities attract capital by minimizing taxes; providing low cost, high quality public goods (infrastructure); and minimizing costs imposed by regulation. Cities attract highly skilled labor by providing public goods (e.g., schools, parks, protection) and by regulating land use to ensure desirable residential settings. By providing these resources, local governments increase the likelihood that productive enterprises will locate (or remain) there.

Improving the economic position of a local jurisdiction increases the prosperity of residents as well as the revenue base for the jurisdiction. Thus, Peterson (1981) argued that local officials will pursue the locality's economic interests by actively pursuing policies that advance the city's economic position, opposing policies that threaten that position, and not taking the initiative on neutral policies.

Peterson (1981) used this analysis to define three types of policies: developmental, redistributive, and allocational. *Developmental* policies enhance the economic position of cities. They increase employment opportunities, land values, and local government revenues. For the average taxpayer, the marginal benefit of developmental policies will be greater than the marginal cost. Such policies often include expansion of the transportation system, development of industrial parks, and construction of athletic facilities. *Redistributive* policies make the city a more costly place to live for the average taxpayer. While Peterson focused on redistributive policies designed to benefit low income residents, some pollution control regulations also fit this category. Such policies increase the costs of doing business and reduce the city's competitiveness in attracting and holding business activity.[5] *Allocational* policies are those with ambiguous effects on the local economy. They provide benefits to particular groups of residents such as neighborhoods. For the average taxpayer, the net benefit of any allocational policy is zero or slightly negative. Siting decisions for public facilities are typical of allocational policies.

Each of the three types of policies is associated with a unique kind of politics. Peterson (1981) characterized developmental policy making as a closed process dominated by local business and professional elites. The most salient attribute of redistributive policy making at the local level is its absence. Redistributive policies pose a threat to the fiscal base of local jurisdictions. The fact that these policies are inimical to the fundamental interests of local governments makes it difficult for redistributive policy proposals to reach local government agendas, much less be adopted and implemented. Peterson argued that the need for redistribution will not increase the likelihood of local adoption of these policies. Rather, the locality's capacity to redistribute will be determinative. Political activity associated with allocational policies will involve interest group conflict, bargaining, and compromise.

How can we use Peterson's framework to analyze forest practice regulation? The first step is to place forest practice regulation into one of the categories. To do this, we must ask how regulation affects the economic position of the jurisdiction. Regulation often increases the costs of harvesting timber. If timber production is an important sector of a local economy, then increasing production costs threatens the economic position of the jurisdiction. This is contrary to the interests of the locality. Thus, in areas where timber production is economically important, forest practice regulation would best fit Peterson's redistributive category.

However, what if the local economy is heavily dependent on tourism? Regulation might protect scenic resources and thus contribute to the local tourism sector. In this case, forest practice regulation could be considered a developmental policy. In suburban communities, regulation might also be considered a developmental policy. Such communities' economic positions are dependent on residential rather than business attractions. Residential quality is related to amenity values of forest environments. Unregulated logging may diminish or even destroy these values.

Finally, what if forest resources constitute a minor component of the local economy? Then forest practice regulation fits the allocational category. Thus, how we classify forest practice regulation depends on the role of forest resources in the local economy (Table 1). I have described four types of localities, each corresponding to three policy classifications for forest practice regulation. For *timber* counties, regulation is a redistributive policy; for *tourist* and *suburban* counties, regulation may be a developmental policy; and for *urban* counties that are not dependent on forest resources, forest practice regulation is an allocational policy. The relative economic importance of various forest resources determines the nature of local policies regarding forest practices on private lands.

Table 1 shows predictions of each type of county's policy with regard to forest practices. We expect that timber counties will not adopt regulations. Furthermore, regulatory proposals will seldom reach the legislative agendas of timber counties. In tourist and suburban counties forest practice regulations may serve a developmental function and thus are likely to be enacted. We should expect little controversy to be associated with adoption of regulations in these two types of

Table 1. Forest Practice Regulation in Four Types of Counties

County Type	Role of Forest Resources	Policy Type	Adoption of Forest Practice Regulations
Timber	economy dependent on wood production	Redistributive	NO
Tourism	economy dependent on scenic and recreational values of forest land	Developmental	YES (focused on practices that affect scenic values)
Suburban	tax base and local business dependent on forest values that support residential quality of life	Developmental	YES (focused on scenery, noise, soil erosion, and road safety)
Urban	economy not dependent on forest resources	Allocational	AMBIGUOUS

counties. As Table 1 indicates, regulations in tourism and suburban counties should be designed to protect particular forest values. Finally, we cannot make unambiguous predictions with regard to forest practice regulation in urban counties. Forest practice policies in these counties are likely to emerge from bargaining among interest groups. Prediction of policy outcomes would require assessment of the relative political resources of interest groups in particular counties.

LOCAL REGULATION OF FOREST PRACTICES IN OREGON AND CALIFORNIA

Local regulation of forest practices has been an issue in both Oregon and California. These states were studied because of the political importance of the issue and the availability of information about local regulations. The author conducted interviews with state and local public officials and with representatives of interest groups in Oregon in early 1986. The interviews and county planning documents provided data for Oregon counties. Data for California were derived from unpublished papers and from the county rules published by the California Department of Forestry (1986).

The fourteen counties in the two states were selected because regulation has been on the policy agenda in all of these counties. By classifying each county as a timber, tourism, suburban, or urban county, we can use Table 1 to predict whether or not regulations would actually be adopted in the county. Data for classifying the counties were derived from the USDA Forest Service, forest survey reports, and from U.S. Bureau of the Census reports.

Table 2 displays data used to classify timber counties. Counties were classified as timber counties if at least 10 percent of 1980 total employment was in the wood products sector. Six of the seven Oregon counties and three of the seven California counties were classified as timber counties.

Table 2. Classification of Timber Counties*

State/ County	CFL/[1] Total Area	Private CFL/[1] Total CFL	1980[2] Wood Prod/ Wood Empl	County Type
Oregon				
Clatsop	.81	.67	.12	Timber
Douglas	.82	.41	.32	Timber
Hood River	.67	.21	.11	Timber
Klamath	.64	.42	.28	Timber
Lincoln	.88	.62	.21	Timber
Multnomah	.41	.42	.01	——
Tillamook	.85	.33	.24	Timber
California				
Marin	.02	1.00	.00	——
Mendocino	.58	.84	.19	Timber
Monterey	.03	.43	.00	——
San Mateo	.15	.98	.00	——
Santa Clara	.02	.86	.00	——
Santa Cruz	.48	.96	.22	Timber
Trinity	.63	.32	.32	Timber

*Commercial Forest Land acreage for Oregon is based on 1977 data; for California, 1968, 1970, 1973, and 1975 data.
Sources: [1] Bassett and Choate (1974); Bolsinger (1976, 1980); Gedney (1983); Oswald (1972); [2] U.S. Bureau of the Census (1982a).

Table 3 displays data used to classify urban and suburban counties. Only counties that were part of standard metropolitan statistical areas (SMSA) were classified as either urban or suburban. An additional requirement for urban counties was that the proportion of the local labor force employed locally exceed 80 percent. Only two counties were classified as urban. The remainder of SMSA counties were classified as suburban. It was assumed that for suburban counties a large proportion of residents would be employed outside of the county.

Evaluation of the importance of tourism in the local economy was the difficult step in the classification process. For Oregon, planning documents and interviews were used to identify two tourism counties. A variety of published and unpublished material was used to identify tourism counties in California. With the exception of Hood River County in Oregon, all of the tourism counties are coastal. Hood

Table 3. Classification of Urban and Suburban Counties

State/ County	1980[1] Part of SMSA	1980 Empl/[2] Labor Force	Urban or Suburban
Oregon			
Clatsop	No	.52	——
Douglas	No	.63	——
Hood River	No	.57	——
Klamath	No	.58	——
Lincoln	No	.56	——
Multnomah	Portland	1.03	Urban
Tillamook	No	.48	——
California			
Marin	SF-Oakl.	.48	Suburban
Mendocino	No	.57	——
Monterey	Salinas	.45	Suburban
San Mateo	SF-Oakl.	.71	Suburban
Santa Clara	San Jose	.88	Urban
Santa Cruz	Santa Cruz	.50	Suburban
Trinity	No	.26	——

Sources: [1] U.S. Bureau of the Census (1982b); [2] U.S. Bureau of the Census (1982a).

River County includes the Columbia River Gorge, which is a popular area for a variety of outdoor recreational pursuits.

Table 4 displays the final classification of each county along with predictions about the adoption of forest practice regulations. No predictions are displayed for urban counties or for counties dependent on both timber and tourism.

The remaining step in the analysis is to examine regulatory policies in each of the fourteen counties. But first, I will describe relevant state policies that provide the context for local regulation. Oregon has a state forest practices act that authorizes the state Board of Forestry to promulgate forest practice rules. Oregon also has a state land use planning law that requires counties to adopt zoning ordinances in order to protect natural resources. All of the Oregon counties examined in this paper have considered regulating private forestry as part of the required planning process.[6]

The California Forest Practices Act allows counties to request that the Board of Forestry promulgate special county rules. The Board must adopt and enforce requested local rules if they are consistent with the forest practice act and necessary to protect the county . As of the end of 1987, the Board has approved special rules for five counties (Marin, Monterey, San Mateo, Santa Clara, Santa Cruz). All of these counties were included in the study reported here. Two counties (Mendocino

Table 4. County Types and Predicted Policy Outcomes

State/County	County Type	Adoption of Regulations?
Oregon		
Clatsop	Timber	No
Douglas	Timber	No
Hood River	Timber/Tourist	Ambiguous
Klamath	Timber	No
Lincoln	Timber/Tourist	Ambiguous
Multnomah	Urban	Ambiguous
Tillamook	Timber	No
California		
Marin	Suburban	Yes
Mendocino	Timber/Tourist	Ambiguous
Monterey	Suburban/Tourist	Yes
San Mateo	Suburban	Yes
Santa Clara	Urban	Ambiguous
Santa Cruz	Suburban/Tourist	Yes
Trinity	Timber	No

and Trinity) that adopted herbicide restrictions by initiative during the late 1970s also were included.

Table 5 displays the results of the empirical analysis and evaluates the consistency of policy outcomes with the predictions in Table 4. The second column in Table 5 presents the stage in the policy-making process that the issue reached. Four stages were used: (1) the issue reached the public policy *agenda*; (2) a specific *proposal* was developed; (3) a law was *adopted*; and (4) a law was *implemented*.

The third column describes issues, proposals, or ordinances. While scenery and wildlife habitat are consistently important in the Oregon counties, use of public roads, noise, and watershed protection are the major issues in the California counties. This finding is consistent with the different resource values that are economically important in the two states (Tables 1 and 4). The Oregon counties in the study are dependent on timber and *tourism*; the California counties are also concerned about residential habitat because many are *suburban*.

The fourth column in Table 5 indicates whether actual policy outcomes were consistent with predictions from Table 4. Two patterns emerge from an examination of this column. First, only two counties had policy outcomes that were inconsistent with predictions. Klamath County, Oregon, adopted a zoning ordinance to protect bald eagle nest sites. Merchants in the county sponsor an annual bald eagle festival, and the zoning ordinance protects the resource on which this financially lucrative festival is based.[7]

Table 5. Policy Outcomes in the Counties

State/ County	Stage in Policy Process	Nature of Ordinance or Proposal	Consistent with Prediction?
Oregon			
Clatsop	proposal	-restrict herbicide use in municipal watershed	YES
Douglas	proposal	-restrict harvest methods along scenic corridor	YES
Hood River	implemented	-restrict harvest methods along scenic corridor	no prediction
Klamath	adopted	-protect bald eagle nest sites	NO
Lincoln	agenda	-protect scenic values, wetlands, nesting areas	no prediction
Multnomah	adopted	-restrict harvest methods along scenic corridor	no prediction
Tillamook	agenda	-protect wildlife habitat	YES
California			
Marin	implemented	-restrict use of public roads, noise, require scenic buffers, protect watersheds	YES
Mendocino	implemented	-prohibit aerial application of phenoxy herbicides	no prediction
Monterey	implemented	-restrict use of public roads, require scenic buffers, protect wildlife habitat	YES
San Mateo	implemented	-restrict use of public roads, noise	YES
Santa Clara	implemented	-restrict use of public roads, noise, require scenic buffers	no prediction
Santa Cruz	implemented	-restrict use of public roads, noise, watershed protection	YES
Trinity	implemented	-prohibit use of phenoxy herbicides	NO

Trinity County, California, accounted for the second inconsistent outcome. Both Trinity and Mendocino Counties enacted restrictions on herbicide use during the late 1970s. These restrictions were contrary to the interests of the timber economy in the two counties. However, marijuana cultivation is also an important economic sector in these counties and restrictions on herbicide use would clearly benefit this sector. Thus, even in the two counties with outcomes contrary to predictions, one could make a case that the policies enacted protected the counties' economic interests.

The second pattern that may be discerned from Table 5 is that all but one of the urban and timber/tourist counties enacted regulatory ordinances. The model did not yield a predicted policy outcome for these counties. The only prediction was that the political process would be characterized by interest group bargaining and that the outcome would reflect the relative political resources of opposing groups. Further research is necessary to test hypotheses regarding political processes in the counties.

In general, results of this study are consistent with Peterson's (1981) analysis of local politics. This study has not subjected Peterson's model to a systematic test. Such a test would require a larger and representative sample. Furthermore, a test should employ continuous measures rather than the types defined here. The purpose of the typology is to identify the types of independent variables that should be examined. Indicators of these variables could be measured and used to quantitatively explain variation in local forest practice policies. Some of those indicators have been used here to identify timber, suburban, and urban counties. Measurement of the tourism component of local economies remains problematic. While further research is necessary for a systematic test, the plausibility of Peterson's explanation has been demonstrated. The counties studied have generally acted to promote and protect their economic interests.

CONCLUSIONS

Perhaps the primary insight generated by the sociology of natural resources is that natural resources are socially defined. Furthermore, resource definitions change. The values of forest attributes change with tastes, wealth, and technology. The western Oregon and northern California counties examined in this paper illustrate the political/legal consequences of changing resource values. The economies of these counties have become relatively less dependent on the production of wood fiber and more reliant on the production of forest outputs related to tourism and residential habitat. Changes in the local economic role of forest outputs are reflected in the adoption of local ordinances that regulate forest practices on private lands.

Changes in resource values will also affect other areas of local politics. The results reported in this paper suggest that analysis of the relative economic importance of forest resources will yield insights useful for policy makers as well as for social scientists. Understanding the economic relationship between forests and adjacent human communities can help us to anticipate and guide local political decisions that will shape the legal context of the management of private forest lands in the future.

ACKNOWLEDGMENTS

The author would like to thank Stefan Ruchti, Robert G. Lee, Jeff Romm, and an anonymous reviewer for helpful comments.

NOTES

1. See especially Kaufman and Kaufman (1946) and Carroll and Lee (1989).

2. Schallau (1989) and Waggener (1977) discuss the conceptual bases for and policy implications of this field of research.

3. Some local governments in urban areas did regulate logging before this period. Two California counties adopted logging ordinances before the state enacted its first forest practice statue in 1945 (Arvola, 1976). Similarly, several New York towns adopted logging ordinances during the 1950s and 1960s (New York State Department of Environmental Conservation, 1985). However, the 1970s and 1980s have witnessed a notable increase in the numbers of local governments that have enacted such ordinances.

4. During the same year, Marin County and local governments in the Lake Tahoe Basin also considered proposals to regulate logging. See Arvola (1976) and Cox and Soper (1970).

5. Pollution control regulations may also increase the attractiveness of a city as a place to live. Peterson (1981) acknowledged that particular policies may include elements of more than one type. The net effect of a policy for the average taxpayer should determine how political decision making proceeds.

6. Since the mid-1970s there has been controversy regarding whether or not the forest practices act prohibits counties from using their land use planning authority to regulate forest practices. During 1987, the Oregon Supreme Court, the governor, and legislature were involved in resolution of the issue. The Oregon forest practices act now clearly preempts local authority to regulate forest practices.

7. While Klamath County did adopt zoning restrictions, the county relied on

the Oregon Department of Forestry for enforcement. The department declined to enforce the ordinance, arguing that the forest practices act prohibits counties from regulating private forestry.

REFERENCES

Arvola, T.F. 1976. *Regulation of Logging in California 1945-1975*. Sacramento, CA: State of California, The Resources Agency.

Bassett, P.M. and G.A. Choate. 1974. *Timber Resource Statistics for Oregon, January, 1973*. Portland, OR: USDA Forest Service, Resource Bulletin PNW-56.

Bolsinger, C.L. 1976. *Timber Resources of Northern California, 1970*. Portland, OR: USDA Forest Service, Resource Bulletin PNW-65.

———. 1980. *California Forests: Trends, Problems and Opportunities*. Portland, OR: USDA Forest Service, Resource Bulletin PNW-89.

California Department of Forestry. 1986. Special Treatment (Coastal) Rules and County Rules. Sacramento, CA: The Resources Agency.

Carroll, M.S. and R.G. Lee. 1989. "Adaptability of Northwestern Loggers to Labor Market Shifts." In R.G. Lee, W.R. Burch, and D.R. Field (eds.), *Community and Forestry: Continuities in the Sociology of Natural Resources*. Boulder, CO: Westview Press.

Clepper, H. 1971. *Professional Forestry in the United States*. Washington, DC: Resources for the Future.

Cox, A. and D. Soper. 1970. *Logging in Urban Counties*. Palo Alto, CA: Stanford University.

Cubbage, F. and W. Siegel. 1985. "Public Regulation of Private Forestry in the East." Paper presented at the Western Forest Economists' Meeting, Wemme, OR.

DeMaria, S.L. 1983. "The Legislative and Regulatory Environment for Forestry Enterprises in California." The S.J. Hall Memorial Lectureship in Industrial Forestry. University of California, Berkeley.

Gedney, D.R. 1983. *The Privately Owned Timber Resources of Western Oregon.* Portland, OR: USDA Forest Service, Resource Bulletin PNW-99.

Greeley, W. 1951. *Forests and Men.* Garden City, NY: Doubleday and Company.

Kaufman, H.F. and L.C. Kaufman. 1946. *Toward the Stabilization and Enrichment of a Forest Community.* Missoula MT: The University of Montana.

Lundmark, T. 1975. "Regulation of Private Logging in California." *Ecology Law Quarterly* 5(1):139-188.

New York State Department of Environmental Conservation. 1985. Town Ordinances Restricting Timber Harvest. (Unpublished data). Albany, NY.

Oswald, D.D. 1972. *Timber Resources of Mendocino and Sonoma Counties, California.* Portland, OR: USDA Forest Service, Resource Bulletin PNW-40.

Peterson, P.E. 1981. *City Limits.* Chicago: The University of Chicago Press.

Salazar, D.J. 1985. "Political Processes and Forest Practice Legislation." Ph.D. dissertation, University of Washington.

Schallau, C.H. 1989. "Community Stability: Issues, Institutions, and Instruments." In R.G. Lee, W.R. Burch and D.R. Field (eds.), *Community and Forestry: Continuities in the Sociology of Natural Resources.* Boulder, CO: Westview Press.

State of California. 1973. Statutes of California. Chapter 880. Sacramento.

U.S. Department of Commerce (Bureau of the Census). 1982a. County Business Patterns, 1980. Washington, DC: U.S. Government Printing Office.

———. 1982b. 1980 Census of the Population. Vol. 1, Characteristics of the Population. Washington, D.C.: U.S. Government Printing Office.

Waggener, T.R. 1977. "Community Stability as a Forest Management Objective." *Journal of Forestry* 75(11):710-714.

IV

Conclusions and Implications

18

Community Stability and Timber-Dependent Communities: Future Research

Gary E. Machlis
Jo Ellen Force
Department of Forest Resources
College of Forestry, Wildlife and Range Sciences
University of Idaho

Resource development and its impact upon community stability have long been of interest to rural sociologists. Most results have reflected Hansen's (1923) finding that employment declines are a driving factor (see Brown and Webb 1941; Kolb and Polson 1933; Landis 1933; Lively 1932; Zimmerman 1930). Timber-dependent communities were part of these early studies of rural communities (see Gibson 1944; Kaufman and Kaufman 1946).

Today, the relationship between the forest industry and community stability is of renewed importance. During recent years the migration of the timber industry to the southeastern United States and increasing Canadian lumber exports have had a substantial impact on traditional Pacific Northwest markets. Nearly 40 percent of the sawmills that have closed in the northern Rocky Mountain region during the past 20 years have done so since 1980 (Blasing 1986). This change in the timber industry has had many social and economic impacts upon local communities (Machlis 1981; Machlis and Ellis 1985), yet linkages between the forest industry and community stability are not well understood, and empirical evidence on this relationship is incomplete (Field and Burch 1988; Muth 1986).

Contemporary sociological literature, as Summers and Branch (1984:184) point out, has focused on boomtowns and "the rapid and massive introduction of economic activities that are often alien to the social and cultural organization of the host communities." Several reviews of this literature are available (see, for example, Detomasi and Gartrell 1984; Murdock and Leistritz 1979; Summers and Branch 1984); much of the current research concerns boomtowns associated with energy developments (see, for example, Bates 1978; Davenport and Davenport 1979; Freudenburg 1981; Gartrell et al. 1984; Krannich and Greider 1984). Yet, the engines of social change faced by timber-dependent communities may be, if not less dramatic, different from those driving the boomtown syndrome: timber-dependent towns may represent a variant on the motif of resource-dependent communities. A critique of how their analysis has been approached can enrich our understanding of rural communities in general. In addition, the broader question of how communities dependent on natural resources react to changes in their resource base has local and national policy implications and is central to issues of international development, rural development, and social change.

Literature on timber dependency and community stability has slowly emerged, and a few policy-related overviews exist (see, for example, O'Leary 1975; Schallau 1986; Zinn 1976). This paper reviews and evaluates the relevant literature and suggests potential avenues for future inquiry. The review is representative of the literature, rather than exhaustive, and the scope is generally limited to the United States (for a general bibliography on communities and natural resources, see Field et al. 1986).

ISSUES IN THE LITERATURE

Community studies have been directed around several key concerns that also confront researchers specifically interested in timber dependent communities. Our discussion is organized around the basic conceptual problem—coherent definition of critical variables. Three major concerns are raised: How is community defined? What is meant by "community stability"? And, how is timber dependency measured?

Issue 1. The definition of community has been inconsistent and atheoretical
Definitions of community are legion, each with consequences for operationalizing and measuring the concept. Wilkinson (1986) makes clear the futility of achieving a "supra-definition" of community and instead suggests three essential criteria for identifying community within a population: a territorial presence, a structural organization, and a set of shared actions. Where these converge, *community* is likely.

Kin, clan and class all share features of community: widely-held values, shared sentiments, interdependency, identity and so forth. Occupational groups are one of the primary institutional structures within which individuals may find attachments and meanings that engender a sense of community, and the literature includes numerous examples from resource-based occupations (Colfer and Colfer 1978; Muth 1985). Significantly, these definitions of community are neither mutually exclusive nor contradictory: communities of affiliation can coexist and even flourish within communities of place. What is crucial is that the social scientist clearly define, a priori, the community under study.

Researchers examining the relationship between forest activities and community stability have defined communities in a number of ways. In establishing the Lakeview Sustained Yield Management Unit, Beuter and Olson (1980) noted that the USDA Forest Service set specific boundaries by considering the area within a given radius from the county courthouse to be the community targeted for stabilization. Since many of the studies have been conducted by economists, the delineation of "economic regions" is common (Maki and Schweitzer 1973; Schallau et al. 1969).

Though many of the studies focus on towns, the unit of analysis is often the county, the level at which the data are often gathered. Presumably this is because of the difficulty in obtaining adequate data at the town level. The list of studies in Table 1 shows that counties are the most common unit of analysis and that some studies use data from a very wide geographical area. Jackson and Flowers (1983) found the study of a broad area to be justified because the timber supply for one community can come from any forest in an entire Forest Service Region.

Two general problems arise from the methods used to operationalize communities in the above studies. First, the results are difficult to compare. Timber flows are increasingly intercounty and even interregional. Effects from changes in timber supply or demand may differ depending on the area under consideration. For example, Dickerman and Butzer (1975) noted that a multiplier effect from forest activities can spread benefits throughout a region. In contrast, Kromm (1972) focused on a small town and found that many of the benefits of forest activities flowed out of the community. This finding suggests the second problem. When broad areas are examined, localized impacts may be masked, and inequities in the distribution of costs and benefits may not be detected.

Issue 2. The theoretical construct of community stability has remained unclear, and economic measures have dominated the literature

"Stability" is an elusive term whose meaning varies with academic discipline. In ecology, stability is conceptualized as a dynamic equilibrium; the actual variables of a system are in constant flux (Lewontin 1969; for a review, see Odum 1983; Van Voris et al. 1980). Stability has also been defined as the resilience of ecosystems in the face of external stress (Bayne 1975) or the ability of populations to accommodate change (Ricklefs 1973). Further, ecologists differentiate among dimensions of stability: two examples are *persistence* (the number of species in an ecosystem remains the same) and *constancy* (the size of a population remains the same [Lewin 1986]).

Table 1. Operational definitions of community used in recent forestry/community stability
studies

Author	Unit of Analysis
Beuter and Olson 1980	county
Byron 1978	city/town
Daniels and Daniels 1986	town
Darr and Fight 1974	county
Dickerman and Butzer 1975	region/county
Drielsma 1984	county
Flacco 1978	county
Jackson and Flowers 1983	Forest Service Region I
Kromm 1972	town
Machlis and Ellis 1985	county
Maki and Schweitzer 1973	economic regions
Netting and Elias 1980	town
Schallau and Polzin 1983	county
Schallau et al. 1969	economic regions (collections of counties)

In the social sciences, stability has often been treated as multidimensional.
Dessauer (1949), in his encyclopedic study of the topic, broadly defines stability
as "the continuity of the existing social and political conditions." He emphasizes
the relative aspects of stability:

> A state of stability is consequently characterized by the inter-
> play of two sets of conditions. On the one side social changes
> must not go beyond a certain limit, must not be too many or too
> fast or too radical. On the other, the minds of men must be able
> to bear those changes. . . . Social conditions are stable if the
> changes which are taking place do not frighten the affected.
> (Dessauer 1949:125)

Definitions of community stability are extremely varied. Burch and DeLuca
(1984) characterize a "stable" community as 1) having a diversity of functions, 2)
having well-defined personal roles, and 3) changing slowly enough to allow for
adaptation. Other sociologists have viewed community stability in terms of social
conflict (Gamson 1966), population change (Beale 1974; Krannich and Greider
1984; Richardson and Larson 1976), environmental perceptions (Kersey and
Machlis 1986), and structural change (Muth 1986; Muth and Lee 1985).

In the literature on forest-dependent communities, the term "community
stability" is used frequently, but is rarely rigorously defined (Byron 1978) and
often refers to maintaining the status quo (Schallau and Alston 1987). Waggener

(1977) noted that community stability can be conceptualized as constancy or as modulated change and growth. Kaufman (1953:117) conceptualized community stability as "orderly change rather than a fixed condition."

Echoing Kaufman, Porterfield (1978) suggests a dynamic definition—perturbations need not a priori reflect community instability. Following classical definitions of social stability, the USDA Forest Service (1982) defines community stability dynamically as "the rate of change with which people can cope without exceeding their capacity to deal with it." The difficulties with operationalizing these definitions are evident.

Muth (1986), in a study of southeastern Alaska, argues that community stability is best understood in terms of the stability of community institutional structure. He found a significant relationship between structural differentiation (the proportion of specialized institutions within the community) and several measures of what he calls "social pathology," such as mental health admissions and divorce. Muth cautions that methodologies for careful analysis of structural change are often difficult to apply in resource-dependent communities.

In general, indicators of economic stability dominate the research on stability and forest communities. Lönnstedt (1978:1), for example, in a study of Nordic countries states that

> Stability of communities means that all branches of industry in a district shall give a stable means of subsistence for the population.

Examples of the forest industry's response to several predictable fluctuations are general business cycles (as described by Schumpeter 1939), building cycles (Zivnuska 1952), and seasonal variations (Koroleff 1951). Since economic stability must be considered relative to a normatively chosen constant (Samuelson 1947), McKetta (1984) compared forest-industry sectors with other industries for the years 1970–1979. Using indices of price and employment, he found some sectors (logging and lumber) to be relatively unstable, others (such as pulp and paper) to be relatively stable.

The most frequently used indicators of stability are employment, income, and price levels (Beuter and Olson 1980; Hyde and Daniels 1986; Waggener 1977, 1980). Other measures include timber-company profits (Daniels and Daniels 1986), bank deposits and property valuations (Schallau 1980), and even the level of nonmarket goods and services (Power 1983). Like the sociologists, economists have also used population change as a measure (see, for example, Netting and Elias 1980).

Just as the choice of indicators has varied, so have the techniques used for measurement. Employment has most often been measured as the percentage of total employment in the wood-products industry (Hyde and Daniels 1986; Jackson and Flowers 1983; Waggener 1977). Byron (1978) measured the numbers of registered unemployed and vacancies each month for 10 major occupational groups. Income has generally been measured as the percentage of wage income from wood-products industries.

Several issues arise when researchers attempt to measure the stability of a community or region, particularly the fact that stability is often a relative assessment. For example, Dessauer (1949) and later Waggener (1977) noted that stability in one variable may mean instability in another. If federal supplies of timber are maintained at some historical level, prices will adjust. Burch (1977) observed that whereas isolated resource towns may have socially unstable conditions, the towns have served to isolate potentially disruptive groups from the larger society. Freden (1978) found that although employment in forest-products industries had dropped rapidly, for those who remained employed, conditions were actually more stable.

Issue 3. Like community stability, resource-dependency has predominantly been measured in economic terms

Researchers interested in studying community organization and response have often focused on "resource towns" (Chapple 1973; Roberge 1977). These are communities "dependent on a single industry or company engaged in resource extraction or processing activities" (Robinson, 1984:3). Often the dependency of a town is obvious, such as the case of Temesaming, Quebec, where nearly everyone in town, including the school teachers, was employed by Canadian International Paper (Roberge 1977).

In other cases, such dependency is less clear-cut, and operational definitions are required. Drielsma (1984) developed a variety of indices to measure community specialization in agricture, tourism, mining, and forestry. In their study of rural agricultural communities, Brunner et al. (1927) define agriculture- dependent communities as those having a population between 250 and 2,500, located in a strictly agricultural area, and mainly providing services for local farmers. In a similar sense, Sanders and Lewis (1976) characterize a rural community as a "primacy economy".

Studies of communities in forested regions have measured timber dependency in numerous ways (Beuter and Schallau 1978). Economic measures predominate. Several researchers have measured dependency as the percentage of excess employment in forest industries (Beuter and Olson 1980; Flacco 1978; Maki and Schweitzer 1973; Schallau et al. 1969). Excess employment is determined by first assuming that any industry with a percentage of total employment above the national average (for that industry) is part of the community's economic export base. Employment in these industries is excess employment; dependency is the portion of total excess employment attributed to the timber industry.

Darr and Fight (1974) measured timber dependency as the percentage of industry sales directly and indirectly dependent on demand for products from eight forest-oriented sectors. Others have measured dependency as the percentage of total income earnings (Maki et al. 1985; Schallau 1986; Schallau and Polzin 1983). Drielsma (1984) produced an innovative measure of industrial specialization by computing an index based on per capita harvest of timber, portion of county forested, and area in forest per capita.

Dependency has also been defined in terms of quality of life or social meaning. For example, community residents may be dependent on a forested area for "clean air and water, unspoiled recreational opportunities, security from violence and crime" (Power 1983). Burch (1977) noted that societies may also depend on forests as places of social meaning, such as for escape, sanctuary, or spiritual rejuvenation. Generally though, timber dependency has been measured in economic terms.

The literature on timber dependency and community stability is diverse; it involves several disciplines, little explicit theory, and a range of methodological strategies. Nevertheless, some generalizations can be made regarding methodological problems and theoretical possibilities.

METHODOLOGICAL PROBLEMS

1). *The definition of community* has often been determined by available data rather than a theoretical rationale; this has weakened the comparability of studies and testing of hypotheses. It is difficult to compare, for example, studies that use town or city and economic regions as operational definitions of community. Further, combining geographic- and affiliation-based definitions has not been widely attempted.

2). Economic measures of *community stability* have dominated the forest-related literature. Sociocultural measures of stability have not been used, nor have authors focused on instability and the social impacts of change, except in the extreme cases of boom towns and mill closures.

A long tradition of research and a large literature exist on the use of social indicators (for a review, see Burch and DeLuca 1984; Rossi and Gilmartin 1980), and these efforts provide direction for the measurement of community stability. A historical example is Odum's (1936) exhaustive list of indicators for development in the American South; a contemporary example is the discussion by Andrews et al. (1979) of indicators of community cohesion regarding water development in the West.

3). Economic conceptualizations of *timber dependency* dominate the literature; sociological measures have not been used; noneconomic dependencies have not been widely considered.

The issue of what constitutes resource dependency is important for both methodological and theoretical reasons. Treating dependency as unidimensional (i.e., excess employment) oversimplifies the relationship between local cultures and resources; woodsworking has lifestyle as well as economic implications. The excess employment measure also minimizes income transfers, indirect employment, shadow (unpaid) labor, and changes in productivity per worker.

Methodologically, one cannot define timber dependency as excess employment in the timber industry, measure community stability as changes in employment, and hope to find much variation in the relationship between variables—an important question has been defined away. For example, measures of income may inaccurately reflect the importance of timber industries in relation to other industries, if wage scales are not similar. Most of the studies used statistics of the wood-products industry and did not differentiate between primary extraction activities and secondary processing. These two types of forest industry may have different impacts on community characteristics and economic stability (Drielsma 1984). Income also may not reflect the number and proportion of people with jobs, and such variables may have implications for (1) welfare requirements, (2) individual and collective self-esteem, and (3) equity issues. Finally, economic measures may not assess dependency for quality of life or social meaning.

A short-term perspective minimizes the opportunities to identify cycles of social stability if they exist. It may also lead to an overestimation of local versus global effects: recessions, depressions, and world wars may be imprudently omitted from the analysis.

THEORETICAL POSSIBILITIES

1. Definition of timber communities will be most robust when they encompass those major elements of community described by Wilkinson (1986). As Muth (1985) and others point out, the importance of communities of affiliation cannot be ignored without consequences. Such communities, nested within communities of place, may react differentially to changes in resource flows. One occupational group may be dramatically destabilized while others may exhibit resiliency; the relationships that are subsequently altered may reflect instability at a different level of social organization. We suggest, as others have, that a hierarchical conception of community is worth exploring—a useful analogy is the hierarchical approach to ecosystems suggested by ecologists O'Neill et al. (1986). For example, data could be collected for each community of affiliation *and* aggregated at town or county levels.

2. Community stability is a form of dynamic equilibrium, and can best be discerned relative to specific situations. Since the definition of stability is a

judgment placed upon rates of social change, the choice of criteria should be clearly grounded in theory.

One approach is to treat the number of institutional types as a measure of persistence, the number of institutions of each type as a measure of constancy, and the relationship between the two relative to a normative standard as a measure of stability. The standard could be similar extractive sectors (i.e., ratios of persistence to constancy in mining- or agriculture-dependent communities) or to a regional, if not national, norm. Communities having divergent rates of institutional persistence and/or constancy would be characterized as unstable.

A second approach is to operationalize definitions that stress the resiliency (i.e., the ability to cope with the change) of timber-dependent communities. This requires careful study of community perceptions (both social psychology and ethnography are useful to such work), but "threshholds of coping" might be discovered. The ability of a timber-dependent community to adjust to change would be considered as a nonlinear step function. As threshholds are reached and then exceeded, communities experience lower levels of stability.

CONCLUSION: AN AGENDA FOR RESEARCH

The above concerns represent perils and opportunities in the study of timber-dependent communities. An important challenge is to add to our sociological understanding of rural communities in transition. Resource dependency is a general environmental condition; its study casts a wide net on social phenomena. We believe a necessary strategy is to carefully examine the specific role of resource use as the engine of change that impacts community stability through its effects upon social systems.

First, the *kind* of resource dependency is likely to have significant impacts, and hence comparative studies of timber, mining, fishing, tourism and farming communities are needed. Will dependence upon mining (with its lack of renewable stock and its centralized technology) be expressed differently than timber dependency? And if so, how will that impact community stability? And just as we have suggested that different forest industries may have variant influences on local communities, tourism-dependent towns and regions may respond differently to destination-resort versus national-park-gateway forms of the industry. Again, comparative studies are appropriate.

Second, how does the *structure* of a particular resource industry influence community stability? What happens when outside experts gain control? The relationship between local and external interests can be expressed in terms of insularity and power; conflict and cooptation are likely consequences. Studies of such histories in timber-dependent communities will contribute to a major concern of rural sociology.

Third, the rate of change in timber-dependent communities may be significantly slower than in the "boomtown" context, and the influence of different *rates* of social change merits examination. If jobs, families, shops, churches, and other institutions "turn over" at slower levels, how do communities respond? What rates of system change will be debilitating, robust, or of little consequence? Timber-dependent communities represent important natural laboratories for answering such questions.

Fourth, the *scale* of change in timber-dependent communities may often be smaller than in energy-related locales. Large projects such as coal-fired power plants may inundate small communities with a population of transient workers, and the boom and bust cycle of construction is often severe. Change in timber-dependent communities may be of smaller and subtler scale, though certainly mill closures and land withdrawals may have impacts intensely felt. Are different forest processing technologies substitutes for one another at the community level? If only a portion of a timber town's human resources (sharing networks, churches, banks) are pressured or removed, can other resources be found? There is value in studying the small-scale adjustments that are the more typical phenomena of timber-dependent communities.

Finally, the literature has most often focused on communities dependent upon a single resource: the fishing village, tourist resort, timber town, farming community and so forth. Yet timber-dependent communities tend to be found in multi-use environments (such as Forest Service lands), and hence many such communities rely on *several* simultaneous resource bases. While this is clearly a methodological complication, the analysis of communities involved in a matrix of resource systems offers special insights. For example, will dependency upon a mix of resources have an amplifying or dampening effect upon social system change? Which mix of resource dependencies leads to a vulnerability to external control and which to insularity? Sociological theory abounds to deal with these questions, and our preferences seem less important than the need for a series of studies from different theoretical perspectives. We do argue that answering such questions is likely to be fruitful, surprising, sometimes counterintuitive. The implications for rural development are potentially significant, and the results can surely add to our understanding of rural life.

ACKNOWLEDGEMENTS

Reprinted from *Rural Sociology* 53(2), 1988, pp. 220-234. The editors thank the Rural Sociological Society for permission to reprint this article.

REFERENCES

Andrews, W. H., G. E. Madsen, and C. W. Hardin. 1979. "Testing Social Indicators in the Techcom Model for Water Development." Logan, UT: Utah State University. ISSR Research Monograph 8.

Bates, E. V. 1978 "The Impact of Energy Boom-Town Growth on Rural Areas." *Social Casework* 59:74-83.

Bayne, B. L. 1975. "Aspects of Physiological Condition in *Mytilus Edulis* L. with Respect to the Effects of Oxygen Tension and Salinity." pp. 213-38 In *Proceedings of the Ninth European Marine Biology Symposium*, October 2-8, 1974, Oban, Scotland. Aberdeen, Scotland: Aberdeen University Press.

Beale, C. L. 1974. "Quantitative Dimensions of Decline and Stability among Rural Communities." pp. 3-21 In L. R. Whiting (ed.), *Communities Left Behind: Alternatives for Development*. Ames, IA: Iowa State University Press.

Beuter, J. H. and D. C. Olson. 1980. "Lakeview Federal Sustained Yield Unit, Fremont National Forest: A Review 1974-1979." Corvallis, OR: Oregon State University, Department of Forest Management.

Beuter, J. H. and C. H. Schallau. 1978. "Forests in Transition: Relationship to Economic and Social Stability." Paper presented at Eighth World Forestry Congress, Jakarta, Indonesia.

Blasing, L. B. 1984. "Summary Report Sawmill Closures." Memorandum to Inland Forest Resource Council Members. January 28, 1986.

Brown, M. and J. N. Webb (eds.). 1941. *Seven Stranded Coal Towns*. Washington, DC: U.S. Government Printing Office, Works Projects Administration, Federal Works Agency, Research Monograph 23:188.

Brunner, E. D., G. S. Hughes, and M. Patten. 1927. *American Agricultural Villages*. New York: George H. Doran Co.

Burch, W. R. 1977. "Social Aspects of Forest Research Policy." pp. 329-82 In M. Clawson (ed.), *Research in Forest Economics and Forest Policy*. Washington, D.C.: Resources for the Future, Research Paper R-3.

Burch, W. R. and D. R. DeLuca (eds.). 1984. *Measuring the Social Impact of Natural Resource Policies*. Albuquerque, NM: University of New Mexico Press.

Byron, R. N. 1978. "Community Stability and Forest Policy in British Columbia." *Canadian Journal of Forest Research* 8:61-6.

Chapple, D. L. 1973. "Small Forest Communities." pp. 125-34 In K. W. Thomson and A.D. Trlin (eds.), *Contemporary New Zealand: Essays on the Human Resource, Urban Growth and Problems of Society.* Wellington, New Zealand: Hicks Smith and Sons, Ltd.

Colfer, C. P. and A. M. Colfer. 1978. "Inside Bushler Bay: Lifeways in Counterpoint." *Rural Sociology* 43(2):204-20.

Daniels, S. E. and B. J. Daniels. 1986. "The Impact of Below-Cost Sales on Community Stability." Western Wildlands 12(1):26-30.

Darr, D. R. and R. D. Fight. 1974. *Douglas County, Oregon: Potential Economic Impacts of a Changing Timber Resource Base.* Portland, OR: USDA Forest Service, Pacific Northwest Forest and Range Experiment Station Research Paper PNW-179.

Davenport, J. A. and J. Davenport III (eds.). 1974. *Boom Towns and Human Services.* Laramie, WY: University of Wyoming.

Dessauer, F. E. 1949. *Stability.* New York: MacMillan Company.

Detomasi, D. D. and J. W. Gartrell. 1984. *Resource Communities: A Decade of Disruption.* Boulder, CO: Westview Press.

Dickerman, A. R. and S. Butzer. 1974. "The Potential of Timber Management to Affect Regional Growth and Stability." *Journal of Forestry* 73(5):268-69.

Drielsma, J. H. 1984. "The Influence of Forest-based Industries on Rural Communities." Ph.D. dissertation, Yale University, New Haven, CT.

Field, D. R. and W. R. Burch, Jr. 1988. *Rural Sociology and the Environment.* New York: Greenwood Press.

Field, D. R., D. Hospodarsky, and R. S. Converse. 1986. "Rural Communities and Natural Resources: A Working Bibliography." Corvallis, OR: Oregon State University, Cooperative Park Studies Unit, College of Forestry.

Flacco, P. R. 1978. "Projected Income and Employment Impacts of a Decline in the Timber Resource Base of a Highly Timber-Dependent Economy." Master's thesis, Oregon State University, Corvallis, OR.

Freden, E. 1978. "The Interaction Between Stability in Forestry and the Stability of Communities in Northern Sweden." Paper presented at the Eighth World Forestry Congress, Jakarta, Indonesia.

Freudenburg, W. R. 1981. "Women and Men in an Energy Boomtown: Adjustment, Alienation, and Adaptation." *Rural Sociology* 46(2):320-344.

Gamson, W. A. 1966. "Rancorous Conflict in Community Politics." *American Sociological Review* 31(1):71-81.

Gartrell, J. W., H. Krahn, and T. Trytten. 1984. "Boom Towns: The Social Consequences of Rapid Growth." pp. 85-100 In D. D. Detomasi and J. W. Gartrell (eds.), *Resource Communities: A Decade of Disruption*. Boulder, CO: Westview Press.

Gibson, D. C. 1944. *Socioeconomic Evolution in Timbered Area in Northern Michigan: A Case Study of Sheboygon, Michigan, 1890-1940*. East Lansing, MI: Michigan State College Agricultural Experiment Station Technical Bulletin No. 193.

Hansen, T. A. 1923. *Second Growth on Cut-over Lands in St. Louis County*. St. Paul, MN: University of Minnesota Agricultural Experiment Station Bulletin No. 203.

Hyde, W. F. and S. E. Daniels. 1984. "Below-Cost Timber Sales and Community Stability." Paper presented at the Conference on Below-Cost Timber Sales, Spokane, WA.

Jackson, D. H. and P. J. Flowers. 1983. "The National Forests and Stabilization: A Look at the Factual Record." *Western Wildlands* 8(4):20-27.

Kaufman, H. F. 1953. "Sociology in Forestry." pp. 113-19 In W. A. Duerr and H. J. Vaux (eds.), *Research in the Economics of Forestry*. Washington, DC: Charles Lathrop Pack Forestry Foundation.

Kaufman, H. F. and L. C. Kaufman. 1946. *Toward the Stabilization and Enrichment of a Forest Community: The Montana Study*. Missoula, MT: University of Montana.

Kersey, B. and G. E. Machlis. 1986. "Perceptions of Forest Stability in a Canadian Village." Paper presented at First National Symposium on Social Science in Resource Management, Corvallis, OR.

Kolb, J. H. and R. A. Polson. 1933. *Trends in Town-Country Relations*. Madison, WI: University of Wisconsin Agricultural Experiment Station Bulletin No. 117.

Koroleff, A. M. 1951. *Stability as a Factor in Efficient Forest Management*. Montreal, Canada: Pulp and Paper Research Institute of Canada.

Krannich, R. S. and T. Greider. 1984. "Personal Well-Being in Rapid Growth and Stable Communities: Multiple Indicators and Contrasting Results." *Rural Sociology* 49(4):541-52.

Kromm, D. E. 1972. "Limitations on the Role of Forestry in Regional Economic Development." *Journal of Forestry* 70:630-33.

Landis, P. H. 1933. *The Growth and Decline of South Dakota Trade Centers 1901-1933*. Brookings, SD: South Dakota State University Agricultural Experiment Station Bulletin No. 279.

Lewin, R. 1986. In "Ecology, Change Brings Stability." *Science* 234 (November):1071-73.

Lewontin, R. C. 1969. "The Meaning of Stability." pp. 13-24 in *Diversity and Stability in Ecological Systems*, Brookhaven Symposia in Biology, #22, New Haven, CT: Brookhaven National Laboratory.

Lively, C. E. 1932. *Growth and Decline of Farm Trade Centers in Minnesota 1905-1930*. St. Paul, MN: University of Minnesota Agricultural Experiment Station Bulletin No. 187.

Lönnstedt, L. 1978. "The Interaction Between Stability in Forestry and Stability of Communities in Nordic Countries." Paper presented at Eighth World Forestry Congress, Jakarta, Indonesia.

Machlis, G. E. 1981. "The Social Impact on Communities of Resource-Based Boom and Decline." Paper presented at Governor's Economic Outlook Conference, Boise, ID.

Machlis, G. E. and D. J. Ellis. 1985. "The Social Impacts of the Timber Industry Downturn: Opinions of Community Leaders in Clearwater County." Moscow, ID: University of Idaho, College of Forestry, Wildlife and Range Sciences Report.

Maki, W. R. and D. L. Schweitzer. 1973. *Importance of Timber-based Employment to the Douglas-fir Region, 1954 to 1971*. Portland, OR: USDA Forest

Service, Pacific Northwest Forest and Range Experiment Station, Res. Note PNW-196.

Maki, W. R., D. Olson, and C. H. Schallau. 1985. *A Dynamic Simulation Model for Analyzing the Importance of Forest Resources in Alaska.* Portland, Oregon: USDA Forest Service, Pacific Northwest Forest and Range Experiment Station, Research Note PNW-432.

McKetta, C. W. 1984. "The Stability Rationale in Forest Management: Short-Run Economic Implications of Even Flow Harvest Constraints." Ph.D. dissertation, University of Washington, Seattle.

Murdock, S. H., and F. L. Leistritz. 1979. *Energy Development in the Western United States:Impact on Rural Areas.* New York: Praeger Publishers.

Muth, R. M. 1985. "Structural Differentiation and Community Growth: A Case Study of Natural Resource Development and Social Change in Selected Alaskan Communities." Ph.D. dissertation, University of Washington, Seattle.

Muth, R. M. 1986. "Community Stability as Social Structure: The Role of Subsistence Uses of Natural Resources in Southeast Alaska." Paper presented at the First National Symposium on Social Science and Resource Management, Corvallis, OR.

Muth, R. M. and R. G. Lee. 1985. *Social Impact Assessment in Natural Resource Decision-making: Toward a Structural Paradigm.* Paper presented at the Annual Conference of the International Association of Impact Assessment, Utrecht, the Netherlands.

Netting, R. M. and W.S. Elias. 1980. "Balancing on the Alp: Population Stability and Change in a Swiss Peasant Village." pp. 69-108 In P.C. Reining and B. Lenkerd (eds.), *Village Viability in Contemporary Society.* Boulder, CO: Westview Press.

Odum, H. W. 1936. *Southern Regions of the United States.* Chapel Hill, NC: University of North Carolina Press.

Odum, H. T. 1983. *Systems Ecology: An Introduction.* New York: Wiley and Sons.

O'Leary, J. T. 1975. "The Pursuit of Community Stability in Natural Resource Management." Paper presented at 1975 Annual Meeting of Rural Sociological Society, San Francisco, CA.

O'Neill, R. V., D. L. DeAngelis, J. B. Waide, and T. F. H. Allen. 1986. "A Hierarchical Concept of Ecosystems." *Monographs in Population Biology #23*. Princeton, NJ: Princeton University Press.

Porterfield, R. L. 1978. "Planning for Community and Forest Stability." Paper presented at Eighth World Forestry Congress, Jakarta, Indonesia.

Power, T. M. 1983. "Another Dimension of Community Stability: Local Quality of Life." *Western Wildlands* 8(4):28-32.

Richardson, J. L. and O. Larson. 1976. "Small Community Trends: A Fifty Year Perspective on Social-Economic Change in Thirteen New York Communities." *Rural Sociology* 41(1):45-59.

Ricklefs, R. E. 1973. *Ecology*. Portland, OR: Chiron Press.

Roberge, R. A. 1977. "Resource Towns: The Pulp and Paper Communities." *Canadian Geographical Journal* 94(1):28-35.

Robinson, I. M. 1984. "New Resource Towns on Canada's Frontier: Selected Contemporary Issues." pp. 1-22 in D. D. Detomasi and J. W. Gartrell (eds.), *Resource Communities: A Decade of Disruption*. Boulder, CO: Westview Press.

Rossi, R. J. and K. J. Gilmartin. 1980. *Handbook of Social Indicators: Sources, Characteristics, and Analysis*. New York: Garland STPD Press.

Samuelson, P. A. 1947. *Foundations of Economic Analysis*. Cambridge: Harvard University Press.

Sanders, I. T. and G. F. Lewis. 1976. "Rural Community Studies in the United States: A Decade in Review." *Annual Review of Sociology* 2:35-53.

Schallau, C. H. 1980. *Stages of Growth Theory and Money Flows from Commercial Banks in Timber-dependent Communities*. Corvallis, OR: Pacific Northwest Forest and Range Experiment Station, PNW-279.

Schallau, C. H. 1986. "Community Stability: Issues, Institutions, and Instruments." Paper presented at First National Symposium on Social Science in Resource Management, Corvallis, OR.

Schallau, C. H. and R. M. Alston. 1987. "The Commitment to Community Stability: A Policy or Shibboleth?" 17 *Environmental Law*: 430-81.

Schallau, C. H. and P. E. Polzin. 1983. *Considering Departures from Current Timber Harvesting Policies: Case Studies of Four Economies in the Pacific Northwest.* Portland, OR: USDA Forest Service, Pacific Northwest Forest and Range Experiment Station, Research Paper PNW-306.

Schallau, C. H., W. Maki, and J. Beuter. 1969. "Economic Impact Projections for Alternative Levels of Timber Production in the Douglas-fir Region." *Annals of Regional Science* 3(1):96-106.

Schumpeter, J. A. 1939. *Business Cycles: A Theoretical Historical and Statistical Analysis of the Capitalist Process.* New York: McGraw-Hill.

Summers, G. F. and K. Branch. 1984. "Economic Development and Community Social Change." *Annual Review of Sociology* 10:141-66.

USDA Forest Service. 1982. "Guidelines for Economic and Social Analysis of Programs, Resource Plans, and Projects: Final Policy." *Federal Register* 47(80):17940-54.

Van Voris, P. R., V. O'Neill, W. R. Emanuel, and H. H. Shugart. 1980. "Ecological Stability: An Ecosystem Perspective—Classical and Current Thought. A Review of Selected Literature." Oak Ridge, TN: Oak Ridge National Laboratory, ORNL/TM-5517.

Waggener, T. R. 1977 "Community Stability as a Forest Management Objective." *Journal of Forestry* 75:710-14.

Waggener, T. R. 1980. "Timber Sales, Uncut Inventory, and Timber Dependent Communities." Seattle, WA: College of Forest Resources,University of Washington.

Wilkenson, K. P. 1986. "In Search of the Community in the Changing Countryside." *Rural Sociology* 51(1):1-17.

Zimmerman, C. C. 1930. *Farm Trade Centers in Minnesota, 1905-1929.* St. Paul, MN: University of Minnesota Agricultural Experiment Station Bulletin No. 269.

Zinn, G. W. 1976. "Community Stability and its Value." Paper presented for the Society of American Foresters Workshop on Analysis of Forest-Related Sectors in Regional and Local Economies, Keystone Center, CO.

Zivnuska, J. A. 1952. *Business Cycles, Building Cycles and Commercial Forestry*. New York: Institute for Public Administration.

19

Conclusions: Past Accomplishments and Future Directions

Robert G. Lee
College of Forest Resources
University of Washington

William R. Burch, Jr.
School of Forestry and Environmental Studies
Yale University

Donald R. Field
School of Natural Resources
College of Agriculture and Life Sciences
University of Wisconsin

In this book we have entered the forest through the door of the human community only to discover that the wall separating communities from forests is imposed by the way we think. Contrary to conventional wisdom, we have discovered that we are of the forest and the forest is a reality constructed by us.

Just as Walter Firey reminded us in Chapter 2, the sociological study of natural resources has shown repeatedly that there are no clear boundaries between people and places, nature and society, degraded forests and degraded human communities. Forests increasingly function as extensions of human society and serve as the repositories for many of its cultural values, just as human organizations are patterned by the ways in which people treat forests.

The chapters we selected for sections on the forest industry and forest-based communities clearly demonstrate that the forest enterprise is as much one of skill in social organization as it is an application of technical skills and biophysical knowledge. The management of forest resources is not simply a biological or physical issue, and human organizations are not simply sociological phenomena. Communities necessarily include the biological and physical processes by which they are sustained, and forests and other resource systems cannot be managed effectively without an appreciation for how they are affected by communities and other human organizations.

Continuity in the sociological study of natural resources is clearly reflected in these studies of forest-based communities. However, like Firey, we conclude that most social scientists who study natural resources are relatively unself-conscious of this continuity. We believe that more self-consciousness will lead to greater academic discipline and will result in more efficient accumulation of knowledge.

Therefore, we conclude this volume with some suggestions for advancing the sociological study of natural resource systems. Our concern will focus on forest-based communities, and seek to extend issues raised in several of our chapters. We will begin with discussion of how emphasis on spatial, temporal, and social scales can productively build on previous sociological studies of natural resources. A discussion of community research issues will follow. We will close with suggestions for future sociological studies of forest-based communities.

SCALES OF NATURAL RESOURCE SYSTEMS

The interaction between human societies and biological and physical processes has been the primary focus for the sociological study of natural resources. Interest in forest-based communities has historically revolved around the rise and fall of local populations and institutions in response to timber resource development and depletion. The Kaufmans' 1946 study of Troy and Libby, Montana (summarized in Chapter 3) was anticipated by Paul Landis' 1938 study, *Three Iron Mining Towns* (Landis, 1938). Both studies illustrate the close correlation between resource utilization and the social cycles of local populations dependent on the extraction of natural resources. However, most of these earlier studies, as well as more recent work, would have benefited from more detailed analysis of interactions between social and biophysical processes. There is a need to look more broadly for studies of interactions that have focused on scale.

Scientists studying interactions in other complex systems have recently emphasized the importance of specifying temporal and spatial scales (Chisholm, 1980; Clark, 1985; MacArthur and Levins, 1967). Long term trends provide very different conditions for interactions than sudden increases. Also, highly localized processes will result in very different interactions than events taking place over very large areas.

Careful deliberation about spatial and temporal scales has long been a concern to foresters who prepare silvicultural prescriptions and plan timber harvests

(Davis, 1954). Decisions must be made about the size of treatment or harvest units and the harvest age of individual trees or stands of trees. Decisions about the size and location of "working circles" (the geographic area of forest land required to provide a sustained supply of wood to a sawmill) have depended on changes in rates of resource formation, efficient transportation distances, sawmill capacities, and other issues of scale. Also, scale has been a concern in managing natural disturbances such as fire, insects, disease, wind, and landslides (Clark, 1978). The rate of spread and the size of the area covered are key considerations when prescribing responses to forest disturbances. Similar concerns arise in range and watershed management. Scale has not until recently been as conscious a concern in recreation management.

Issues of scale in social organization have, correspondingly, been underlying concerns of sociologists who have studied natural resource systems (Field and Burch, 1988). The size of local populations, geographic focus of community cohesion and identification, and rate of growth or decline have been considerations in assessing community vitality and well-being. The social correlates of boom and bust cycles associated with resource extraction are implicitly issues of scale (Murdock and Leistritz, 1979). Nonurban population growth and decline, together with residential settlement patterns, also involve issues of scale (Lee, 1984).

However, neither foresters nor sociologists have explicitly addressed issues of scale when connecting social change with biophysical events and processes. Foresters have largely ignored social concerns and assumed that "wise forest management" would automatically produce social benefits—best illustrated by the maxim that sustained yield wood production will result in stable communities. Sociologists studying natural resources have gone much further in considering issues of scale in social and biophysical systems, but have seldom made scale a matter of self-conscious deliberation. Although many rural sociologists have followed in the steps of Paul Landis and connected social cycles with production cycles, they have generally fixed their attention on a local community and have ignored corresponding forms of social organization arising from production activities that are geographically dispersed (Field and Burch, 1988). Occupational communities of loggers are only one example of how geographically dispersed populations form communities of affiliation in addition to communities of locality. Consequently, we suggest that explicit consideration of temporal and spatial scale will significantly advance the study of interactions between human communities and forests, as well as the broader set of interactions between societies and the biophysical systems of which they are a part.

We will illustrate how attention to scale can be used to specify interactions by reviewing several of the community studies reported in the preceding chapters. Advances in the study of community-forest interactions will be stimulated by paying even greater attention to scale.

COMMUNITY-FOREST INTERACTIONS

Figure 1 displays characteristic time scales for selected social and ecological processes reported in preceding chapters. We have followed Clark (1985:10) by defining the characteristic time scale as T_e, in years: "the time required for the state of the system to change by a factor equal to the base of the natural logarithms, e (i.e., about 2.7 fold)." This "natural" time scale reflects rates of exponential growth and decay in living systems. Although there are scaling problems in applying any definition of scale to a wide range of social and ecological phenomena, this definition will suffice for making simple comparisons.

Time scales for events summarized in Figure 1 range across seven orders of magnitude. Biophysical events range from weeks (animal reproduction cycles) to millennia (rate at which some tree species expand their ranges). Social events range from hours (recreation visits) to hundreds of years (persistence of some local

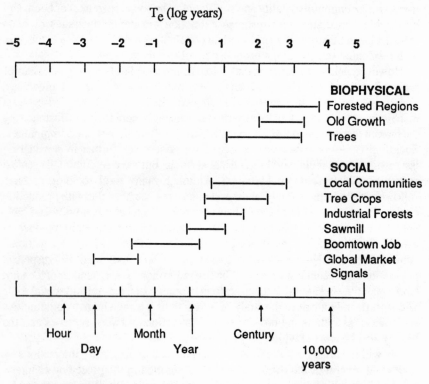

Figure 1. Characteristic time scales for interacting social and biophysical events.

communities). Patterns of interaction among these events are governed by their relative time scales.

Interaction among events operating in different time scales is illustrated by several of the studies reported in this book. Muth (Chapter 15) discusses how the relatively rapid reproduction cycles of game species has permitted subsistence to function as an institutionalized mechanism for helping people cope with the boom and bust cycles of a succession of unstable extractive industries (furriering, fishing, petroleum construction, and timber harvesting). He illustrates how people have perpetuated local community affiliations in the face of relatively rapid cycles of resource exploitation, including three such cycles within the last century.

Most Alaskan communities are long-lived social organizations relative to resource extraction industries. There is a persistent Native culture in Alaska mixed with strong non-Native traditions of rural frontier settlement characterized by commitment to place. Hence, there is a small core of Alaskan society that looks upon cycles of industrial exploitation and the waves of laborers they attract as so much "background noise" in the continuing life of "true" Alaskans. Similarly, Hays' (Chapter 4) account of the continuity of Great Lakes communities in the face of three major industrial cycles suggests the possibility of underlying stability in community institutions. While his historical account does not attempt to reveal such underlying structure, his observations invite sociological inquiry when compared with Muth's work on Alaska.

Mitsuda (Chapter 14) offers a contrasting interpretation of the attempts of Japanese mountain villagers to recover from economic and population decline resulting from the substitution of imported oil for charcoal and fuel wood. Penetration by an external, world economy interrupted hundreds of years of social continuity in mountain villages. Timber production has not provided a stable substitute, and only a few communities have succeeded in developing new industries in tourism, specialized food production, and wood products manufacturing. Substitutions of foreign energy and wood resources have occurred on time scales one to two order of magnitude shorter than comparable demographic and cultural adjustments.

Characteristic spatial scales are displayed in Figure 2. This scale is defined as a "characteristic length" equal to the square root of any geographic area (Clark, 1985). We are most concerned with the size of geographic units ranging from residential properties to global marketing networks—a range of almost six orders of magnitude. Local residential communities are relatively small geographic units relative to the regional forest land base or the global markets with which they may interact.

Interaction among people or processes operating at different spatial scales is also illustrated by studies reported in this volume. Marchak's account of timber towns in British Columbia (Chapter 8), together with related studies in the Pacific

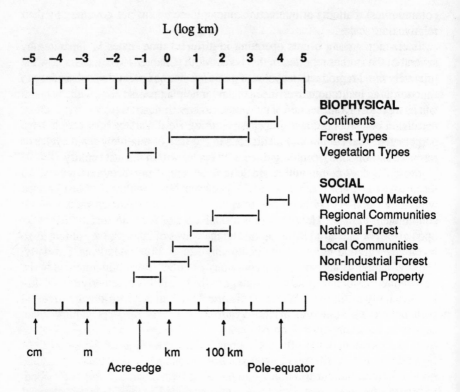

Figure 2. Characteristic spatial scales for interacting social and biophysical events.

Northwest by Brunelle (Chapter 9), Weeks (Chapter 10), and Carroll and Lee (Chapter 11), illustrates patterns of spatial interaction.

Towns formed as laborers migrated to remote logging camps and sawmills. Residential communities emerged when people made long term commitments to settling, marrying, and raising a family. However, Marchak and Drielsma, Miller, and Burch (Chapter 5) identified a number of factors that inhibited community formation, including boom and bust production cycles, unstable employment opportunities, rapid population turnover, low pay, harsh and unsafe working conditions, remote locations, poor schools, lack of opportunities for women, and the unavailability of property for building homes. These disadvantages caused potential long term residents to move in search of better opportunities.

The study by Carroll and Lee points out that occupational communities of loggers can emerge where attachments to residential communities are weak. Such occupational communities have in recent years become the basis for a regional social movement consisting of woods workers seeking to preserve their jobs by lobbying for increased timber harvesting on public lands. Machlis and Force (Chapter 18) refer to such geographically dispersed groupings as "communities of affiliation," as contrasted with "communities of locality." People who identify primarily with logging may find greater stability by affiliating with an occupational community spread across a whole region. Local vulnerability to fluctuations in wood supplies, markets, and local enterprises is reduced by the formation of regionally based occupational communities. Personal reputations once limited to a locality are transmitted through extended social networks to a region as large as several states. Adaptation has occurred through expansion of the spatial scale of work-related community identifications rather than by changing occupation as a means to remain in a residentially defined community.

Similar patterns of regional community formation have been observed among people concerned with recreation, amenity values, and environmental preservation. Shannon (Chapter 16) and Salazar (Chapter 17) discuss the role of these broader concerns in national forest planning and private forest practices regulation, respectively. The many recreation and environmental interest groups are made up of members who share identifications with particular activities, places, and preferred forest conditions. There is a clear sense of common spirit, group boundary, and geographic provinces of common concern. These groups parallel loggers in responding to undesirable changes in a particular locality (i.e., clearcutting) by expanding the geographic scale of leisure-related community identifications. National forest planning becomes an opportunity for using public involvement to build trust relationships with regional and national communities of affiliation that share interests in a particular forest. Similarly, forest practice regulations tend to reflect the preferences of the politically dominant communities of interest in a county, region, or state.

Traditional arguments for sustained yield were based almost exclusively on considerations of the geographic area needed for sustaining local wood supplies. Schallau (Chapter 6), together with Drielsma, Miller, and Burch (Chapter 5), describe how temporal cycles in communities were thought to be stabilized by regularizing rates of resource formation and annual harvest. The Kaufmans (Chapter 3) demonstrated how foresters ignored social dynamics of communities and market cycles and fixed their attention on rationalizing space. Area regulation (cutting the same amount of land for every year it takes to grow a crop of trees) was the purest expression of this attempt to eliminate the influences of social and economic variations.

Contrary to the claim that sustained yield only works in closed economies, Lee (Chapter 7) has suggested that adoption of sustained yield is a response to social instability. Social turbulence such as riots, war, revolts, depression, and rapid institutional change has preceded the adoption of sustained yield policies in both

Germany and the United States. Foresters have overlooked this fact because of their fixation with regulating the spatial and temporal scales of biophysical events. Aside from concern with interest rates as means for setting time horizons in forest planning, foresters have ignored how forests are affected by the variation of surrounding societies in space and time (Duerr, Teeguarden et al., 1982).

Current efforts to require sustained yield on state and private lands can be seen as a product of intense social conflict over extensive clearcutting, accelerated rates of harvesting, and the anticipated decline in jobs that will occur when most of the available commercial wood is harvested. Now that foresters are beginning to abandon sustained yield as a guiding principle, critics are responding to accelerated harvesting and its threats to scenery, water quality, wildlife, recreation, and future wood products jobs by demanding that it be institutionalized on private as well as public lands.

Some of the more complex patterns of interaction were described by Blahna (Chapter 12) and Fortmann and Starrs (Chapter 13). A blending of long-term rural residents and recent migrants from urban areas has altered the way rural communities respond to large scale economic enterprises and changes in the resource base. Rapid demographic changes accompanying the arrival of urbanites did not necessarily result in conflict with locals or the substitution of urban ways for local lifestyles. Newcomers brought political skills that enabled them to exercise local leadership in expanding the control over natural resources from conventional property rights to community control over a large geographic area of concern to the community as a whole—generally lands owned by government agencies or large firms. Throughout the United States new residents living adjacent to forests exercise substantial control over a geographic area extending well beyond their property boundaries. Institutional change in property rights has not kept pace with the rapid expansion of territorial dominance accompanying reverse migration.

IMPLICATIONS FOR FUTURE RESEARCH

Machlis and Force (Chapter 18) have suggested a number of productive directions for future research on forest-based communities. They recommend that research focus on the kinds of resources upon which communities depend and the political structure of resource industries, as well as on the rate and geographic scale of social change. We endorse these recommendations and urge researchers to extend concern with variation in local communities to the resource industries and biophysical environment upon which they depend.

Explicit consideration of scale in the development of theories and alternative hypotheses will stimulate the advancement of community research. Following are suggestions for advances in theory and methods.

Established analogs to these sociological observations can be found in ecological studies of plants and animals. Ecological studies show that populations of organisms tend to track environmental changes where generation times are short relative to the time scale of environmental variations (Hutchinson, 1953; MacArthur and Levins, 1967). Populations grow rapidly under favorable environmental conditions and decline during unfavorable conditions. Such populations are highly unstable. Interactions among species are far less important in influencing population size and distribution than are environmental influences and reproductive rates. These studies may help us understand patterns of human organization that are found in boom towns.

The boom and bust cycles associated with resource exploitation are an example of how relatively short job opportunities track longer cycles of resource exploitation. This pattern has been observed in energy boom towns, mining and timbering camps, and other relatively unstable industries (Murdock and Leistritz, 1979). While the cases presented in this book were drawn from British Columbia, Alaska, and the Pacific Northwest, far more cases can be found in developing nations where resource stocks are extracted to provide foreign exchange and capital for industrial development.

Interactions between people become much more important when short-term job opportunities are extended and people develop enduring ties to one another and attachments to a place. Ecological theory also tells us that interactions take on a very different pattern when generation times are long relative to environmental variations. Populations do not track on extremes in environmental fluctuations, but instead follow average environmental conditions. Such populations are relatively stable, but can have long recovery periods in the event of major disturbances. Social interactions among organisms and demographic processes are far more important for determining population size and distribution than when quickly breeding organisms adjust to longer term environmental changes.

These patterns corroborate sociological observations and help us to differentiate boom towns from the traditional communities of the upper Midwest, Alaska, Japan, and other regions where strong attachments to place and local people have replaced frontier turbulence with long-term commitments.

When there is a close match between temporal scales of environmental variation and generations these generalizations do not hold. Interactions become far more complex, and ecological outcomes are the joint product of social, environmental, and other factors.

Such ecological analogs can help us to hypothesize about complex patterns of interaction between human social organization and environmental conditions across the full range of social and environmental variation. Research could most productively begin with communities where there is a mismatch between rates of social and environmental change. Alaska, British Columbia, and similar frontier regions in developing nations provide opportunities to compare long standing subsistence based communities with ephemeral resource exploitation camps. More complex patterns of interaction exist where social organization has increased in spatial and temporal scale, as is found in regional occupational, recreational, and environmental communities of affiliation. These complex interactions are the sources of many modern forest management conflicts.

Finally, our understanding of communities will advance more rapidly if hypotheses derived from these emerging generalizations are properly tested. We recommend a strategy for challenging multiple alternative working hypotheses (Salazar and Lee, forthcoming). Inherited generalizations, such as the idea that sustained yield results in community stability, are often untested "ruling theories" that people have sought to support by citing favorable evidence and testimony. It is an unacceptable scientific practice to attempt to prove things true. Scientific advance will be far more rapid if hypotheses are stated in a fashion that permits them to be challenged and evidence is gathered with the objective of falsifying hypotheses (Platt, 1964).

CONCLUSIONS

Knowledge of forest-based communities is daily becoming more important to both the people who manage forests and those who decide how they should be managed. Following are some trends that have contributed to this change:

1. There have been massive alterations of vegetative cover and land use on a regional scale, and these alterations are having significant consequences for local communities, national economies, and the global environment. Tropical forests are being converted to pastures, farms, towns, roads, hydroelectric sites, and wastelands. Productive temperate forests are being converted to highways, residential developments, industrial parks, and many small leisure forests, and old growth forests are being converted to secondary and young growth forests. Economic gain from forests now requires significant investment and costly management. Carbon released from burning forest cover has contributed significantly to the accumulation of "greenhouse gases" in the atmosphere.

2. Localized human communities dependent on forests are no longer regulated by the natural cycles of natural resource production. The global economic system relies on the manipulation of information about quantities and prices, not land and the people attached to it. This has had two effects on communities. Economic signals are far less stable than natural cycles of production. Erratic behavior of markets is illustrated by the October 19, 1987 stock market crash triggered by electronic trading between commodity markets (real goods) and stock portfolios (speculative ventures). Secondly, a system driven primarily by information

manipulation tends to convert all people and land to abstractions. Hence, square-mile clearcuts, conversion of forest land to thousands of mini-estates, and destruction of a forest village in Thailand or Washington State are all reduced to profit and loss statements appearing on a distant computer screen. Hungry villagers, proud loggers, endangered species, and the smell of moss-covered glens are lost in the swirling relativity of economic computations.

3. Globalization and abstraction are accompanied by a loss of accountability for those ultimately involved in making resource decisions. Decisions that affect local communities and resources are increasingly not part of the local normative structure and networks of social control. Consequently, local customs and sanctions that have traditionally maintained social order are not available. This is illustrated by the decisions of banks and large corporations to shift capital investment away from land, resources, and manufacturing enterprises in rural communities.

Local investors play only a minor role in industries that could generate local wealth by diversifying the economic base or adding value to wood before it is exported. U.S. landowners who export raw logs escape local and regional accountability and shift the blame for loss of sawmilling jobs to "environmentalists" who seek to preserve old growth on public lands. Correspondingly, environmentalists who would reserve the forests of Southeast Alaska or the Amazon basin are not accountable to the people who depend on utilization of these forests for their livelihood. An overarching national and international normative structure is needed to ensure accountability between ownership and action, but the development of a new normative order has lagged well behind the development of the abstract, global, and political economy.

4. Economic change and its accompanying lag in the development of accountability for decision makers is reflected in changes in the social role of professional resource managers. Villagers, peasants, voters, and taxpayers want more participation in decisions about forest management planning and practices. Yet professionals find it difficult to accommodate these demands when hegemony over resource utilization and conservation is no longer localized and concentrated, but has instead been globalized and dispersed. Managers have resisted sharing control with diverse interest groups that have become involved in guiding policy development and implementation. Moreover, resource managers find it increasingly difficult to rationalize resource regulation when they are affected by stochastic events such as wildfires and insect outbreaks, breakthroughs in biotechnology, fluctuations in distant markets, or the uncertain impacts of global climate change.

5. There is an emerging realization that economic growth will not cure all of the problems created by population growth and associated resource exploitation. Although it is reasonable to expect substantial increases in the productivity of food, fodder, and forests, reductions in consumption are going to be absolutely neces-

sary. A combination of the marginality of less exploited lands, climate change, and ecosystem disruptions associated with new technologies will impose ecological limits to economic expansion. Reductions in energy consumption will limit human mobility. Locality will become more important with reduced consumption and efficiencies brought about by local production and recycling. Communities of locality can be expected to grow in importance.

These trends, together with the contributions provided by the contributors to this volume, suggest that human community, organization, participation, and values will become an even more essential component of future forest and natural resource planning and management. One of the pioneers of American forestry, H. H. Chapman, hinted at the theme of this book in 1925. He argued that in the final analysis it is not the professional manager who will determine the disposition and use of forest land, but the public. Public professions, such as forestry and natural resources management, are looked upon as a means for resolving problems of the political economy, not simply as technicians for satisfying the interests of government agencies or private investors. This contribution to an understanding of forest-based communities can help foresters and other natural resource professionals to assume greater responsibility for fulfilling the public's expectation.

ACKNOWLEDGEMENTS

The comments of Debra Salazar are gratefully acknowledged.

REFERENCES

Chisholm, M. 1980. "The Wealth of Nations." *Transactions of the Institute of British Geography, New Series* 5:255-275.

Clark, W. C. 1978. "Patches, Movements, and Population Dynamics in Ecological Systems: A Territorial Perspective." In J. H. Steele, (ed.), *Spatial Pattern in Plankton Communities.* New York: Plenum.

Clark, W. C. 1985. "Scales of Climate Impacts." *Climate Change* 7:5-27.

Davis, K. P. 1954. *American Forest Management.* New York, Toronto, London: McGraw-Hill Book Company, Inc.

Duerr, W. A., D. E. Teeguarden, N. B. Christiansen and S. Guttenberg. 1982. *Forest Resource Management: Decision-Making Principles and Cases.* Corvallis, Oregon: Oregon State University Book Stores, Inc.

Field, D. R. and W. R. Burch Jr. 1988. *Rural Sociology and the Environment*. New York: Greenwood Press.

Hutchinson, G. E. 1953. "The Concept of Pattern in Ecology." *Proceedings of the Academy of Natural Sciences of Philadelphia* 105:1-12.

Landis, P. H. 1938. *Three Iron Mining Towns: A Study in Cultural Change*. Ann Arbor, MI: Edwares Brothers, Inc.

Lee, R. G. 1984. "Implications of Contemporary Community Organization and Social Values for Forest Management on the Residential/Wildland Interface." In G. A. Bradley (ed.), *Land Use and Forest Resources in a Changing Environment*. Seattle, Washington: University of Washington Press.

MacArthur, R. H. and R. Levins. 1967. "The Limiting Similarity, Convergence and Divergence of Coexisting Species." *American Naturalist* 101:377-385.

Murdock, S. H. and F. L. Leistritz. 1979. *Energy Development in the Western United States: Impacts on Rural Areas*. New York: Praeger Publishers.

Platt, J. R. 1964. "Strong inference." *Science* 146(3642):347-353.

Salazar, D. J. and R. G. Lee. forthcoming. "Natural Resource Policy Analysis and Public Choice Theory: A Strategy for Empirical Research." *Natural Resources Journal* (Winter 1990).

Profiles of the Authors

Dale J. Blahna is Assistant Professor in the Department of Geography and Environmental Studies at Northeastern Illinois University. He received his Ph.D. in Environment and Behavior from the University of Michigan in 1985 and has worked as a consulting sociologist with the U.S. Forest Service. His current research interests include natural resource sociology, public participation, and outdoor recreation.

Andy Brunelle is a Special Assistant in the office of Governor Cecil D. Andrus of Idaho where he works on natural resource and rural development issues. He received a bachelor's degree in 1983 from Boise State University and earned a master's degree in public policy from the University of Oregon in 1986. While at the University of Oregon he studied the effects of the changing timber industry on small communities in the Pacific Northwest. He is a native of Boise, Idaho.

William R. Burch, Jr. is the Hixon Professor of Natural Resources Management in Forestry and Environmental Studies and the Institution of Social and Policy Studies at Yale University. He is Director of the Tropical Resources Institute at Yale, Research Sociologist with the National Park Service, and Faculty Associate at the College of the Atlantic, Bar Harbor, Maine. Burch is the author or editor of ten books. Representative are: *Daydreams and Nightmares: A Sociological Essay on the American Environment* (Harper & Row, 1971), *Measuring the Social Impact of Natural Resources Policies*, with Don DeLuca (University of New Mexico Press, 1984), and *Rural Sociology and the Environment*, with Donald R. Field (Greenwood Press, 1988).

Matthew S. Carroll is Assistant Professor in the Department of Natural Resource Sciences at Washington State University in Pullman. He holds a bachelor's degree in forest management from the University of Massachusetts and master's and Ph.D. degrees in forest and natural resource sociology from West Virginia University and the University of Washington, respectively. His research interests are in the application of sociology to natural resource problems with a particular emphasis on resource based human communities. He served as chair of the Society of American Foresters National Task Force on Community Stability.

Johannes H. Drielsma is Chief of Management Planning for the Forestry Commission of New South Wales, Australia, where he is responsible for forest planning, environmental matters, education, and information services. From 1976 to 1979 he undertook postgraduate studies and research at Yale University School of Forestry and Environmental Studies in natural resource sociology and was awarded a doctorate in 1984. Current interests include social impact assessment, particularly in the effects of forestry on rural communities.

Donald R. Field is currently Associate Dean, College of Agricultural and Life Sciences at the University of Wisconsin. He has served as senior scientist in the National Park Service and held faculty positions in the College of Forestry at Oregon State University and the College of Forest Resources at the University of Washington. The former Associate Regional Director of Science and Technology and Regional Chief Scientist of the National Park Service in Seattle, he is coauthor of *Rural Sociology and the Environment* and *Leisure and Recreation Places*, coeditor of *Water and Community Development* and *Interpretation*.

Walter Firey is Professor Emeritus of Sociology at the University of Texas at Austin, where he taught from 1946 to 1985. He was a Fellow at the Center for Advanced Study in the Behavioral Sciences, 1959-1960. He is author of *Land Use in Central Boston, Man, Mind and Land: A Theory of Resource Use, Law and Economy in Planning, The Study of Possible Societies*, and articles on land use, planning, and human ecology.

Jo Ellen Force is Associate Professor in the Department of Forest Resources at the College of Forestry, Wildlife and Ranges Sciences, University of Idaho, Moscow, Idaho. She teaches forest land use planning, forest policy, and community forest management. Her research interests include international social forestry issues, public participation activities on national forests in the Pacific Northwest, community stability in timber-dependent communities, and firewood use on national forests. She has consulted on USAID social forestry projects in India and Pakistan.

Louise Fortmann is Associate Professor in the Department of Forestry and Resource Management at the University of California at Berkeley. She worked for ten years in Tanzania, Botswana, and Kenya specializing in local institutions and resource management systems, agricultural development, and the role of women in development. Her recent work has focused on the proprietary dimensions of natural resource management.

Samuel P. Hays is the author of *Conservation and the Gospel of Efficiency* and many other books and articles dealing with the social analysis of politics in modernizing America. He is Professor and former chairman of the Department of

History at the University of Pittsburgh, and has been a fellow of the Woodrow Wilson International Center for Scholars and Harmsworth Professor at Oxford University.

Harold F. Kaufman is Professor Emeritus of Sociology, Department of Sociology and Anthropology, Mississippi State University. His M.A. thesis, *Social Factors in the Reforestation of the Missouri Ozarks*, established him as the first rural sociologist to systematically study forestry problems. He served as Director of the Social Science Research Center at Mississippi State University, where he established a U.S. Forest Service Southern Station research unit that conducted forest fire prevention research for 20 years. Kaufman also was a leader in the origination of the Natural Resources Research Committee in the Rural Sociological Society in the early 1960s.

Robert G. Lee is Professor of Forestry (specializing in the sociology of natural resources) at the University of Washington. He received a Masters degree from Yale University and a Ph.D. in Wildland Resource Science from the University of California at Berkeley. His current work focuses on forest-dependent communities in the United States and Japan, institutional regulation of ecological processes and multiresource management. He is author of articles on leisure, recreation, community, and forest policy issues. He served as Chair for the Division of Forest Resources Management at the University of Washington from 1983 to 1988.

Gary E. Machlis is Associate Professor of Forest Resources and Sociology at the University of Idaho. He is also Sociology Project Leader of the Cooperative Park Studies Unit, a research station of the National Park Service at the University of Idaho. Dr. Machlis received his B.S. and M.S. degrees in forestry from the University of Washington and his Ph.D. in human ecology from Yale University. He is the author and editor of several books on park management and conservation, including *The State of the World's Parks* and *Interpretive Views*. Dr. Machlis has conducted studies in over 25 national parks, and recently spent 4 months in China working on the Giant Panda Project for the World Wildlife Fund.

M. Patricia Marchak, Ph.D., F.R.S.C., Professor and Head of the Department of Anthropology and Sociology at the University of British Columbia, has written extensively on resource industries and economic development. She is the author of *Green Gold: The Forest Industry in B.C., Ideological Perspectives on Canada,* and *In Whose Interests,* and coeditor of *Uncommon Property: The Fishing and Fish Processing Industry in B.C.* She is currently doing further research on the forest industry in Pacific Rim countries.

Hisayoshi Mitsuda is Professor of Rural Sociology in the Department of Sociology at Bukkyo University in Kyoto, Japan. He holds a Ph.D. from Kyoto University in agriculture economics, and studied mountain villages for over ten years. He has published six books and over two dozen articles, including several articles in academic journals published in the United States. He has traveled widely and is a leader in the campaign to save Japan's ancient forests.

Joseph A. Miller is Librarian of the Yale School of Forestry and Environmental Studies and Lecturer in History. He has served as editor of *Forest History* (now the *Journal of Forest History*) and review editor of *Environmental Management*. His research has centered on the legislative origins of conservation in the nineteenth century, changes in landscapes over time, and the history of American forestry.

Robert M. Muth has been employed by the USDA Forest Service since 1970. He worked with the Wildland Recreation Research Project in Seattle, and as the National Social Impact Assessment Coordinator for the RARE II Project in Washington, D.C. He is presently the Regional Social Scientist with the Alaska Region of the Forest Service in Juneau. He earned his Ph.D. (natural resource sociology) through the College of Forest Resources at the University of Washington. His research interests include social impact assessment and subsistence use of renewable natural resources.

Debra J. Salazar is Assistant Professor of Forestry (specializing in forest policy analysis) and Adjunct Professor of Political Science at the University of Washington. She received M.S. and Ph.D. degrees from the University of Washington. Her research focuses on regulation of forest practices and land use. Her academic publications are significant contributions to the advancement of forest policy analysis.

Con H. Schallau is Research Economist with the Pacific Northwest Research Station, Forestry Sciences Laboratory in Corvallis, Oregon. His research assignment involves the development of complex models for investigating the impacts of public forest resource management policies on regional and local economies. Prior to his present assignment, Dr. Schallau was Deputy Director of the Intermountain Research Station in Ogden, Utah. Schallau holds the rank of Professor (courtesy) in the Forest Management Department at Oregon State University, and is Professor (adjunct) in the Agricultural and Applied Economics Department at the University of Minnesota in St. Paul, Minnesota.

Margaret A. Shannon is Assistant Professor of Forest Policy at State University of New York, Syracuse. She has also worked as a private consultant. She received a Ph.D. in Wildland Resource Science from the University of California, Berkeley. Her research interests broadly concern natural resource sociology and law, and wildland resource science. She has published in *Western Wildlands* and in *Proceedings: Society of American Foresters Annual Meeting*.

Paul F. Starrs recently completed a Ph.D. in geography at the University of California at Berkeley with a study of western United States cattle ranchers and their relationship with the federal government. Working as a cultural geographer, he has written on the topics of agriculture in the San Joaquin Valley of California, Mormon meetinghouse architecture, western public lands, natural resource use, arid lands, orange crate labels, and images of Southern California.

Edward C. Weeks is Associate Professor and Director of the Graduate Program in Public Affairs in the Department of Planning, Public Policy and Management at the University of Oregon. He is a member of a group of students and faculty who collaborate on research concerned with the community impact of regional economic change and with community economic development.

Index

Alternative hypotheses, 285, 286
Amenities and recreation, 3, 48, 159, 165, 283
Attachments to a place, 285

Beers, Howard, 19
Behan, Richard, 83
Blahna, Dale, 284
Boom towns, 31, 33, 44, 47, 95, 259, 285
    boom and bust cycles, 281
    boom and bust economies, 96
    economies, 215, 216
Brownell, Baker, 27
Brunelle, Andy, 282
Burch, William, 279

California Forest Practices Act, 249
Carroll, Matthew, 282
Change
    scale of, 268
Chapman, H. H., 288
Citizen participation, 230-231
    definition, 231
Clark-McNary Act of 1924, 58
Clary, David, 58
Communities
    of affiliation, 261, 266, 286
    of interest, 246
    of locality, 288
    of place, 261
Communities, dependent, 57
Communities, geographic scale of, 234
Communities, resource dependent, 260
    community decline, 99
    definition, 264, 265

external control, 99, 142, 191, 201, 218, 244, 267
    institutional change, 129
    institutional structure, 212, 263
    institutions, 136
    long term residents, 163
    migration patterns, 130, 182, 195
    migration problems, 97
    newcomers, 161, 189
    population instability, 98
    subsistence, 214
Community, 32, 33
    economic, 73
    natural resource, 231
    of interests, 234
    visions of the future, 235
Community choices
    resources based communities-external control, 46
Community control movements, 100
Community infrastructure, 203
Community instability
    small firms and, 37, 59, 64, 70, 91, 112
Community institutions, 35, 135
Community management of reources, 191
Community stability, 19, 34, 39, 57, 58, 69-78, 107, 211, 259, 261
    as dynamic change, 74
    as dynamic equilibrium, 261, 266
    definition, 32, 74, 262-264
    plant ownership, 117
    responsibility for, 72
    small firms and, 120
Community structure, 204

Community, and political
   jurisdictions
   economic development, 49
   environmental amenities, 49
Community, definition of, 6, 7, 260
Community, economic base, 75
Community, occupational, 141-152,
   283
   adaptability, 150
   logger identity, 147
   logger reputation, 149
   shared meaning, 148
   socialization, 145
   terminology, 146
Community, resource-based
   economies, 75
Community-forest interactions, 280
Conflict
   geographic scope of, 188
Country Life Commission, 58
Cultural complex and nature, 21
Culture clash and migration, 160

Dana, Samuel, 57
Dependency ratio, 196
Depopulation and community
   structure
   depopulation problem, 196
Depopulation, impacts of rapid, 197
Drielsma, Johannes, 282, 283
Duerr, William, 85, 87
DuWors, Richard, 20

Economic abstractions, 287
Economic impacts, measuring, 76
Economic region, 71, 261
Economic stability, 72
Environmental issues, 49

Farm forestry households, 197
Fernow, Bernard, 89
Field, Donald, 279
Firey, Walter, 9, 277, 278

Folkman, William, 22
Forest community, 31
Forest industry, 259
   labor productivity, 74, 109, 127
   size and scale, 119, 121
   structural change, 108, 110, 114,
      125, 128
   technological change, 109
   unionization, 117
   vertical integration, 118
   work force change, 109, 129, 151,
      205
Forest management, conflicts over,
   45, 286
   amenity values, 250
   clearcutting, 48, 166, 169
   herbicides, 252
   pesticides and herbicides, 48
   residential settlement, 246
Forest policy, 37, 246
Forest practice regulation, 241
   amenity values, 243
   local, 243
Forest program, 37
Forestry, definition of, 4
Forests
   and human choice, 41
   and human values, 42
Fortmann, Louise, 284
Frey, John, 20
Fuelwood gathering, 180

Global economic system, 287
Greeley, William, 57
Greenhouse effect, 286

Harvest regulation, regionalization
   of, 62
Harvest schedules, departures from,
   73, 91
Hays, Samuel, 10, 281
Heating fuel revolution, 195

Heflin, Catharine, 19
Heske, Franz, 90
Hypes, J. L., 19

Industrial society, advanced, 3, 11, 42, 198
Institutional persistence, 267
Intergenerational equity, 70

Kaso Act, 200
Kaufman, Harold, 8, 10, 19, 278, 283
Kirkland, B. A., 57

Labor force structure, 198
Land management organizations
  conflict, 147, 162
  human choice, 43
  lack of social science expertise, 5
  natural resource systems, 28
  participation, 231
  personal relationships, 232
  U.S. Forest Service, 181, 182, 190, 230
  workforce diversity, 5
Land management planning, 234
Landis, Paul, 8, 18, 278, 279
Lee, Robert, 279, 284
Lively, Charles, 21
Local resources, rights to, 180

Machlis, Gary, 283, 284
Marchak, Patricia, 282
Mason, David, 59, 70
"Micro" social world, 142
Migration, rural-urban, 200
Miller, Joseph, 282, 283
Mitsuda, Hisayoshi, 281
Moe, Edward, 20
Montana Study, 27
Mukerjee, Radhakamal, 15
Muth, Robert, 281

National Forest Management Act, 1976, 62, 71

National forest planning, 283
National Recovery Administration, 59
Natural resources, and culture, 18
Natural resources, definition of, 21
Natural resources, sociology, 9
  definitions, 16
  dynamics of resource practices, 17
  equilibrium, 16
  holistic viewpoint, 17, 23
  resource system, 23
  social system, 23
Networks of social control, 287
New energy technologies, 181
"Nimby" (not-in-my-back-yard)
  protests, 170, 180
Nonstatutory claims, 191
Normative structure, 287

Odum, Howard, 17
Oregon and California Railroad
  Lands Act, 59
Ownership, 20, 101, 179

Pinchot, Gifford, 56, 58
Policy and science, 27
Population change and community
  structure, 131
Population growth, 288
Population growth and environmental
  conflict, 167
Population migration, 130, 132, 159
Preexisting community organization
  Protest and, 186, 187
Property rights, 21, 179, 191
  and forest management, 22
Public dialogue, 236
Public involvement processes, 232
Public lands, claims to, 179
Public Law 273, 36
Public participation, 38, 46, 172, 209, 229, 287
Push-pull theory, the, 202

Recreation, 42
Recreational planning, 35
Reforestation, 242
Regional analysis, 18
Regional economic system, 73
Regional systems, 130
Residential settlement, 42, 98, 163,
    171, 180
Resource cycles, 215, 217
Resource management organizations
    U.S. Forest Service, 185
Resource management, conflicts over
    nonstatutory claims, 180
Resource managers
    social role of professional, 287
Resource sharing
    social meanings of, 222
Retirement settlement, 134
Reverse migration, 4, 160, 164, 190,
    201
    cultural infusion, 170
    environmental conflict, 160, 168,
        189
Rural depopulation process, 199

Salazar, Debra, 283
Scale
    space, 281
    time, 280, 285
Scales
    social, spatial, temporal, 278
Schallau, Con, 283
Service-based economy, 4
Shannon, Margaret, 283
Shelton Cooperative Sustained Yield
    Unit, 60
Single industry towns, 95
Small business set-aside program, 115
Social and biophysical processes
    interactions between, 278
Social change, 31, 260
    rates of, 268

Social contracts, 237
Social decision processes
    social contracts, 229
Social indicators, 265
Social stability
    cycles of, 266
Sociology and conservation
    conservation practices, 20
    forest, 21
    practice, 21
Stages-of-growth theory, 76
Structural changes, 203
Subsistence
    specialized knowledge, 223
    to a mixed economy, 215
Subsistence resource use, 212-213
    definition, 213
Sustained yield, 59, 61, 70, 73, 84
    "scientific forestry", 56
    and forest-dependent industries, 55
    cooperative sustained yield policy, 60
    critique of, 85
    definition, 56
    federal sustained-yield units, 71
    functional meanings, 87
    German forestry, 56
    German origins of, 83
    marketing areas, 71
    of renewable natural resources, 92,
        223
    origins of definitions, 88
    ownership, 101
    social meaning, 63, 85
    social meanings, 86, 87
    social reform, 88, 90
    technical meanings, 86
    Vallecitos Sustained-Yield Unit, 61
Sustained Yield Forest Management
    Act of 1944, 36, 60, 71, 90
Sustained yield management, 36, 37

Taxfarming, 181

Threshholds of coping, 267
Timber-orientation, 45, 46
    wood production, 45
Tourism and recreation, 47

Unemployment, 96, 129, 187
"Urbanization and Natural
    Resources", 22

Vance, Rupert, 16
Vaux, Henry, 86
Vegetative cover, alternations of, 286

Waggener, Thomas, 62, 71
Water resources, 35
Weeks, Edward, 282
Whetten, Nathan, 20
Workers and plants, 116

Zimmerman, Carle, 17
Zivnuska, John, 61

WIDENER UNIVERSITY
WOLFGRAM
LIBRARY
CHESTER, PA.

MASTER UNIVERSITY
WOLFRAM
LIBRARY